Frommer's®

P o r t a b l e
Chicago

6th Edition

P9-CQA-681

*by Elizabeth Canning Blackwell &
Michael Austin*

Here's what critics say about Frommer's:

"Amazingly easy to use. Very portable, very complete."
—*Booklist*

"Detailed, accurate, and easy-to-read information for all price ranges."
—*Glamour Magazine*

WILEY

Wiley Publishing, Inc.

Published by:

WILEY PUBLISHING, INC.

111 River St.
Hoboken, NJ 07030-5774

ISBN 978-0-470-16906-3
Editor: Anuja Madar
Production Editor: Suzanna R. Thompson
Cartographer: Andrew Murphy
Photo Editor: Richard Fox
Production by Wiley Indianapolis Composition Services

For information on our other products and services or to obtain technical support, please contact our Customer Care Department within the U.S. at 800/762-2974, outside the U.S. at 317/572-3993 or fax 317/572-4002.

Wiley also publishes its books in a variety of electronic formats. Some content that appears in print may not be available in electronic formats.

Manufactured in the United States of America

5   4   3   2   1

Contents

List of Maps

ABOUT THE AUTHORS

Elizabeth Canning Blackwell began life on the East Coast, but 4 years at Northwestern University transformed her into a Midwesterner. She has worked as a writer and editor at *Encyclopaedia Britannica,* Northwestern University Medical School, the *Chicago Tribune,* and *North Shore,* a lifestyle magazine for the Chicago suburbs. She also has written for national magazines on everything from planning the perfect wedding to fighting a duel. She lives just outside the city with her husband, daughter, and an extensive collection of long underwear.

A Chicago-area native and the son of a Trans World Airlines employee, **Michael Austin** caught the travel bug at a profoundly young age (around 9, he guesses). Today he is a freelance writer specializing in food, wine, and, naturally, travel. His stories and personal essays have appeared in *Esquire, GQ, Outside,* and the *Chicago Tribune Magazine.* Most recently he collaborated with Oprah Winfrey's personal chef, Art Smith, on *Back to the Family,* a cookbook featuring reflections on sharing meals with loved ones. A James Beard Award finalist for feature writing, Michael lives in his favorite city, Chicago.

AN INVITATION TO THE READER

In researching this book, we discovered many wonderful places—hotels, restaurants, shops, and more. We're sure you'll find others. Please tell us about them, so we can share the information with your fellow travelers in upcoming editions. If you were disappointed with a recommendation, we'd love to know that, too. Please write to:

Frommer's Portable Chicago, 6th Edition
Wiley Publishing, Inc. • 111 River St. • Hoboken, NJ 07030-5774

AN ADDITIONAL NOTE

Please be advised that travel information is subject to change at any time—and this is especially true of prices. We therefore suggest that you write or call ahead for confirmation when making your travel plans. The authors, editors, and publisher cannot be held responsible for the experiences of readers while traveling. Your safety is important to us, however, so we encourage you to stay alert and be aware of your surroundings. Keep a close eye on cameras, purses, and wallets, all favorite targets of thieves and pickpockets.

FROMMER'S STAR RATINGS, ICONS & ABBREVIATIONS

Every hotel, restaurant, and attraction listing in this guide has been ranked for quality, value, service, amenities, and special features using a **star-rating system.** In country, state, and regional guides, we also rate towns and regions to help you narrow down your choices and budget your time accordingly. Hotels and restaurants are rated on a scale of zero (recommended) to three stars (exceptional). Attractions, shopping, nightlife, towns, and regions are rated according to the following scale: zero stars (recommended), one star (highly recommended), two stars (very highly recommended), and three stars (must-see).

In addition to the star-rating system, we also use **seven feature icons** that point you to the great deals, in-the-know advice, and unique experiences that separate travelers from tourists. Throughout the book, look for:

Finds	Special finds—those places only insiders know about
Fun Fact	Fun facts—details that make travelers more informed and their trips more fun
Kids	Best bets for kids—advice for the whole family
Moments	Special moments—those experiences that memories are made of
Overrated	Places or experiences not worth your time or money
Tips	Insider tips—some great ways to save time and money
Value	Great values—where to get the best deals

The following **abbreviations** are used for credit cards:

AE	American Express	DISC	Discover	V	Visa
DC	Diners Club	MC	MasterCard		

FROMMERS.COM

Now that you have this guidebook to help you plan a great trip, visit our website at **www.frommers.com** for additional travel information on more than 3,600 destinations. We update features regularly to give you instant access to the most current trip-planning information available. At Frommers.com, you'll find scoops on the best airfares, lodging rates, and car rental bargains. You can even book your travel online through our reliable travel booking partners. Other popular features include:

- Online updates of our most popular guidebooks
- Vacation sweepstakes and contest giveaways
- Newsletters highlighting the hottest travel trends
- Online travel message boards with featured travel discussions

The Best of Chicago

Like any great city, Chicago's got something for everyone, whether your tastes run toward world-famous museums and blow-your-budget luxury hotels or family-friendly lodgings and low-key neighborhood restaurants. Narrowing down your choices may seem daunting, but never fear: Here's your cheat sheet to the very best of the city.

1 The Most Unforgettable Travel Experiences

- **Studying the Skyline:** The birthplace of the modern skyscraper, Chicago is the perfect place to learn about—and appreciate—these dramatic buildings. If you're only in town for a short time, get a quick skyscraper fix by strolling through the heart of downtown. If you have more time, take an architectural tour by foot, bus, bike, or boat. See "Sightseeing Tours" on p. 117.

- **Chilling Out on the Lakefront:** Chicagoans treat the Lake Michigan waterfront as our personal playground. Miles of parkland hug the shoreline; walk to Monroe Harbor for picture-perfect views of downtown, or join active Lincoln Park singles for biking or jogging farther north. See "Staying Active" on p. 121.

- **Riding the Rails:** Find out why the Loop is so named by hopping a Brown Line elevated train (or "the El," for short). Watch the city unfold as the train crosses the Chicago River and screeches past downtown high-rises. See "Getting Around" on p. 27 and "Sightseeing Tours" on p. 117.

- **Escaping Downtown:** You won't really experience Chicago unless you leave downtown and explore some residential areas, whether it's the historic wood-framed homes in Old Town or the eclectic boutiques of Wicker Park. It's one of the best ways to get a feeling for how the people here actually live. See "The Neighborhoods in Brief" on p. 26.

Chicago & Vicinity

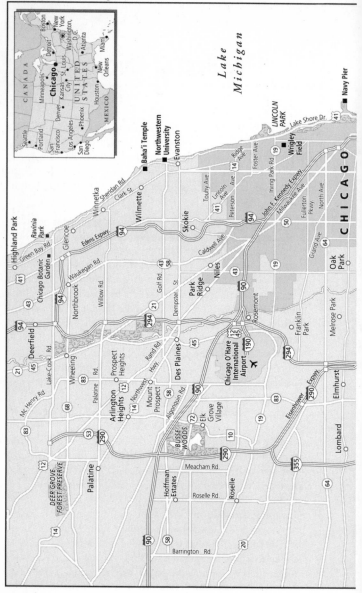

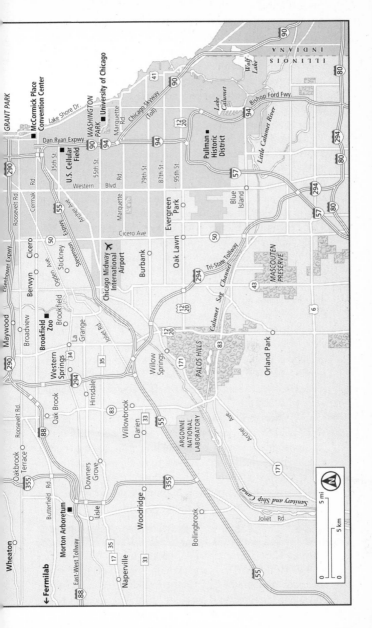

2 The Best Splurge Hotels

- The **Four Seasons** (120 E. Delaware Place; ℂ **800/332-3442;** www.fourseasons.com): A favorite among camera-shy celebrities who want to keep a low profile, the hotel exudes understated luxury; expect discretion, not a lively lobby scene. Where the Four Seasons really shines is its service—the concierges might be the best in town. See p. 39.

- The **Park Hyatt Chicago** (800 N. Michigan Ave.; ℂ **800/ 233-1234;** www.parkchicago.hyatt.com): With its focus on modern design and clean lines, the Park Hyatt feels like one of those cool urban spaces featured in *Architectural Digest.* The coolest feature? Moveable bathroom walls that allow you to soak in the view while you lounge in the tub. See p. 40.

- **The Peninsula Chicago** (108 E. Superior St.; ℂ **866/288- 8889;** http://chicago.peninsula.com): The Chicago outpost of this Asian chain is a seamless blend of classic and modern. The grand public spaces may be a throwback to the past, but the hotel's amenities are ultramodern. The top-notch gym, spa, and indoor swimming pool (filled with natural light) make The Peninsula a must for fitness fanatics. See p. 41.

- The **Ritz-Carlton** (160 E. Pearson St.; ℂ **800/621-6906;** www.fourseasons.com): The Ritz has one of the most welcoming lobbies in town, with bird's-eye views of the city. The guest rooms, decorated in warm shades of yellow and blue, have European-style elegance, and the staff prides itself on granting every wish. See p. 41.

- The **W Chicago Lakeshore** (644 N. Lake Shore Dr.; ℂ **877/ W-HOTELS;** www.whotels.com): The city's only hotel with a lakefront address may try a little too hard to be hip, but it offers a nightclubby vibe that sets it apart from the many cookie-cutter convention-friendly hotels in town. The rooms' color scheme—shades of gray, black, and deep red—are a refreshing change from the chain-hotel look. See p. 44.

3 The Best Moderately Priced Hotels

- **Chicago City Centre Hotel & Sports Club** (300 E. Ohio St.; ℂ **800/HOLIDAY;** www.chicc.com): A real find for budget-conscious families, the City Centre scores big for its amenities: two pools (indoor and outdoor) and free access to the

Lakeshore Athletic Club next door. The location is great, too—just a few blocks from kid-friendly Navy Pier. See p. 45.

- **Hampton Inn & Suites Chicago Downtown** (33 W. Illinois St.; ✆ **800/HAMPTON;** www.hamptoninn.com): The Hampton Inn feels more expensive than it is. The rooms have an upscale urban look, and the indoor pool is a draw for families. The hotel's hot breakfast buffet puts the standard coffee-and-doughnut spread at other motels to shame. See p. 47.

- **Red Roof Inn** (162 E. Ontario St.; ✆ **800/733-7663;** www.redroof-chicago-downtown.com): This is your best bet for the cheapest rates downtown. The rooms don't have much in the way of style, but it fits the bill if you want a central location and plan on using your hotel as a place to sleep rather than hang out. See p. 45.

- **Majestic Hotel** (528 W. Brompton St.; ✆ **800/727-5108;** www.cityinns.com): This neighborhood hotel is tucked away on a residential street just a short walk from Wrigley Field and the lakefront. You won't find lots of fancy amenities, but the atmosphere here has the personal touch of a B&B. See p. 49.

4 The Most Unforgettable Dining Experiences

- **Charlie Trotter's** (816 W. Armitage Ave.; ✆ **773/248-6228**): Charlie Trotter is the city's original celebrity chef, and his intimate restaurant is the first place I steer foodie visitors. The service lives up to Trotter's legendary perfectionism; the chef himself has been known to come out of the kitchen and ask diners why they didn't finish a certain dish. See p. 75.

- **Alinea** (1723 N. Halsted St.; ✆ **312/867-0110**): Widely considered the town's top restaurant of the moment, Alinea has gotten national press for chef Grant Achatz's revolutionary twist on contemporary dining. An added bonus: service that's friendly, not snobby. See p. 74.

- **Gibsons Bar & Steakhouse** (1028 N. Rush St.; ✆ **312/266-8999**): This is the kind of place to live large (literally): The portions are enormous, so you're encouraged to share, which adds to the party atmosphere. See p. 61.

- **foodlife** (Water Tower Place, 835 N. Michigan Ave.; ✆ **312/335-3663**): This is my top pick for a quick, affordable, family-friendly meal downtown. Leaps and bounds beyond the standard mall food court, foodlife offers a wide range of nonchain food stations at affordable prices. See p. 66.

- **The Village** (71 W. Monroe St.; ✆ 312/332-7005): Eating at this Chicago landmark is like taking a trip back in time, from the so-tacky-they're-cool twinkling "stars" embedded in the ceiling to the vintage waiters (some of whom look like they've been working here since the place opened in 1927). See p. 55.

5 The Best Museums

- **Art Institute of Chicago** (111 S. Michigan Ave.; ✆ 312/443-3600): Internationally known for its French Impressionist collection, the Art Institute can also transport you to Renaissance Italy, ancient China, or any number of other worlds. See p. 86.
- **Field Museum of Natural History** (Roosevelt Rd. and Lake Shore Dr.; ✆ 312/922-9410): The Field can easily entertain for an entire day. Exhibits include ancient Egyptian mummies, a full-size Maori meetinghouse, and stuffed figures of the notorious man-eating lions of Tsavo. See p. 97.
- **John G. Shedd Aquarium** (1200 S. Lake Shore Dr.; ✆ 312/939-2438): Sure, you'll find plenty of tanks filled with exotic fish, but the Shedd is also home to some wonderful large-scale re-creations of natural habitats. See p. 98.
- **Museum of Science and Industry** (57th St. and Lake Shore Dr.; ✆ 800/468-6674): Although the exhibits promote scientific knowledge, most have an interactive element that makes them especially fun for families. Some of the classic exhibits— the underground re-creation of the coal mine and the World War II German U-boat—have been attracting crowds for generations. See p. 104.
- **Frank Lloyd Wright Home and Studio** (951 Chicago Ave., Oak Park; ✆ 708/848-1976): The Midwest's greatest architect started out in the Chicago suburb of Oak Park, and his house—now a museum with guided tours—gives a firsthand look at his genius and his influence. See p. 111.

6 The Best Nightlife Experiences

- **Getting the Blues:** Here, in the world capital of the blues, you've got your pick of places to feel them, from the touristy but lively atmosphere of Kingston Mines in Lincoln Park to the roadhouse feel of Buddy Guy's Legends. See "The Music Scene" on p. 156.

- **Taking in a Show:** Chicago is home to a downtown Broadway-style district anchored by beautifully restored historic theaters. Beyond downtown, you'll find a number of innovative independent companies, where the pure love of theater makes up for the low budgets. See "The Performing Arts" on p. 147.
- **Taking in Some Cool Jazz at the Green Mill:** This atmospheric Uptown jazz club is the place to go to soak up smooth sounds from some of the hottest up-and-coming performers on the jazz scene, while the club itself is a living museum of 1930s Chicago. See p. 157.
- **Watching Improv Come Alive:** Chicago is a comedy breeding ground through improv hot spots such as Second City and iO. The shows may soar or crash, but you just might catch one of comedy's future stars. See "Comedy & Improv" on p. 155.

7 The Best Places to Hang with the Locals

- **Shopping the Town:** Michigan Avenue is often touted as a shopper's paradise. For more distinctive items, head to the city's residential districts, where trendy independent clothing boutiques sit next to eclectic home-design stores filled with one-of-a-kind treasures. See chapter 9.
- **Soaking Up Sun at Wrigley Field:** It's a Chicago tradition to play hooky for an afternoon, sit in the bleachers at this historic baseball park, and watch the Cubbies try to hit 'em onto Waveland Avenue. Even if you can't get in, you can still soak in the atmosphere at one of the neighborhood's many watering holes. See "In the Grandstand: Watching Chicago's Athletic Events" on p. 123.
- **Playing in the Sand:** If you're staying at a downtown hotel, you can hit the sands of Chicago's urban beaches almost as quickly as your elevator gets you to the lobby. Oak Street Beach (at Michigan Ave. and Lake Shore Dr.) is mostly for posing; North Avenue Beach, a little farther north along the lakefront path, is home to weekend volleyball games, family beach outings, and a whole lot of eye candy. See "Beaches" on p. 121.

8 The Best Free (or Almost Free) Things to Do

- **Bonding with the Animals at Lincoln Park Zoo:** Occupying a prime spot of Lincoln Park close to the lakefront, the zoo is small enough to explore in an afternoon and varied enough to make you feel as though you've traveled around the world. See p. 102.

- **Listening to Music Under the Stars:** The Grant Park Music Festival presents free classical concerts from June through August in Millennium Park. A few blocks south, you'll find the outdoor dance floor that's home to Chicago SummerDance, where you can learn new dance moves and swing to a variety of live acts. See "Classical Music" on p. 148.
- **Exploring Millennium Park:** This downtown park is Chicago's newest great showcase (and it's an easy walk from downtown hotels). See p. 93.

9 The Best One-of-a-Kind Shops

- **ArchiCenter Shop** (224 S. Michigan Ave.; ✆ **312/922-3432**): Looking for unique, well-designed souvenirs? This store, run by the Chicago Architecture Foundation, should be your first stop. See p. 144.
- **Uncle Fun** (1338 W. Belmont Ave.; ✆ **773/477-8223**): This old-fashioned storefront is crammed with a random assortment of classic dime-store gadgets (hand buzzers, Pez dispensers, rubber chickens) along with an equally eclectic selection of retro bargain-bin items (where else can you pick up a Mr. T keychain?). See p. 139.
- **The T-Shirt Deli** (1739 N. Damen Ave.; ✆ **773/276-6266**): Got a soft spot for those cheesy 1970s "Foxy Lady" T-shirts? Head to the T-Shirt Deli, where the staff will customize shirts while you wait. Come up with your own message, or browse the hundreds of in-stock iron-on decals. See p. 138.

10 The Best Chicago Websites

- **www.metromix.com**: A good place to check restaurant reviews and get an early look at new bars and nightclubs.
- **www.chicagoreader.com**: At the site of the *Chicago Reader,* the city's alternative weekly paper, you'll find extensive coverage of local music and lots of reviews of smaller theater productions.
- **www.cityofchicago.org/exploringchicago**: The official site of the Chicago Office of Tourism gives a good overview of what's happening in town.
- **http://chicago.citysearch.com**: This local edition of the national Citysearch sites offers reviews of restaurants, bars, shows, and shops. Reviews tend to be fairly short, but they keep readers up-to-date on openings.

- **www.chicagoist.com**: Want to see what issues have Chicagoans riled up? Check out this sounding board for local news, which covers everything from government corruption scandals to the latest celebrity sightings.

2

Planning Your Trip to Chicago

After choosing a destination, most prospective travelers have two fundamental questions: "What will it cost?" and "How will I get there?" This chapter answers those and other questions you might have about planning your trip to Chicago.

1 Visitor Information

The **Chicago Office of Tourism,** Chicago Cultural Center, 78 E. Washington St., Chicago, IL 60602 (© **877/CHICAGO** or TTY 866/710-0294; www.choosechicago.com), will mail you a packet of materials with information on upcoming events and attractions. The **Illinois Bureau of Tourism** (© **800/2-CONNECT** or TTY 800/406-6418; www.enjoyillinois.com) will also send you information about Chicago and other Illinois destinations.

2 When to Go

THE CLIMATE

The winters here are no worse than in other northern cities, but it still isn't exactly prime tourist season. The ideal time to visit is summer or fall. Summer offers a nonstop selection of special events and outdoor activities, but you'll also be dealing with the biggest crowds and periods of hot, muggy weather. Autumn days are generally sunny, and the crowds at major tourist attractions grow thinner—you don't have to worry about snow until late November at the earliest. Spring is extremely unpredictable, with dramatic fluctuations of cold and warm weather, and usually lots of rain. If your top priority is indoor cultural sights, winter's not such a bad time to visit: no lines at museums, the cheapest rates at hotels, and the pride that comes with slogging through the slush with the natives.

As close to your departure as possible, check the local weather forecast at the websites of the *Chicago Tribune* newspaper (www.chicagotribune.com) or the **Weather Channel** (www.weather.com).

Chicago's Average Temperatures & Precipitation

	Jan	Feb	Mar	Apr	May	June	July	Aug	Sept	Oct	Nov	Dec
High (°F)	20	34	44	59	70	79	85	82	76	64	48	35
High (°C)	–7	1	7	15	21	26	29	28	24	18	9	2
Low (°F)	14	18	28	39	48	58	63	62	54	42	31	20
Low (°C)	–10	–8	–2	4	9	14	17	17	12	6	–1	–7
Rainfall (in.)	1.6	1.3	2.6	3.7	3.2	4.1	3.6	3.5	3.4	2.3	2.1	2.1

CHICAGO CALENDAR OF EVENTS

The best way to stay on top of the city's current crop of special events is to ask the **Chicago Office of Tourism** (☎ **877/CHICAGO;** www.choosechicago.com) or the **Illinois Bureau of Tourism** (☎ **800/2-CONNECT;** www.enjoyillinois. com) to mail you a copy of the *Chicago Visitor's Guide,* a quarterly publication that surveys special events, including parades, street festivals, concerts, theatrical productions, and museum exhibitions. Also request the latest materials produced by the **Mayor's Office of Special Events** (☎ **312/744-3315,** or call the Special Events Hot Line at 312/744-3370, TTY 312/744-2964; www.cityofchicago. org/specialevents), which keeps current with citywide and neighborhood festivals.

January

Winter Delights. Throughout January and February, the city's Office of Tourism (☎ **877/CHICAGO;** www.choosechicago.com) offers special travel deals to lure visitors during tourism's low season. Incentives include bargain-priced hotel packages, affordable prix-fixe dinners at downtown restaurants, and special music and theater performances. Early January through February.

February

Chicago Auto Show, McCormick Place, 23rd Street and Lake Shore Drive (☎ **630/495-2282;** www.chicagoautoshow.com). More than 1,000 cars and trucks, domestic and foreign, current and futuristic, are on display. The event draws nearly a million visitors. Look for special weekend packages at area hotels that include show tickets. February 8 to 17.

March

St. Patrick's Day Parade. In a city with a strong Irish heritage (and a mayor of Irish descent), this holiday is a big deal. The Chicago River is even dyed green for the occasion. The parade route is along Columbus Drive from Balbo Drive to Monroe Street. The Saturday before March 17.

April

Opening Day. For the **Cubs,** call ☎ **773/404-CUBS** or visit **www.cubs.mlb.com**; for the **White Sox,** call ☎ **312/674-1000**

or go to **www.whitesox.mlb.com**. Make your plans early to get tickets for this eagerly awaited day. Early April.

Chicago Improv Festival. Big names and lesser-known (but talented) comedians converge for a celebration of silliness, with large main-stage shows and smaller, more experimental pieces. Most performances are at the Athenaeum Theater on the North Side (2936 N. Southport Ave.; © **773/935-9810;** www.chicagoimprov festival.org). Last week of April.

May

The Ferris Wheel and Carousel begin spinning again at Navy Pier, 600 E. Grand Ave. (© **312/595-PIER;** www.navypier.com). The rides operate through October. From Memorial Day through Labor Day, Navy Pier also hosts twice-weekly fireworks shows Wednesday nights at 9:30pm and Saturday nights at 10:15 pm.

June

Printers Row Book Fair, Dearborn Street from Congress Parkway to Polk Street (© **312/222-3986;** www.chicagotribune.com/about/custom/events/printersrow). One of the largest free outdoor book fairs in the country, this weekend event celebrates the written word with everything from readings and signings by big-name authors to panel discussions on penning your first novel. First weekend in June.

Chicago Blues Festival, Petrillo Music Shell, Randolph Street and Columbus Drive, Millennium Park (© **312/744-3315**). Muddy Waters would scratch his noggin over the sea of suburbanites who flood into Grant Park every summer to accompany local legends Buddy Guy and Lonnie Brooks on air guitar. Blues Fest is free, with dozens of acts performing over 4 days, but get there in the afternoon to get a good spot on the lawn for the evening show. Second weekend in June.

Ravinia Festival, Ravinia Park, Highland Park (© **847/266-5100;** www.ravinia.com). This suburban location is the open-air summer home of the Chicago Symphony Orchestra and the venue of many first-rate visiting orchestras, chamber ensembles, pop artists, and dance companies. June through September.

Old Town Art Fair, Lincoln Park West and Wisconsin Street, Old Town (© **312/337-1938;** www.oldtowntriangle.com). This juried fine arts fair has drawn crowds to this historic neighborhood for more than 50 years with the work of more than 250 painters, sculptors, and jewelry designers from the Midwest and around the country on display. Second weekend in June.

Grant Park Music Festival, Pritzker Music Pavilion, Randolph Street and Columbus Drive, Millennium Park (℃ **312/742-7638;** www.grantparkmusicfestival.com). The free outdoor musical concerts in the park begin the last week in June and continue through August.

Taste of Chicago, Grant Park (℃ **312/744-3315**). The city claims that this is the largest free outdoor food fest in the nation. Over 10 days of feasting in the streets, scores of Chicago restaurants cart their fare to food stands set up throughout the park. To avoid the heaviest crowds, try going on weekdays earlier in the day. Admission is free; you pay for the sampling. June 27 through July 6.

July

Independence Day Celebration (℃ **312/744-3315**). Chicago celebrates the holiday on the 3rd of July. Concerts and fireworks are the highlights of the festivities in Grant Park. Expect huge crowds. July 3.

Sheffield Garden Walk, starting at Sheffield and Webster avenues (℃ **773/929-9255;** www.sheffieldfestivals.org). Here's your chance to snoop in the lush backyards of Lincoln Park homeowners. Bands, children's activities, and food and drink tents attract lots of singles and young families. July 19 and 20.

Dearborn Garden Walk & Heritage Festival, North Dearborn and Astor streets (℃ **312/632-1241;** http://dearborngardenwalk.com). This event allows regular folks to peer into private gardens on the Gold Coast, one of the most expensive and exclusive neighborhoods in the city. July 13.

Chicago SummerDance, east side of South Michigan Avenue between Balbo and Harrison streets (℃ **312/742-4007**). From July through late August, the city's Department of Cultural Affairs transforms a patch of Grant Park into a lighted outdoor dance venue on Thursday, Friday, and Saturday from 6 to 9:30pm, and Sunday from 4 to 7pm. One-hour lessons are offered from 6 to 7pm. Free admission.

Venetian Night, Monroe Harbor to the Adler Planetarium (℃ **312/744-3315**). This carnival of illuminated boats on the lake is complete with fireworks and synchronized music by the Grant Park Symphony Orchestra. Last Saturday in July.

August

Northalsted Market Days, Halsted Street between Belmont Avenue and Addison Street (℃ **773/868-3010;** www.northalsted. com). The largest of the city's street festivals, held in the heart of this gay neighborhood, Northalsted Market Days offers music on three stages, lots of food and offbeat merchandise, and the best people-watching of the summer. August 2 and 3.

Chicago Air & Water Show, North Avenue Beach (© 312/744-3315). The U.S. Air Force Thunderbirds and Navy Seals usually make an appearance at this hugely popular aquatic and aerial spectacular. Free admission. August 16 and 17.

September

Chicago Jazz Festival, Petrillo Music Shell, Jackson Drive and Columbus Drive, Grant Park (© 312/744-3315). Several national headliners are always on hand at this steamy gathering, which provides a swell end-of-summer bookend opposite to the gospel and blues fests in June. The event is free; come early and stay late. First weekend in September.

Mexican Independence Day Parade, Dearborn Street between Wacker Drive and Van Buren Street (© 312/744-3315). This parade is on Saturday; another takes place the next day on 26th Street in the Little Village neighborhood (© 773/521-5387). September 13.

World Music Festival Chicago, various locations around the city (© 312/742-1938; www.cityofchicago.org/worldmusic). Held at venues around town, the festival brings in top performers from Hungary, Sri Lanka, Zimbabwe, and more to perform traditional, contemporary, and fusion music. Late September.

October

Chicago International Film Festival (© 312/683-0121; www.chicagofilmfestival.org). The oldest U.S. festival of its kind screens films from around the world at various theaters, over 2 weeks, beginning the first Thursday in October.

Chicago Marathon (© 312/904-9800; www.chicagomarathon.com). Sponsored by LaSalle Bank, Chicago's marathon is a major event on the international long-distance running circuit. It begins and ends in Grant Park, but can be viewed from any number of vantage points along the route. October 5.

November

The **Chicago Humanities Festival** takes over locations throughout downtown, from libraries to concert halls (© 312/661-1028; www.chfestival.org). Over a 2-week period, the festival presents cultural performances, readings, and symposiums tied to an annual theme. Early November.

Dance Chicago (© 773/989-0698; www.dancechicago.com). All of the city's best-known dance troupes (including Hubbard

Street and Joffrey Ballet) and many smaller companies participate in this month-long celebration of dance.

Christmas Tree Lighting, Daley Center Plaza, in the Loop (© 312/744-3315). The switch is flipped the day after Thanksgiving, around dusk.

December

A Christmas Carol, Goodman Theatre, 170 N. Dearborn St. (© 312/443-3800; www.goodman-theatre.org). This seasonal favorite, performed for more than 2 decades, runs from about Thanksgiving to the end of December.

3 Getting There

BY PLANE
O'HARE INTERNATIONAL AIRPORT
Chicago's **O'Hare International Airport** (© 773/686-2200; www.flychicago.com; online airport code ORD) has long battled Atlanta's Hartsfield for the title of the world's busiest airport. O'Hare is about 15 miles northwest of the Loop. Depending on traffic, the drive to or from downtown can take anywhere from 30 minutes to more than an hour.

MIDWAY INTERNATIONAL AIRPORT
On the opposite end of the city, the southwest side, is Chicago's other major airport, **Midway International Airport** (© 773/838-0600; www.flychicago.com; online airport code MDW). Although it's smaller than O'Hare and handles fewer airlines, Midway is closer to the Loop and attracts more discount airlines, so you may be able to get a cheaper fare flying into here. (Always check fares to both airports if you want to find the best deal.) A cab ride from Midway to the Loop usually takes about 20 minutes. You can find the latest information on both airports at the city's Department of Aviation website: www.flychicago.com.

ARRIVING AT THE AIRPORT
IMMIGRATION & CUSTOMS CLEARANCE International visitors arriving by air, no matter what the port of entry, should cultivate patience and resignation before setting foot on U.S. soil. U.S. airports have considerably beefed up security clearances in the years since the terrorist attacks of 9/11, and clearing Customs and Immigration can take as long as 2 hours.

People traveling by air from Canada, Bermuda, and certain Caribbean countries can sometimes clear Customs and Immigration at the point of departure, which is much faster.

GETTING INTO TOWN FROM O'HARE & MIDWAY

Taxis are plentiful at both O'Hare and Midway, but getting to town is easily accessed by public transportation as well. A cab ride into the city will cost about $30 to $35 from O'Hare (20 miles from downtown), and $25 to $30 from Midway (10 miles from downtown). *One warning:* Rush hour traffic can be horrendous, especially around O'Hare. If you have to get downtown in a hurry, the El can actually be faster than driving.

If you're not carting enormous amounts of luggage and want to save money, I highly recommend taking public transportation, which is convenient from both airports. For $2, you can take the El (vernacular for the elevated train) straight into downtown.

O'Hare is on the Blue Line; a trip to downtown takes about 40 minutes. Trains leave every 6 to 10 minutes during the day, and every half-hour in the evening and overnight.

Getting downtown from Midway is even faster; the ride on the Orange Line takes 20 to 30 minutes.

Continental Airport Express (© **888/2-THEVAN;** www.airport express.com) serves most first-class hotels in Chicago with its blue-and-white vans. The cost is $25 one-way ($45 round-trip) to or from O'Hare, and $20 one-way ($36 round-trip) to or from Midway. Group rates for two or more people traveling together are less expensive than sharing a cab. The shuttles operate from 4am to 11:30pm.

For limo service from O'Hare or Midway, call **Carey Limousine of Chicago** (© **773/763-0009;** www.ecarey.com) or **Chicago Limousine Services** (© **312/726-1035**). The service will cost about $100 to $150 from Midway and $150 to $200 from O'Hare, excluding gratuity and tax.

BY CAR

Interstate highways from all major points on the compass serve Chicago. Here are approximate driving distances in miles to Chicago: from **Milwaukee,** 92; from **St. Louis,** 297; from **Detroit,** 286; from **Denver,** 1,011; from **Atlanta,** 716; from **Washington, D.C.,** 715; from **New York City,** 821; and from **Los Angeles,** 2,034.

BY TRAIN

When you arrive in Chicago, the train will pull into **Union Station,** 210 S. Canal St., between Adams and Jackson streets (© **312/655-2385**). Bus nos. 1, 60, 125, 151, and 156 all stop at the station, which is just west across the river from the Loop. The nearest El stop is at Clinton Street and Congress Parkway (on the Blue Line), which is a fair walk away, especially when you're carrying luggage.

4 General Travel Resources

SAFETY

Chicago has all the crime problems of any urban center, so use your common sense and stay cautious and alert. At night, you might want to stick to well-lit streets along the Magnificent Mile, River North, Gold Coast, and Lincoln Park, which are all high-traffic areas late into the night. That said, Chicago is still a big city; muggings can—and do—happen anywhere.

Late at night, avoid wandering dark residential streets on the fringes of Hyde Park and Pilsen, which border areas with more troublesome reputations. You can also ask your hotel concierge or an agent at the tourist visitor center about the safety of a particular area.

The El is generally quite safe, even at night, although some of the downtown stations can feel eerily deserted late in the evening. Buses are a safe option, too, especially nos. 146 and 151, which pick up along North Michigan Avenue and State Street and connect to the North Side via Lincoln Park.

5 Specialized Travel Resources

TRAVELERS WITH DISABILITIES

Most disabilities shouldn't stop anyone from traveling in the U.S. There are more options and resources out there than ever before. Most of Chicago's sidewalks, as well as major museums and tourist attractions, are fitted with wheelchair ramps. Many hotels provide special accommodations such as ramps and large bathrooms for visitors in wheelchairs, as well as telecommunications devices for visitors with hearing impairments; inquire when you make your reservation.

Pace, the company that runs bus routes between Chicago and its suburbs, offers paratransit services throughout the area for travelers with disabilities. For information, call ✆ **800/606-1282,** or visit **www.pacebus.com**.

Several **Chicago Transit Authority (CTA)** El stations on each line have elevators. Call the CTA at ✆ **312/836-7000** for a list of accessible stations. All city buses are equipped to accommodate wheelchairs.

For specific information on facilities for people with disabilities, contact the **Mayor's Office for People with Disabilities,** 121 N. LaSalle St., Room 1104, Chicago, IL 60602 (✆ **312/744-7050** or TTY 312/744-4964; www.cityofchicago.org/disabilities). The office is staffed from 8:30am to 4:30pm Monday through Friday.

GAY & LESBIAN TRAVELERS

While it's not quite San Francisco, Chicago is a very gay-friendly city. The neighborhood commonly referred to as "Boys Town" (roughly from Belmont Ave. north to Irving Park Ave., and from Halsted St. east to the lakefront) is the center of gay nightlife—and plenty of daytime action, too. **Gay and Lesbian Pride Week** (✆ 773/348-8243; www.chicagopridecalendar.org), highlighted by a lively parade on the North Side, is a major event each June. In the Lakeview neighborhood, you can pick up several gay publications, including the weekly *Chicago Free Press* (www.chicagofreepress.com) and *Windy City Times* (www.windycitymediagroup.com/index.html), which both cover local news and entertainment. **Horizon Community Services** (✆ 773/929-HELP; www.horizonsonline.org), a gay social service agency with counseling services, support groups, and an antiviolence project, provides referrals daily from 6 to 10pm; you can also call the main switchboard at ✆ 773/472-6469 during the day.

STUDENT TRAVEL

The best resource for students in Chicago is **STA Travel** (www.statravel.com). There is an STA office in Lincoln Park at 2570 N. Clark St., Chicago, IL 60614 (✆ 773/880-8051).

Chicago also has several hostels offering students and other travelers inexpensive, no-frills lodging. The best is **Hostelling International Chicago,** 24 E. Congress Pkwy., in the Loop (✆ 312/360-0300; fax 312/360-0313; www.hichicago.org). Other hostels open year-round include **Arlington House International Hostel,** 616 W. Arlington Place, Chicago, IL 60614 (✆ 800/HOSTEL-5 or 773/929-5380; fax 773/665-5485; www.arlingtonhouse.com), in Lincoln Park, and **Chicago International Hostel,** 6318 N. Winthrop Ave., Chicago, IL 60660 (✆ 773/262-1011; fax 773/262-3632; www.hostelinchicago. com), on the North Side.

6 Staying Connected

INTERNET/E-MAIL
WITHOUT YOUR OWN COMPUTER

To find cybercafes in your destination, check **www.cybercaptive. com** and **www.cybercafe.com**. In Chicago, try **Screenz,** 2717 N. Clark St., 1 block south of Diversey Ave. in Lincoln Park (✆ 773/ 348-9300), a computing center where you can check e-mail, burn CDs of your digital photos, and print out your favorite pictures.

Aside from formal cybercafes, most **youth hostels** and **public libraries** offer Internet access, and though **hotel business centers** are accessible to guests, they can be expensive.

WITH YOUR OWN COMPUTER

In downtown Chicago, both Starbucks and the sandwich chain Cosí have numerous locations with Wi-Fi access. In the southern part of the Loop, the **Harold Washington Library Center,** 400 S. State St. (*C* **312/747-4300**), also has wireless access. Wireless hotspots in Lincoln Park include **Panera Bread,** 616 W. Diversey Pkwy. (*C* **773/528-4556**), and **Argo Tea,** 958 W. Armitage Ave. (*C* **773/388-1880**).

7 Tips on Accommodations

SURFING FOR HOTELS

In addition to the online travel booking sites **Travelocity, Expedia, Orbitz, Priceline,** and **Hotwire,** you can book hotels through **Hotels.com, Quikbook** (www.quikbook.com), and **Travelaxe** (www.travelaxe.net).

HotelChatter.com is a daily webzine offering smart coverage and critiques of hotels worldwide. Go to **TripAdvisor.com** or **Hotel Shark.com** for helpful independent consumer reviews of hotels and resort properties.

It's a good idea to **get a confirmation number** and **make a printout** of any online booking transaction.

FAST FACTS: Chicago

Area Codes The 312 area code applies to the Loop and the neighborhoods closest to it. The code for the rest of the city is 773. Suburban area codes are 847 (north), 708 (west and southwest), and 630 (far west). You must dial "1" plus the area code for all telephone numbers, even if you are making a call within the same area code.

Babysitters Many of the top hotels work with **American ChildCare Service** (*C* **312/644-7300**; www.americanchildcare. com), a state-licensed and insured babysitting service that can match you with a sitter.

Currency The most common bills are the $1 (a "buck"), $5, $10, and $20 denominations. There are also $2 bills (seldom encountered), $50 bills, and $100 bills (the last two are usually not welcome as payment for small purchases).

Coins come in eight denominations: 1¢ (1 cent, or a penny); 5¢ (5 cents, or a nickel); 10¢ (10 cents, or a dime); 25¢ (25 cents, or a quarter); 50¢ (50 cents, or a half-dollar); the gold-colored Sacagawea coin, worth $1; the Presidential $1 coin; and the rare silver dollar.

Customs **What You Can Bring into the United States:** Every visitor more than 21 years of age may bring in, free of duty, the following: (1) 1 liter of wine or hard liquor; (2) 200 cigarettes, 100 cigars (but not from Cuba), or 3 pounds of smoking tobacco; and (3) $100 worth of gifts. These exemptions are offered to travelers who spend at least 72 hours in the United States and who have not claimed them within the preceding 6 months. It is altogether forbidden to bring into the country foodstuffs (particularly fruit, cooked meats, and canned goods) and plants (vegetables, seeds, tropical plants, and the like). International tourists may carry in or out up to $10,000 in U.S. or foreign currency with no formalities; larger sums must be declared to U.S. Customs on entering or leaving, which includes filing form CM 4790. For details regarding U.S. Customs and Border Protection, consult your nearest U.S. embassy or consulate, or **U.S. Customs** (✆ **202/927-1770**; www.customs.ustreas.gov).

What You Can Take Home from the United States:

Canadian Citizens: For a clear summary of Canadian rules, write for the booklet *I Declare,* issued by the **Canada Border Services Agency** (✆ **800/461-9999** in Canada, or 204/983-3500; www.cbsa-asfc.gc.ca).

U.K. Citizens: For information, contact **HM Customs & Excise** at ✆ **0845/010-9000** (from outside the U.K., 020/8929-0152), or consult their website at **www.hmce.gov.uk**.

Australian Citizens: A helpful brochure available from Australian consulates or Customs offices is *Know Before You Go.* For more information, call the **Australian Customs Service** at ✆ **1300/363-263**, or log on to **www.customs.gov.au**.

New Zealand Citizens: Most questions are answered in a free pamphlet available at New Zealand consulates and Customs offices: *New Zealand Customs Guide for Travellers, Notice no. 4.* For more information, contact **New Zealand Customs,** The Customhouse, 17–21 Whitmore St., Box 2218,

Wellington (© **04/473-6099** or 0800/428-786; www.customs. govt.nz).

Dentists The referral service of the **Chicago Dental Society** (© **312/836-7300**; www.cds.org) can help you find an area dentist; you can also get a referral online through their website. Your hotel concierge or desk staff may also keep a list of dentists.

Doctors In the event of a medical emergency, your best bet— unless you have friends who can recommend a doctor—is to rely on your hotel physician or go to the nearest hospital emergency room. **Northwestern Memorial Hospital** also has a **Physician Referral Service** (© **877/926-4664**). Also see "Hospitals" below.

Hospitals The best hospital emergency room in downtown Chicago is, by consensus, at **Northwestern Memorial Hospital,** 251 E. Huron St. (© **312/926-2000**; www.nmh.org), a state-of-the-art medical center right off North Michigan Avenue. The emergency department (© **312/926-5188** or 312/944-2358 for TDD access) is located at 251 E. Erie St., near Fairbanks Court. For an ambulance, dial © **911,** which is a free call.

Internet Access Many Chicago **hotels** have business centers with computers available for guests' use. Computers with Internet access are also available to the public at the **Harold Washington Library Center,** 400 S. State St. (© **312/747-4300**), and at the Internet cafe inside the **Apple** computer store, 679 N. Michigan Ave. (© **312/981-4104**). Most Starbucks coffee shops and McDonald's restaurants in downtown Chicago also have wireless Internet access available. See "Internet/E-Mail" under "Staying Connected" on p. 18.

Laundry The closest laundromat to downtown is **Sudz Coin Laundry,** 1246 N. Ashland Ave. (© **773/218-9630**; www.sudz laundry.com), about a block north of Division Street.

Pharmacies **Walgreens,** 757 N. Michigan Ave. (© **312/664-4000**), is open 24 hours. Both Walgreens and **CVS,** another major chain, have a number of downtown locations.

Police For emergencies, call © **911.** This is a free call (no coins required). For nonemergencies, call © **311.**

Post Office The main post office is at 433 W. Harrison St. (© **312/983-8182**); free parking is available. You'll also find convenient branches in the Sears Tower, the Federal Center

Plaza at 211 S. Clark St., the James R. Thompson Center at 100 W. Randolph St., and a couple of blocks off the Magnificent Mile at 227 E. Ontario St.

Taxes In Chicago, the local sales tax is 9%. Restaurants in the central part of the city, roughly the 312 area code, are taxed an additional 1%, for a total of 10%. The hotel room tax is a steep 14.9%.

Transit Info The CTA has a useful number to find out which bus or El train will get you to your destination: ℂ **836-7000** (from any area code in the city or suburbs) or TTY 836-4949.

Visas For information about U.S. Visas, go to **http://travel. state.gov** and click on "Visas."

3

Getting to Know the Windy City

The orderly configuration of Chicago's streets and the excellent public transportation system make the city quite easy to get around—once you identify and locate a few basic landmarks.

1 Orientation

VISITOR INFORMATION

The **Chicago Office of Tourism** runs a toll-free visitor hot line (© **877/CHICAGO** or TTY 866/710-0294; www.choosechicago. com) and operates two visitor information centers staffed with people who can answer questions. The main visitor center, located in the Loop and convenient to many places that you'll likely be visiting, is on the first floor of the **Chicago Cultural Center,** 77 E. Randolph St. (at Michigan Ave.).

A second, smaller center, the **Chicago Water Works Visitor Center,** is in the old pumping station at Michigan and Chicago avenues in the heart of the city's shopping district. The entrance is on the Pearson Street side of the building, across from the Water Tower Place mall.

The **Illinois Bureau of Tourism** (© **800/2CONNECT** or TTY 800/406-6418; www.enjoyillinois.com) can provide general and specific information 24 hours a day. Many of the bureau's brochures can be ordered online or picked up at the Water Works Visitor Center (see above).

INFORMATION BY TELEPHONE The **Mayor's Office of Special Events** operates a recorded hot line and website (© **312/ 744-3370** or TTY 312/744-2964; www.cityofchicago.org/special events) listing current special events, festivals, and parades occurring throughout the city.

PUBLICATIONS Chicago's major daily newspapers are the *Tribune* and the *Sun-Times. Chicago* magazine is an upscale monthly with good restaurant listings. Even better for short-term visitors is the weekly magazine *Time Out Chicago,* which lists just about everything going on around town during the week, from art openings to theater performances.

CITY LAYOUT

The **Chicago River** forms a Y that divides the city into its three geographic zones: North Side, South Side, and West Side (Lake Michigan is where the East Side would be). The downtown financial district is called **the Loop.** The city's key shopping street is **North Michigan Avenue,** also known as the **Magnificent Mile.** In addition to department stores and vertical malls, this stretch of property north of the river houses many of the city's most elegant hotels. North and south of this downtown zone, Chicago stretches along 29 miles of Lake Michigan shoreline that is, by and large, free of commercial development, reserved for public use as green space and parkland from one end of town to the other.

Today, Chicago proper has about three million inhabitants living in an area about two-thirds the size of New York City; another five million make the suburbs their home.

FINDING AN ADDRESS   Chicago is laid out in a **grid system,** with the streets neatly lined up as if on a giant piece of graph paper.

Point zero is located at the downtown intersection of State and Madison streets. **State Street** divides east and west addresses, and **Madison Street** divides north and south addresses. From here, Chicago's highly predictable addressing system begins. Making use of this grid, it's relatively easy to plot the distance in miles between any two points in the city.

Virtually all of Chicago's principal north-south and east-west arteries are spaced by increments of 400 in the addressing system—regardless of the number of smaller streets nestled between them—and each addition or subtraction of 400 numbers to an address is equivalent to a half-mile. Thus, starting at point zero on Madison Street and traveling north along State Street for 1 mile, you will come to 800 N. State St., which intersects Chicago Avenue. Continue uptown for another half-mile, and you arrive at the 1200 block of North State Street at Division Street. And so it goes, right to the city line, with suburban Evanston located at the 7600 block north, 9½ miles from point zero.

STREET MAPS   Maps are available at the city's visitor information centers at the **Chicago Cultural Center** and the **Chicago**

Chicago Layout

Water Works Visitor Center (see "Visitor Information" on p. 23). You can also print out maps from the Chicago Convention and Tourism Bureau website, **www.choosechicago.com**.

THE NEIGHBORHOODS IN BRIEF

The Loop & Vicinity

Downtown The Loop refers literally to a core of high-rise buildings contained within a rectangular loop of elevated train tracks. Greater downtown Chicago overflows these confines and is bounded by the Chicago River to the north and west, by Michigan Avenue to the east, and by Roosevelt Avenue to the south.

The North Side

Near North/Magnificent Mile North Michigan Avenue from the bridge spanning the Chicago River to its northern tip at Oak Street is known as the Magnificent Mile. Many of the city's best hotels and shops are to be found on and around elegant North Michigan Avenue.

River North Just to the west of the Mag Mile is an old warehouse district called River North. These formerly industrial buildings have been transformed into one of the city's most vital commercial districts, with many of the city's hottest restaurants, nightspots, and art galleries.

The Gold Coast Some of Chicago's most desirable real estate and historic architecture are found along Lake Shore Drive, between Oak Street and North Avenue and along the adjacent side streets.

Old Town West of LaSalle Street, principally on North Wells Street between Division Street and North Avenue, is the residential district of Old Town, which boasts some of the city's best-preserved historic homes. The neighborhood is one of the most expensive residential areas in the city.

Lincoln Park Chicago's most popular residential neighborhood for young singles and urban-minded families is Lincoln Park. Stretching from North Avenue to Diversey Parkway, it's bordered on the east by the huge park of the same name.

Lakeview & Wrigleyville Midway up the city's North Side is a one-time blue-collar, now mainstream middle-class quarter called Lakeview. It has become the neighborhood of choice for many gays and lesbians, recent college graduates, and residents priced out of Lincoln Park. The main thoroughfare is Belmont Avenue, between Broadway and Sheffield Avenue. Wrigleyville is the name given to the neighborhood in the vicinity of Wrigley Field.

The West Side

West Loop Also known as the Near West Side, the neighborhood just across the Chicago River from the Loop is the city's newest gentrification target, as old warehouses and once-vacant lots are transformed into trendy condos.

Bucktown/Wicker Park Centered near the confluence of North, Damen, and Milwaukee avenues, where the Art Deco Northwest Tower is the tallest thing for miles, this resurgent area has hosted waves of immigrants (not to mention writer Nelson Algren). In recent years, it has morphed into a bastion of hot new restaurants, alternative culture, and loft-dwelling yuppies surfing the gentrification wave that's washing over this still-somewhat-gritty neighborhood.

The South Side

South Loop The South Loop—stretching from Harrison Street's historic Printers Row south to Cermak Road (where Chinatown begins), and from Lake Shore Drive west to the south branch of the Chicago River—is now one of the fastest-growing residential neighborhoods in the city.

Pilsen Originally home to the nation's largest settlement of Bohemian-Americans, Pilsen (which derives its name from a city in Bohemia, the Czech Republic) was for decades the principal entry point in Chicago for immigrants of every ethnic background. Centered at Halsted and 18th streets just southwest of the Loop, Pilsen now contains the second-largest Mexican-American community in the U.S.

Hyde Park Hyde Park is like an independent village within the confines of Chicago, right off Lake Michigan and roughly a 30-minute train ride from the Loop. Fifty-seventh Street is the main drag, and the University of Chicago—with all its attendant shops and restaurants—is the neighborhood's principal tenant.

2 Getting Around

The best way to savor Chicago is by walking its streets. Walking isn't always practical, however, particularly when moving between distant neighborhoods and on harsh winter days. In those situations, Chicago's public train and bus systems can get you almost anywhere you want to go.

BY PUBLIC TRANSPORTATION

The **Chicago Transit Authority (CTA)** operates an extensive system of trains and buses throughout the city of Chicago. The sturdy system carries about 1.5 million passengers a day. Subways and elevated trains (known as the El) are generally safe and reliable, although it's advisable to avoid long rides through unfamiliar neighborhoods late at night.

Fares for the bus, subway, and El are $2, with an additional 25¢ for a transfer that allows CTA riders to make two transfers on the bus or El within 2 hours of receipt. Children 6 and under ride free, and those between the ages of 7 and 11 pay $1. Seniors can also receive the reduced fare if they have the appropriate reduced-fare permit (call ☎ **312/836-7000** for details on how to obtain one, although this is probably not a realistic option for a short-term visitor).

The CTA uses credit card–size fare cards that automatically deduct the exact fare each time you take a ride. The reusable cards can be purchased with a preset value already stored, or riders can obtain cards at vending machines located at all CTA train stations and charge them with whatever amount they choose (a minimum of $2 and up to $100). If within 2 hours of your first ride you transfer to a bus or the El, the turnstiles at the El stations and the fare boxes on buses will automatically deduct from your card just the cost of a transfer (25¢). If you make a second transfer within 2 hours, it's free. The same card can be recharged continuously.

Fare cards can be used on buses, but you can't buy a card on the bus. If you get on the bus without a fare card, you'll have to pay $2 cash (either in coins or in dollar bills); the bus drivers cannot make change, so make sure that you've got the right amount before hopping on board.

CTA INFORMATION   The CTA operates a useful telephone information service (☎ **836-7000** or TTY 836-4949 from any area code in the city and suburbs) that functions daily from 5am to 1am. You can also check out the CTA's website at **www.transitchicago.com**.

BY THE EL & THE SUBWAY   The rapid-transit system operates five major lines, which the CTA identifies by color: The **Red Line** runs north-south; the **Green Line** runs west-south; the **Blue Line** runs through Wicker Park/Bucktown west-northwest to O'Hare Airport; the **Brown Line** runs in a northern zigzag route; and the **Orange Line** runs southwest, serving Midway airport. The **Purple Line,** which runs on the same Loop elevated tracks as the Orange and Green lines, serves north-suburban Evanston and runs only during rush hour.

I highly recommend taking at least one El ride while you're here—you'll get a whole different perspective on the city (not to mention fascinating views inside downtown office buildings and North Side homes as you zip past their windows).

BY BUS Other than on foot or bicycle, the best way to get around Chicago's warren of neighborhoods—the best way to actually see what's around you—is by riding a public bus, especially if you're staying near the lakefront, where the trains don't run. Look for the **blue-and-white signs to locate bus stops,** which are spaced about 2 blocks apart. Each bus route is identified by a number and the name of the main street it runs along; the bus that follows Grand Avenue, for example, is the no. 65 Grand.

A few buses that are particularly handy for many visitors are the **no. 146 Marine/Michigan,** an express bus from Belmont Avenue on the North Side that cruises down North Lake Shore Drive (and through Lincoln Park during nonpeak times) to North Michigan Avenue, State Street, and the Grant Park museum campus; the **no. 151 Sheridan,** which passes through Lincoln Park en route to inner Lake Shore Drive and then travels along Michigan Avenue as far south as Adams Street, where it turns west into the Loop (and stops at Union Station); and the **no. 156 LaSalle,** which goes through Lincoln Park and then into the Loop's financial district on LaSalle Street.

BY TAXI

Taxis are easy to hail in the Loop, on the Magnificent Mile and the Gold Coast, in River North, and in Lincoln Park, but if you go far beyond these key areas, you might need to call. Cab companies include **Flash Cab** (© 773/561-4444), **Yellow Cab** (© 312/TAXI-CAB), and **Checker Cab** (© 312/CHECKER).

The meter in Chicago cabs currently starts at $2.25 for the first mile and costs $1.80 for each additional mile, with a $1 surcharge for the first additional rider and 50¢ for each person after that.

BY CAR

PARKING Parking regulations are vigorously enforced throughout the city. Read signs carefully: The streets around Michigan Avenue have parking restrictions during rush hour—and I know from bitter firsthand experience that your car will be towed immediately. Many neighborhoods have adopted resident-only parking that prohibits others from parking on their streets, usually after 6pm each day (even all day in a few areas, such as Old Town).

A safe bet is valet parking, which most restaurants provide for $7 to $10. Downtown you might also opt for a public garage, but you'll have to pay premium prices. Several garages connected with malls or other major attractions offer discounted parking with a validated ticket.

If you'll be spending an entire day downtown, the best parking deal in the Loop is the city-run **Millennium Park** garage (© **312/ 742-7644**), which charges $17 for up to 8 hours (enter on Columbus Dr., 1 block east of Michigan Ave., between Monroe and Randolph sts.). A little farther south are two municipal lots underneath **Grant Park,** with one entrance at Michigan Avenue and Van Buren Street and the other at Michigan Avenue and Madison Street (© **312/616-0600**). Parking costs $14 for the first hour and $22 for 2 to 8 hours.

4

Where to Stay

Downtown Chicago is packed with hotels, thanks to the city's booming convention trade. The competition among luxury hotels is especially intense, with the Ritz-Carlton and Four Seasons winning international awards even as newer properties (such as the James and the Hard Rock) get in on the action. The bad news: low-price lodgings have become even harder to find. Steadily increasing room rates (especially during peak convention season in late spring and during the busy summer months) mean that Chicago is not exactly a budget destination; all the more reason to do some research before booking.

Many Chicago hotels offer a quintessential urban experience: Rooms come with views of surrounding skyscrapers, and the bustle of city life hits you as soon as you step outside the lobby doors. Although every property listed here caters to business travelers, Chicago attracts lots of tourists as well, and you won't have a problem finding family-friendly hotels in the most convenient neighborhoods; this is not a city where luxury hotels have dibs on all the prime real estate.

Hotel rates can vary enormously throughout the year, but I've divided hotels into four categories based on their average rates. "Very Expensive" hotels are luxury properties where rooms cost an average of $400 and up (and are seldom discounted). At "Expensive" hotels, rooms are at least $200 per night, with an upper price limit of $350 to $400. At a "Moderate" hotel, you can usually find a room for less than $200 per night; "Inexpensive" hotels are usually $150 or less per night. The rates given in this chapter are per night and do not include taxes, which are quite steep at 14.9%, nor do they take into account corporate or other discounts. Prices are always subject to availability and vary according to the time of week and season.

RESERVATION SERVICES   For discounted rooms at more than 30 downtown hotels, try **Hot Rooms** (© **800/468-3500** or 773/468-7666; www.hotrooms.com). For a free copy of the annual *Illinois Hotel-Motel Directory,* which also provides information about weekend packages, call the **Illinois Bureau of Tourism** at © **800/2-CONNECT.**

BED & BREAKFAST RESERVATIONS   A centralized reservations service called **At Home Inn Chicago,** P.O. Box 14088, Chicago, IL 60614 (℃ **800/375-7084** or 312/640-1050; fax 312/640-1012; www.athomeinnchicago.com), lists more than 70 accommodations in Chicago. Options range from high-rise and loft apartments to guest rooms carved from a former private club on the 40th floor of a Loop office building.

A group of local B&B owners has formed the **Chicago Bed and Breakfast Association,** with a website that links to various properties throughout the city: **www.chicago-bed-breakfast.com**.

1 The Loop

Strictly speaking, "downtown" in Chicago means the Loop—the central business district, a 6- by 8-block rectangle enveloped by elevated tracks on all four sides. Within these confines are the city's financial institutions, trading markets, and municipal government buildings, making for a lot of hustle and bustle Monday through Friday.

EXPENSIVE

Fairmont Hotel 𝒜𝒜   The Fairmont ranks right up there with the city's most luxurious hotels, offering an array of deluxe amenities and services and regularly hosting high-level politicians and high-profile fundraisers. The only downside is the hotel's location; although it's only a short walk from bustling Millennium Park, the Art Institute, and Michigan Avenue, it's tucked among anonymous office towers, which makes it feel cut off from the life of the city. The grand circular lobby sets the hotel's tone: upscale and lavish rather than cozy and personal (you might wander a while before finding the check-in desk). Still, the rooms are large and inviting, with plush bedding and comfortable chairs (ask for one with a lake view, although city-view rooms aren't bad, either). The posh bathrooms feature extra-large tubs, separate vanity areas, and swivel TVs. The windows open (a rarity in high-rise hotels), so you can enjoy the breeze drifting off Lake Michigan.

200 N. Columbus Dr. (at Lake St.), Chicago, IL 60601. ℃ **800/526-2008** or 312/565-8000. Fax 312/856-1032. www.fairmont.com. 692 units. $129–$389 double; $229–$539 suite. AE, DC, DISC, MC, V. Valet parking $41 with in-out privileges. Subway/El: Red, Green, Orange, Brown, or Blue line to State/Lake. Small pets accepted for a $25 fee. **Amenities:** Restaurant (eclectic); lounge; access to nearby health club; concierge; business center; 24-hr. room service; babysitting; laundry service; 24-hr. dry cleaning. *In room:* A/C, TV w/pay movies, high-speed Internet access, minibar, hair dryer, iron.

Hard Rock Hotel Chicago ⓕ   The good news: This hotel is not located on top of the super-touristy Hard Rock Cafe (which is about a mile or so away in River North). In fact, it is a relatively restrained rehab of one of the city's historic skyscrapers, the 40-story Carbide and Carbon Building. The overall theme here is music: Pop tunes echo throughout the lobby, TV monitors show videos, and glass cases display pop-star memorabilia. But the mix of old and new can be somewhat jarring—the black-and-gray lobby feels like a night-club, while the marble-and-gold-trimmed elevator bank still feels like an office building. The guest rooms are neutral, with modern furniture; the building's larger-than-average windows let in plenty of natural light. The so-called Hard Rock Rooms on the corners of each floor are larger than the standard double rooms and feature chaise lounges for stretching out.

The lobby starts swinging after dark, when the music gets going at the street-level bar, Base (open until 4am, it hosts live music and DJs most nights).

230 N. Michigan Ave. (at Lake St.), Chicago, IL 60601. ⓒ 866/966-5166 or 312/345-1000. Fax 312/345-1012. www.hardrockhotelchicago.com. 387 units. $169–$349 double; from $1,500 suite. AE, DC, DISC, MC, V. Valet parking $39 with in-out privileges. Subway/El: Red or Blue line to State/Lake. **Amenities:** Restaurant (Asian fusion); bar; exercise room; concierge; business services; 24-hr. room service; same-day laundry service; dry cleaning. *In room:* A/C, TV w/DVD player and video games, free high-speed Internet access, minibar, coffeemaker, hair dryer, iron, safe, CD player.

Hotel Burnham ⓕⓕⓕ   If you're looking for a spot with a sense of history, this is it. The historic Reliance Building—one of the first skyscrapers ever built and a highly significant architectural treasure—has been brilliantly restored as an intimate boutique hotel named for Daniel Burnham, whose firm designed the building in 1895. The Burnham is a must for architecture buffs: Wherever possible, the restoration retained period elements—most obviously in the hallways, with their terrazzo tile floors, white marble wainscoting, mahogany door and window frames, and room numbers painted on the translucent glass doors. Rooms are clubby but glamorous, with plush beds, mahogany writing desks, and chaise lounges. The hotel's 19 suites feature a separate living-room area and CD stereo systems. Don't come to the Burnham if you're looking for extensive amenities—the lobby is tiny, as is the exercise room. But the Burnham is one of Chicago's most distinctive hotels, and it's highly recommended for visitors who want a historic location jazzed up with a dash of colorful modern style.

Where to Stay in Chicago

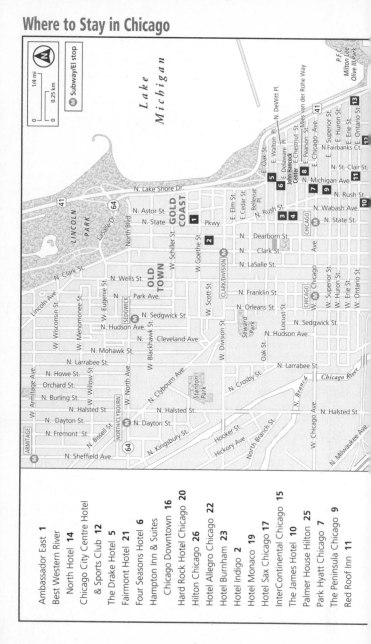

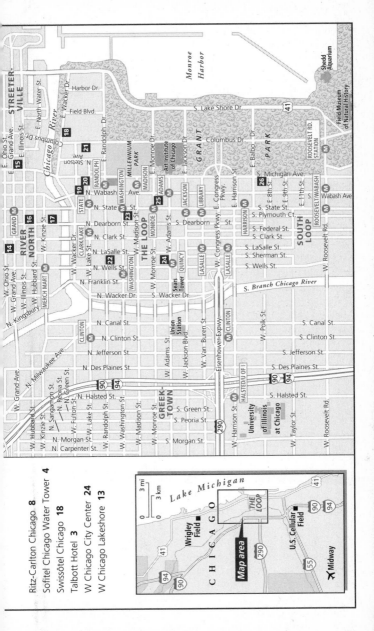

Ritz-Carlton Chicago **8**

Sofitel Chicago Water Tower **4**

Swissôtel Chicago **18**

Talbott Hotel **3**

W Chicago City Center **24**

W Chicago Lakeshore **13**

1 W. Washington St. (at State St.), Chicago, IL 60602. ✆ **866/690-1986** or 312/782-1111. Fax 312/782-0899. www.burnhamhotel.com. 122 units. $299 double; $229–$399 suite. AE, DC, DISC, MC, V. Valet parking $40 with in-out privileges. Subway/El: Red or Blue line to Washington. Pets allowed. **Amenities:** Restaurant (contemporary American); access to nearby health club; concierge; business services; meeting space; 24-hr. room service; laundry service; dry cleaning. *In room:* A/C, TV, free high-speed Internet access, minibar, coffeemaker, hair dryer, iron, safe.

Hotel Monaco 🐟🐟🐟   This 14-story boutique hotel deftly manages to straddle the line between fun and conservative. The stylish decor is a fresh alternative to Chicago's many cookie-cutter business hotels: The rooms feature dramatic deep-red headboards and green-striped walls, while the lobby—with its gold decorative accents and zebra-striped chairs—looks like a 1930s-era salon. Despite the funky feel, the Monaco is rather subdued; it's a place to relax, not pose. The eclectic furniture includes mahogany writing desks and ergonomic chairs; suites come with a two-person whirlpool spa and pull-out queen-size sofa bed. (If you're taller than average, you can request a Tall Room, with longer beds.) All rooms include "meditation stations"—comfy seats tucked into the larger-than-average windows, which are perfect for taking in the cityscape outside (ask for a river view).

225 N. Wabash Ave. (at Wacker Dr.), Chicago, IL 60601. ✆ **800/397-7661** or 312/960-8500. Fax 312/960-1883. www.monaco-chicago.com. 192 units. $169–$329 double; $279–$429 suite. AE, DC, DISC, MC, V. Valet parking $38 with in-out privileges. Subway/El: Brown, Green, or Orange line to Randolph, or Red Line to Washington. Small pets allowed. **Amenities:** Restaurant (American); small fitness room (and access to nearby health club for $10/day); concierge; business center; 24-hr. room service; in-room massage; babysitting; laundry service; dry cleaning. *In room:* A/C, TV w/pay movies, fax, high-speed Internet access, minibar, coffeemaker, hair dryer, iron, safe.

Palmer House Hilton   The longest continually operating hotel in North America (since 1871), the Palmer House was named for legendary State Street merchant prince Potter Palmer. The building's grand Italianate lobby retains a Gilded Age aura (it's worth a look even if you're not staying here), but don't come here expecting to be swept back in time. The massive complex depends heavily on large business groups, so the hotel often feels like an extension of the McCormick Place Convention Center. The good news: Rooms that were previously decorated in drab, motel-worthy colors have been upgraded in the past few years with new, cheerier bedding and carpets. Standard double rooms are quite spacious, with plenty of room to spread out. The bad news: Rooms also feel somewhat spartan, with only two fairly uncomfortable chairs to sit in. Bathrooms are small but serviceable (some rooms come with two bathrooms, a plus for families). Executive Level rooms on the top two floors come with DVD players, thick robes, and complimentary breakfast and afternoon hors d'oeuvres; guests on those floors have use of a lounge and their own concierge.

17 E. Monroe St. (at State St.), Chicago, IL 60603. ℂ **800/HILTONS** or 312/726-7500. Fax 312/917-1797. www.hiltonchicagosales.com. 1,639 units. $129–$350 double; $450–$1,500 suite. AE, DC, DISC, MC, V. Valet parking $35 with in-out privileges; self-parking across the street $25. Subway/El: Red Line to Monroe. **Amenities:** 3 restaurants (the legendary but dated Trader Vic's and 2 American bar and grills); 2 lounges; health club w/indoor pool, Jacuzzi, and sauna for $10/day or $20/entire stay; children's programs; concierge; business center; shopping arcade; room service until 2am; babysitting referrals; laundry service; overnight dry cleaning; executive rooms. *In room:* A/C, TV w/pay movies, high-speed Internet access, minibar, coffeemaker, hair dryer, iron.

Swissôtel Chicago 𝔀𝔀   This sleek, modern hotel is all business and may therefore feel a bit icy to some visitors, but its no-nonsense aura makes it especially attractive to business travelers in search of tranquillity. The hotel's triangular design gives every room a panoramic vista of Lake Michigan, Grant Park, and/or the Chicago River. The spacious rooms have separate sitting areas and warm contemporary furnishings. Business travelers will appreciate the oversize desks (convertible to dining tables), ergonomic chairs, and—in upgraded Business Advantage rooms—CD players and high-speed and Wi-Fi Internet access.

Active travelers will want to break a sweat in the lofty environs of the Penthouse Health Club and Spa, perched on the 42nd floor.

323 E. Wacker Dr., Chicago, IL 60601. ℂ **888/737-9477** or 312/565-0565. Fax 312/565-0540. www.swissotelchicago.com. 632 units. $159–$409 double; $395–$2,500 suite. AE, DC, DISC, MC, V. Valet parking $45 with in-out privileges. Subway/El: Red, Brown, Orange, or Green line to Randolph. **Amenities:** 2 restaurants (steakhouse, American); lounge; penthouse fitness center w/indoor pool, spa, Jacuzzi, and sauna; concierge; business center w/extensive meeting services; 24-hr. room service; massage; babysitting; laundry service; 24-hr. dry cleaning; executive-level rooms. *In room:* A/C, TV w/pay movies, dataport, minibar, coffeemaker, hair dryer, iron.

W Chicago City Center 𝔀   One of two Chicago properties in the hip W hotel chain (the other is the W Chicago Lakeshore; p. 44), this is an oasis of cool in the button-down Loop. Unfortunately, the rooms tend toward the small and dark (most look out into a central courtyard), and the W color scheme—dark purple and gray—doesn't do much to brighten the spaces. Don't stay here if you crave lots of natural light. All W properties pride themselves on their "whatever, whenever" service: Whatever you want, whenever you want it (the modern version of a 24-hr. on-call concierge). If you're the loll-around-in-bed type, this is a great place to do it; the super-comfy beds feature cushiony pillow-top mattresses, soft duvets, and mounds of pillows.

Given its location, this W is foremost a business hotel—although one that's definitely geared toward younger workers rather than crusty old executives.

172 W. Adams St. (at LaSalle St.), Chicago, IL 60603. © 877/W-HOTELS or 312/332-1200. Fax 312/332-5909. www.whotels.com. 368 units. $219–$569 double; $399–$1,500 suite. AE, DC, DISC, MC, V. Valet parking $42 with in-out privileges. Subway/El: Brown Line to Quincy. Pets allowed. **Amenities:** Restaurant (European); bar; exercise room; concierge; business services; 24-hr. room service; in-room massage; babysitting; same-day laundry service; dry cleaning. *In room:* A/C, TV/VCR/DVD w/pay movies, fax, high-speed Internet access, minibar, hair dryer, iron, safe, CD player.

MODERATE

Hotel Allegro Chicago ★ (Value)   Owned by the same company as the Hotel Monaco and the Hotel Burnham (both listed above), the Allegro is my top pick in the Loop for families in search of a fun vibe. Guests enter a lobby with plush, boldly colored furnishings ("Art Deco with punch" is the way one hotel employee described it to me). That whimsical first impression segues into the cheery, pink-walled guest rooms. Most rooms are small (without much space beyond the bed, an armoire, and one chair) but manage to feel cozy rather than cramped; the compact bathrooms, annoyingly, have only pedestal sinks—meaning minimal storage for beauty-product junkies. Suites have separate bedrooms and foldout couches and come with robes, VCRs, and two-person Jacuzzi tubs.

A note to theater fans: The Allegro has access to exclusive seats for many high-profile downtown shows and often promotes special theater packages.

171 W. Randolph St. (at LaSalle St.), Chicago, IL 60601. © 800/643-1500 or 312/236-0123. Fax 312/236-0917. www.allegrochicago.com. 483 units. $149–$299 double; $225–$399 suite. AE, DC, DISC, MC, V. Valet parking $30 with in-out privileges. Subway/El: All lines to Washington. Pets allowed. **Amenities:** Restaurant (northern Italian); lounge; exercise room (and access to nearby health club w/indoor pool for $10/day); concierge; business center; salon; limited room service; same-day laundry service; dry cleaning. *In room:* A/C, TV w/pay movies, free high-speed Internet access, minibar, coffeemaker, hair dryer, iron.

2 South Loop

EXPENSIVE

Hilton Chicago ★★   When it opened in 1927, this massive brick-and-stone edifice billed itself as the largest hotel in the world. Today the Hilton still runs like a small city, with numerous restaurants and shops and a steady stream of conventioneers. The classical-rococo

---

Kids **Family-Friendly Hotels**
_____

Chicago has plenty of options for families on the go. The **Hampton Inn & Suites Chicago Downtown** (p. 47) keeps the kids in a good mood with a pool, Nintendo, and proximity to the Hard Rock Cafe and the Rainforest Cafe. Children 17 and under stay free in their parent's room. Kiddies also stay free at the **Chicago City Centre Hotel & Sports Club** (p. 45), which has a large outdoor pool, access to an indoor pool at an adjoining health club, and is near Navy Pier and the beach. The **Best Western River North Hotel** (p. 47) won't win any prizes for its no-frills decor, but it's one of the best values in River North and lies within walking distance of many family restaurants. The indoor pool and outdoor deck—with great city views—are another big draw.

---

public spaces—including the Versailles-inspired Grand Ballroom and Grand Stair Lobby—are magnificent, but the rest of the hotel falls into the chain-hotel mold: comfortable and well-run but fairly impersonal.

The Hilton is a great choice for families thanks to its vast public spaces, proximity to major museums and Grant Park (where kids can run around), and policy of children 17 and under staying free in their parent's room. Because the Hilton depends heavily on convention traffic, however, those seeking a cozy, romantic getaway should head elsewhere.

720 S. Michigan Ave. (at Balbo Dr.), Chicago, IL 60605. **©** **800/HILTONS** or 312/922-4400. Fax 312/922-5240. www.hilton.com. 1,544 units. $129–$399 double; $179–$7,000 suite. AE, DC, DISC, MC, V. Valet parking $45; self-parking $41. Subway/El: Red Line to Harrison. **Amenities:** 4 restaurants (cafe, American, steakhouse, Irish pub w/live music); 2 lounges; indoor pool; health club w/indoor track, hot tubs, sauna, and steam room; concierge; business center; 24-hr. room service; massage; babysitting; laundry service; 24-hr. dry cleaning. *In room:* A/C, TV w/pay movies, high-speed and Wi-Fi Internet access, minibar, coffeemaker, hair dryer, iron.

3 Near North & the Magnificent Mile
VERY EXPENSIVE
Four Seasons Hotel ✫✫✫ Consistently voted one of the top hotels in the world by frequent travelers, the Four Seasons offers an understated luxury that appeals to publicity-shy Hollywood stars

and wealthy families. The hotel has every conceivable luxury amenity, and in 2007 it underwent a $30-million renovation that changed its look from that of a subdued English country manor to that of a sleek and elegant modern getaway. The hotel's location—hidden between the 30th and 46th floors of the Mag Mile's most upscale vertical mall—epitomizes the hotel's discretion. This is not a place you wander into casually to gawk or people-watch. The elegant rooms feature contemporary furnishings, subdued colors, and modern artworks, and each has windows that open to let in the fresh air. The hotel's elegant fitness center exudes upscale exclusivity (the pool, surrounded by Roman columns, looks like it could be part of an aristocratic private club).

120 E. Delaware Place (at Michigan Ave.), Chicago, IL 60611. © **800/332-3442** or 312/280-8800. Fax 312/280-1748. www.fourseasons.com. 343 units. $495–$695 double; $735–$3,700 suite; weekend rates from $385. AE, DC, DISC, MC, V. Valet parking $36 with in-out privileges; self-parking $30. Subway/El: Red Line to Chicago. Pets accepted. **Amenities:** 2 restaurants (New American, cafe); lounge; indoor pool; fitness center and spa; concierge; business center; 24-hr. room service; babysitting; laundry service; 24-hr. dry cleaning. *In room:* A/C, TV/DVD w/pay movies and video games, free high-speed Internet access, minibar, coffeemaker, hair dryer, iron, safe, CD player.

Park Hyatt Chicago ⭐⭐⭐   For those in search of chic modern luxury, the Park Hyatt is the coolest hotel in town (as long as money is no object). The building occupies one of the most desirable spots on North Michigan Avenue and the best rooms are those that face east, overlooking the bustle of the Mag Mile and the lake in the distance.

Luxury might be the watchword here, but the look is anything but stuffy: Rooms feature Eames and Mies van der Rohe reproduction furniture and window banquettes with stunning city views (another plus: the windows actually open). The comfortable beds are well appointed with several plush pillows. While some hotels might provide a TV and VCR, this is the kind of place where you get a DVD player and flatscreen TV. The spalike bathrooms are especially wonderful: Slide back the cherrywood wall for views of the city while you soak in the tub.

800 N. Michigan Ave., Chicago, IL 60611. © **800/233-1234** or 312/335-1234. Fax 312/239-4000. www.parkchicago.hyatt.com. 198 units. $385–$525 double; $695–$3,000 suite. AE, DC, DISC, MC, V. Valet parking $42 with in-out privileges. Subway/El: Red Line to Chicago. **Amenities:** Restaurant (French/American); lounge; indoor pool; health club w/Jacuzzi and spa; concierge; business center w/computer technical support; 24-hr. room service; massage; babysitting; laundry service; 24-hr. dry cleaning. *In room:* A/C, TV/DVD w/pay movies, free high-speed Internet access, minibar, coffeemaker, hair dryer, iron, safe, CD player, iPod connectivity.

The Peninsula Chicago ★★★★   Taking design cues from the chain's flagship Hong Kong hotel, The Peninsula Chicago mixes Art Deco sensibility with modern, top-of-the-line amenities. Service is practically a religion; when I visit, every staff member I pass makes a point of greeting me. Although the lobby is impressively grand, rooms are average in size (the "junior suites" are fairly small, with living rooms that can comfortably seat only about four people). But the hotel's in-room technology is cutting edge: A small "command station" by every bed allows guests to control all the lights, the TV, and room temperature without getting out from under the covers. The marble-filled bathrooms have separate shower stalls and tubs, vanities with plenty of room to sit, and another "command station" by the bathtub. Add in the flatscreen TVs, and you have a classic hotel that's very much attuned to the present. The bright, airy spa and fitness center fill the top two floors and make a lovely retreat (especially the outdoor deck).

108 E. Superior St. (at Michigan Ave.), Chicago, IL 60611. © 866/288-8889 or 312/337-2888. Fax 312/751-2888. http://chicago.peninsula.com. 339 units. $525–$650 double; $795–$7,500 suite. AE, DC, DISC, MC, V. Valet parking $45 with in-out privileges. Subway/El: Red Line to Chicago. Pets accepted. **Amenities:** 4 restaurants (contemporary, Asian, eclectic, and European bakery); bar; indoor pool w/outdoor deck; fitness center; spa; hot tub; sauna; children's amenities; concierge; business center; 24-hr. room service; in-room massage; babysitting; laundry service; same-day dry cleaning. *In room:* A/C, TV/DVD w/pay movies, fax, free high-speed and Wi-Fi Internet access, minibar, fridge (upon request), coffeemaker, hair dryer, iron, safe.

Ritz-Carlton Chicago ★★★★   Top-notch service and an open, airy setting make this one of Chicago's most welcoming hotels. Perched high atop the Water Tower Place mall, the Ritz-Carlton's lobby is on the 12th floor, with a large bank of windows to admire the city below. Not surprisingly, the quality of the accommodations is of the highest caliber, although the standard rooms aren't very large. Doubles have space for a loveseat and desk but not much more; the bathrooms are elegant but not huge (for extra-large, lavish bathrooms, request a "Premier" room or suite on the 30th floor). Service is the Ritz-Carlton's selling point, whether it's the "compcierge" who helps guests with computer problems, or the "allergy-sensitive" rooms that are cleaned with special nonirritating products and come stocked with nonfeather duvets and pillows and hypoallergenic bath products on request. Lake views cost more but are spectacular (although in all the rooms, you're up high enough that you're not staring into surrounding apartment buildings).

160 E. Pearson St., Chicago, IL 60611. © 800/621-6906 or 312/266-1000. Fax 312/266-1194. www.fourseasons.com. 435 units. $495–$635 double; $710–$4,000

suite; weekend rates from $385. AE, DC, DISC, MC, V. Valet parking $40 with in-out privileges; self-parking $32 with no in-out privileges. Subway/El: Red Line to Chicago. Pets accepted. **Amenities:** 2 restaurants (French, American); 2 lounges; indoor pool; health club w/spa, Jacuzzi, and sauna; children's programs; concierge; business center; 24-hr. room service; in-room massage; babysitting; laundry service; same-day dry cleaning; premier suites. *In room:* A/C, TV/VCR w/pay movies, high-speed Internet access, minibar, hair dryer, iron, safe, CD player.

EXPENSIVE

The Drake Hotel &&& If ever the term "grande dame" fit a hotel, it's The Drake, which opened in 1920. Fronting East Lake Shore Drive, this landmark building is Chicago's version of New York's Plaza or Paris's Ritz. Despite a massive renovation in the 1990s, The Drake feels dated compared to places such as the glitzy Peninsula—but for many, that's part of its charm.

The Drake's public spaces still maintain the regal grandeur of days gone by, but the guest rooms have been modernized with new furniture and linens. Most rooms include a small sitting area with couch and chairs; some have two bathrooms. The lake-view rooms are lovely, and—no surprise—you'll pay more for them. Be forewarned that "city view" rooms on the lower floors look out onto another building, so you'll probably be keeping your drapes shut. Rooms and suites on the Executive Level provide such additional amenities as a generous continental breakfast in a private lounge, free evening hors d'oeuvres, plus a daily newspaper and private concierge assistance.

140 E. Walton Place (at Michigan Ave.), Chicago, IL 60611. © 800/55-DRAKE or 312/787-2200. Fax 312/787-1431. www.thedrakehotel.com. 535 units. $199–$425 double; $279–$495 executive floor; from $545 suite. AE, DC, DISC, MC, V. Valet parking $41 with in-out privileges. Subway/El: Red Line to Chicago. **Amenities:** 3 restaurants (American, steakhouse, seafood); 2 lounges; fitness center; concierge; business center; shopping arcade (including a Chanel boutique); 24-hr. room service; in-room massage; laundry service; 24-hr. dry cleaning; executive-level rooms. *In room:* A/C, TV w/pay movies, high-speed Internet access, minibar, coffeemaker, hair dryer, iron.

InterContinental Chicago && Newer hotels might get all the attention, but the InterContinental remains a sentimental favorite for many Chicagoans. Built as the Medinah Athletic Club in 1929, the building features truly grand details: marble columns, hand-stenciled ceilings, and historic tapestries (for a peek, go in the southern entrance on the corner of Illinois St.).

The guest rooms have two distinct identities, depending on location. Rooms in what's called the Main Building (the '60s addition) have an elegant, urban style, with lots of dark wood, deep yellow walls, and red velvet banquettes. The bathrooms feel brand-new but aren't particularly spacious, with small tubs. Rooms in the Historic

Tower (the original building) have a more old-world feel: elaborately carved headboards, gold accents, and deep-red-and-cream drapes and bedding. The bathrooms, however, are completely modern; most come with both a tub and separate, large shower stall. (You'll pay about $50 more for rooms in the Historic Tower).

The InterContinental's main claim to fame is its junior Olympic-size pool on the top floor, a beautiful 1920s gem surrounded by elegant mosaics (residents of nearby high-rises buy memberships to the hotel's fitness center just so they can swim here).

505 N. Michigan Ave. (at Grand Ave.), Chicago, IL 60611. ℭ **800/327-0200** or 312/944-4100. Fax 312/944-1320. http://chicago.intercontinental.com. 790 units. $235–$350 double; from $500 suite. AE, DC, DISC, MC, V. Valet parking $43 with in-out privileges. Subway/El: Red Line to Grand. **Amenities:** Restaurant (American); 2 lounges; indoor pool; 24-hr. fitness center w/sauna; concierge; 24-hr. business center; 24-hr. room service; massage; babysitting; laundry service; same-day dry cleaning. *In room:* A/C, TV w/pay movies, high-speed and Wi-Fi Internet access, minibar, coffeemaker, hair dryer, iron, safe.

Sofitel Chicago Water Tower ☆☆

The Sofitel aims to impress by drawing on the city's tradition of great architecture. French architect Jean-Paul Viguier created a building that's impossible to pass without taking a second look: a soaring, triangular white tower that sparkles in the sun. But the place doesn't take itself too seriously, as you'll see when you walk in the airy lobby and check out the luminescent floor tiles that change color in a never-ending light show. The hotel's bright, stylish Café des Architects has become a favorite business lunch spot for locals.

The guest rooms feature contemporary decor with natural beechwood walls and chrome hardware. All the rooms enjoy good views of the city (but the privacy-conscious will want to stay on the upper floors, where they won't be on display to surrounding apartment buildings). The standard doubles are fairly compact—but thanks to large picture windows, the spaces don't feel cramped. The luxurious marble bathrooms are quite spacious.

20 E. Chestnut St. (at Wabash St.), Chicago, IL 60611. ℭ **800/SOFITEL** or 312/324-4000. Fax 312/324-4026. www.sofitel.com. 415 units. $240–$555 double; $370–$685 suite. AE, DC, DISC, MC, V. Valet parking $40. Subway/El: Red Line to Chicago. Small pets accepted. **Amenities:** Restaurant (French cafe); bar; fitness center; concierge; business center; 24-hr. room service; babysitting; laundry service; same-day dry cleaning. *In room:* A/C, TV w/pay movies, high-speed Internet access, minibar, hair dryer, iron, safe.

Talbott Hotel ☆☆ *Finds*

With the feel of an upscale European inn—and service that competes with upscale properties such as the Ritz-Carlton—the Talbott is one of the city's best small, independent hotels. The cozy, wood-lined lobby has the secluded, intimate feel of a private English club, with roaring fireplaces in the winter and leather couches perfect for curling up with a cup of tea. Proprietor Basil Kromelow takes a keen personal interest in the hotel's decor: Most of the gorgeous antiques strewn throughout are purchases from Kromelow's European shopping trips.

The larger-than-average rooms—which were completely renovated in 2006—are decorated in soothing neutral tones, with furniture chosen for its residential feel (such as carved-wood desks), European linens, and plasma TVs. Perhaps surprising for a property that feels so traditional, the Talbott is also at the forefront of guest-service technology; the lights turn on automatically when guests enter their rooms, and a high-tech sensor system shows housekeeping when a room is occupied—so no one will barge in to make up your room while you're enjoying a late-morning sleep-in.

20 E. Delaware Place (between Rush and State sts.), Chicago, IL 60611. © 800/TALBOTT or 312/944-4970. Fax 312/944-7241. www.talbotthotel.com. 149 units. $169–$449 standard kings; $260–$671 suites. AE, DC, DISC, MC, V. Valet parking $40 with in-out privileges; self-parking $30. Subway/El: Red Line to Chicago. **Amenities:** Restaurant (Italian); lounge; complimentary access to nearby health club; concierge; business services; 24-hr. room service; laundry service; dry cleaning. *In room:* A/C, TV, high-speed and Wi-Fi Internet access, minibar, coffeemaker, hair dryer, iron, safe.

W Chicago Lakeshore ★★   If you've had your fill of cookie-cutter chain hotels, the W has a fun, relaxed vibe that appeals to younger travelers. The compact rooms are decorated in deep red, black, and gray—some visitors have told me they find the color scheme gloomy, while others think it's a welcome change from the sterile, neutral decor that fills so many other hotels. Although the Asian-inspired bathrooms are stylish, the wooden shades that separate them from the bedroom don't make for much privacy. In W-speak, rooms and suites are designated "wonderful" (meaning standard, with a city view) or "spectacular" (meaning a lake view, for which you'll pay more). I actually prefer the "wonderful" rooms with their dramatic city views. Although the W boasts of being the only hotel in Chicago with a location on the lake, it is separated from the water by busy Lake Shore Drive, so don't expect to step onto a sandy beach from the lobby. Still, the hotel is within easy reach of the lakefront walking paths and tourist magnet Navy Pier.

644 N. Lake Shore Dr. (at Ontario St.), Chicago, IL 60611. © 877/W-HOTELS or 312/943-9200. Fax 312/255-4411. www.whotels.com. 520 units. $219–$429 double; from $399 suite. AE, DC, DISC, MC, V. Valet parking $44 with in-out privileges. Subway/El: Red Line to Grand. Pets accepted. **Amenities:** Restaurant (Mediterranean);

bar; pool; exercise room; spa; concierge; business center; 24-hr. room service; in-room massage; babysitting; same-day laundry service; dry cleaning. *In room:* A/C, TV/VCR/DVD w/pay movies, high-speed and Wi-Fi Internet access, minibar, cof-feemaker (on request), hair dryer, iron, safe, CD player.

MODERATE

Chicago City Centre Hotel & Sports Club ★★ *Kids* *Value*   The soaring modern atrium lobby is impressive, as is the location east of the Magnificent Mile and close to the Ohio Street Beach and Navy Pier. Although the public spaces have the impersonal feel of a con-ference center, the rooms are cheerily decorated, and the large win-dows allow sweeping city views from the upper floors. (I recommend the rooms on the north side of the building, which look toward the Hancock Building.) But it's the amenities that help this hotel stand out, making it one of the best values in the city.

Fitness devotees will delight in the fact that the hotel adjoins the Lakeshore Athletic Club, where guests may enjoy the extensive facil-ities free of charge (including an indoor pool, fitness classes, and sauna); you don't even have to go outside to get there. The hotel also has its own spacious outdoor pool and sun deck; in the summer you can sit back and enjoy a drink at the outdoor bar, Breezes. (Be fore-warned, however, that the hotel fills up during summer vacation; book as far in advance as possible for July–Aug).

300 E. Ohio St. (at Fairbanks Court), Chicago, IL 60611. ✆ **800/HOLIDAY** or 312/787-6100. Fax 312/787-6259. www.chicc.com. 500 units. $109–$270 double. AE, DC, DISC, MC, V. Self-parking $38. Subway/El: Red Line to Grand. **Amenities:** 3 restaurants (American, cafe); bar; outdoor and indoor pools; complimentary access to nearby health club w/whirlpool and sauna; concierge; business center; 24-hr. room service; babysitting; laundry room; dry cleaning; executive-level rooms. *In room:* A/C, TV w/pay movies and video games, high-speed Internet access, cof-feemaker, hair dryer, iron, safe.

INEXPENSIVE

Red Roof Inn ★ *Value*   This is your best bet for low-price lodgings in downtown Chicago. The location is the main selling point: right off the Magnificent Mile (and within blocks of the Ritz-Carlton and The Peninsula, where rooms will cost you at least three times as much). The guest rooms are stark and small, but the linens and car-peting are clean and relatively new. Ask for a room facing Ontario Street, where at least you'll get western exposure and some natural light (rooms in other parts of the hotel look right into neighboring office buildings). The bathrooms are tiny but spotless. You're not going to find much in the way of style or amenities here—but then you don't stay at a place like this to hang out in the lobby (except, maybe, to sip the free coffee that's available there 24 hr.).

162 E. Ontario St. (half-block east of Michigan Ave.), Chicago, IL 60611. © 800/733-7663 or 312/787-3580. Fax 312/787-1299. www.redroof-chicago-downtown.com. 195 units. $100–$140 double. AE, DC, DISC, MC, V. Valet parking $33 with in-out privileges. Subway/El: Red Line to Grand. *In room:* A/C, TV w/pay movies and video games, dataport, hair dryer, iron.

4 River North

EXPENSIVE

Hotel Sax Chicago 🎭🎭 In 2007, a $17-million renovation transformed the former House of Blues Hotel into the new Hotel Sax Chicago, a luxury property with a bohemian boutique feel. While the lobby is certainly grand—with Italian marble floors and *trompe l'oeil* candelabras—the adjoining lounge, Crimson, goes for a Middle-Eastern vibe, with exotic rugs, jewel tones, and floor-to-ceiling screens and mirrors. This eclectic sensibility carries over to the guest rooms, which feature wingback chairs covered in snakeskin and side tables constructed entirely of mirrored panels. Despite the eye-catching decor, one of the hotel's biggest selling points remains its location in the entertainment-packed Marina Towers complex. Within steps of the hotel, you've got a bowling alley, a marina with boat rentals, the riverside Smith & Wollensky steakhouse (an outpost of the New York restaurant), the innovative Bin 36 wine bar and restaurant (p. 68), and the House of Blues music hall and restaurant (p. 161; don't miss its gospel brunch on Sun).

333 N. Dearborn St. (at the river), Chicago, IL 60610. © 877/569-3742 or 312/245-0333. Fax 312/923-2444. www.hotelsaxchicago.com. 353 units. $269–$449 double; $629–$849 suite. AE, DC, DISC, MC, V. Valet parking $40 with in-out privileges. Subway/El: Brown Line to Clark/Lake, or Red Line to Grand. Pets accepted. **Amenities:** Lounge; access to Crunch fitness center for $15 per day; concierge; business center; 24-hr. room service; babysitting; laundry service; same-day dry cleaning. *In room:* A/C, TV w/pay movies and video games, Wi-Fi, minibar, coffeemaker, hair dryer, iron, safe, multiline telephone.

The James Hotel One of the city's newest hotels (opened in 2006), The James blurs the line between upscale luxury and stylish boutique. Because of its close proximity to North Michigan Avenue shopping, River North nightlife, and the Loop theater district, The James attracts even locals to its sleek, secluded J Bar. Guest rooms get a modern treatment, with private dining niches, reproductions of Mies Van der Rohe chairs and Saarinen tables, plasma TVs, and an iPod/mp3-player docking station. If your view is an interior one, don't fret; what looks like a dismal wall during the day becomes a giant screen for a delightfully frantic black and white animated film when the sun goes down. Bathrooms are well appointed with slate and marble accents and thick robes for lounging.

55 E. Ontario St. (at Rush St.), Chicago, IL 60611. © **877/526-3755** or 312/337-1000 www.jameshotels.com. 297 units (including 52 studios). $189–$529 double; $229–$569 studio; $289–$629 loft; $329–$669 apartment; $1,400–$2,000 penthouse loft. AE, DISC, MC, V. Valet parking $42. Subway/El: Red Line to Grand. Pets welcome. **Amenities:** Restaurant (steakhouse); fitness room; concierge; business center; 24-hr. room service; laundry; dry cleaning. *In room:* AC, TV w/pay movies, fax, high-speed Internet access, minibar, coffeemaker, hair dryer, iron, safe, stereo with iPod/mp3-player dock.

INEXPENSIVE

Best Western River North Hotel *Value Kids*   This former motor lodge isn't going to win any design prizes, but it's got some of the most affordable rates to be found in this busy neighborhood. Rooms are spacious if rather generic (with comfortable bedding and down pillows); the bathrooms, though no-frills, are spotless. One-room suites have a separate sitting area, while other suites have a separate bedroom; all suites come with a sleeper sofa (the Family Suite has two separate bedrooms and two bathrooms). A big selling point for families is the indoor pool, with an adjoining outdoor roof deck (a small fitness room looks out onto the pool, for parents who want to work out while the kids splash around). The almost unheard-of free parking in the hotel's parking lot can add up to significant savings for anyone who drives here for a visit. There's a 2-night minimum for weekend stays May through October.

125 W. Ohio St. (at LaSalle St.), Chicago, IL 60610. © **800/528-1234** or 312/467-0800. Fax 312/467-1665. www.rivernorthhotel.com. 150 units. $159–$199 double; $225–$295 suite. AE, DC, DISC, MC, V. Free parking for guests (1 car per room) with in-out privileges. Subway/El: Red Line to Grand. **Amenities:** Restaurant (pizzeria); lounge; indoor pool; exercise room; room service; laundry service; same-day dry cleaning. *In room:* A/C, TV w/pay movies and video games, high-speed and Wi-Fi Internet access, coffeemaker, hair dryer, iron, safe.

Hampton Inn & Suites Chicago Downtown *Value Kids*   This family-friendly hotel manages to appeal to both adults and kids—the Prairie-style lobby and breakfast lounge give the place a tranquil feel, while the indoor pool and free hot breakfast are a plus for families. Built in 1998, the hotel still feels brand-new; the rooms have an urban look, with dark wood furniture and plush duvets. You can book a standard room, which includes a desk, armchair, and ottoman; a studio, which has a microwave, sink, and minifridge along one wall; or a suite, which includes a kitchenette, separate bedroom, and VCR. The complimentary continental breakfast with two hot items per day, served in an attractive second-floor lounge, can save families money on food; you won't need much lunch if you fill up here each morning.

33 W. Illinois St. (at Dearborn St.), Chicago, IL 60610. © **800/HAMPTON** or 312/832-0330. Fax 312/832-0333. www.hamptoninn.com. 230 units. $159–$299 double; $199–$309 suite. Children 17 and under stay free in parent's room. AE, DC, DISC, MC, V. Valet parking $38 with in-out privileges. Subway/El: Red Line to Grand. **Amenities:** Restaurant (Italian); indoor pool w/Jacuzzi and sun deck; exercise room w/sauna; business center; room service; laundry and dry-cleaning service. *In room:* A/C, TV w/pay movies and video games, high-speed Internet access, coffeemaker, hair dryer, iron, safe.

5 The Gold Coast

EXPENSIVE

Ambassador East ★★   The glory days of the Ambassador East, when stars shacked up here during layovers or touring stops in Chicago, are ancient history.

Although it's now more low profile than in the past, the Ambassador still retains a sense of elegance, from the large floral arrangements in the lobby to the mahogany four-poster beds in the king-size rooms. Executive suites have separate sitting areas; celebrity suites (named for the stars who have crashed in them) come with a separate bedroom, two bathrooms, a small kitchen, and a dining room. Most extravagant is the Presidential Suite, which boasts a canopied terrace, marble fireplace, oval dining room, and full-size refrigerator. One nod to modern times is the "Get Fit" rooms, which come with treadmills and a minibar stocked with healthy snacks.

1301 N. State Pkwy. (1 block north of Division St.), Chicago, IL 60610. © **888/506-3471** or 312/787-7200. Fax 312/787-4760. www.theambassadoreasthotel.com. 285 units. $189–$299 double; from $400 suite. AE, DC, DISC, MC, V. Valet parking $34 with in-out privileges. Subway/El: Red Line to Clark/Division. **Amenities:** Restaurant (contemporary American); small fitness room; concierge; business center; 24-hr. room service; babysitting; 24-hr. laundry service; dry cleaning. *In room:* A/C, TV w/pay movies, high-speed Internet access, minibar, coffeemaker, hair dryer, iron, safe.

MODERATE

Hotel Indigo ★   An accessible version of the boutique hotel concept, the Indigo is perfect for anyone looking for a cool (but not too edgy) alternative to the cookie-cutter business hotel. The bright, beachy decor makes the place feel more like a tropical resort than an urban hotel.

But it's the guest rooms that really make an impact. Rather than the dark wood furniture and generic carpeting found in so many chain hotels, rooms here are light and bright with blonde hardwood floors and white wood furniture. The king rooms on the north side of the building tend to be larger, but they also look out on neighboring buildings (and, in some cases, the fire escape). If you don't need a lot of room to spread out, the queen rooms (on the south side of the building) are small but have lovely views of downtown and plenty of natural light.

1244 N. Dearborn St. (1 block north of Division St.), Chicago, IL 60610. © **866/2-INDIGO** or 312/787-4980. Fax 312/787-4069. www.goldcoastchicagohotel.com. 165 units. $169–$269 double. AE, DC, DISC, MC, V. Valet parking $35 with in-out privileges. Subway/El: Red Line to Clark/Division. Pets accepted. **Amenities:** Restaurant (American); lounge; exercise room; spa services; concierge; business center; room service; same-day dry cleaning. *In room:* A/C, TV w/pay movies and video games, high-speed and Wi-Fi Internet access, coffeemaker, hair dryer, iron, safe.

6 Lincoln Park & the North Side

INEXPENSIVE

Best Western Hawthorne Terrace *(Value)* If you're looking for a neighborhood inn away from the tourist hordes, this independently-owned spot fits the bill. Located in Lakeview—within walking distance of Wrigley Field, Lake Michigan, and the Lincoln Park walking and bike paths—the hotel is set back from busy Broadway Avenue, thanks to a charmingly landscaped terrace (a good spot to enjoy your complimentary continental breakfast when the weather's nice). Inside, the relatively large rooms—decorated in standard motel decor—won't win extra style points, but most are bright and cheery, with spotless bathrooms (another plus: many rooms have two windows, a bonus if you crave natural light). The ground-level exercise room is especially welcoming, with large windows to let in light and a glass-enclosed hot tub. The hotel's extremely varied clientele— from business travelers in search of a homey environment, to diehard baseball fans, to gay travelers in town for the annual Gay Pride Parade—is part of its charm.

3434 N. Broadway Ave. (at Hawthorne Place), Chicago, IL 60657. © **888/401-8781** or 773/244-3434. Fax 773/244-3435. www.hawthorneterrace.com. 59 units. $149–$229 double and suites. Rates include continental breakfast. AE, DC, DISC, MC, V. Valet parking $20 with in-out privileges. Subway/El: Red Line to Addison. **Amenities:** Exercise room w/hot tub and sauna; business services; concierge; same-day dry cleaning. *In room:* A/C, TV w/pay movies, free Wi-Fi, fridge, microwave, coffeemaker, hair dryer, iron.

Majestic Hotel *(Finds)* Located on a charming tree-lined street—but convenient to the many restaurants and shops of Lincoln Park—this is a good choice for anyone who wants a quiet retreat rather than a see-and-be-seen spot. Guests receive a complimentary continental breakfast, 24-hour coffee and tea service, and afternoon cookies in the lobby. Some of the larger suites—the most appealing are those with sun porches—offer butler's pantries with a fridge, microwave, and wet bar. Most of the other rooms are fairly dark (since you're surrounded by apartment buildings on almost all sides), and you should avoid the claustrophobic single rooms with alley views. Ideally suited for enjoying the North Side, the Majestic is only a short walk from both Wrigley Field and the lake.

528 W. Brompton St. (at Lake Shore Dr.), Chicago, IL 60657. ℂ **800/727-5108** or 773/404-3499. Fax 773/404-3495. www.cityinns.com. 52 units. $99–$179 double; $129–$219 suite. Rates include continental breakfast. AE, DC, DISC, MC, V. Self-parking $22 in nearby garage with no in-out privileges. Subway/El: Red Line to Addison; walk several blocks east to Lake Shore Dr. and then 1 block south. **Amenities:** Free passes to nearby Bally's health club; secretarial services; limited room service; laundry service; same-day dry cleaning. *In room:* A/C, TV w/pay movies, dataport, free Wi-Fi, minibar, hair dryer, iron.

5

Where to Dine

Joke all you want about bratwurst and deep-dish pizza; Chicago is a genuine culinary hot spot. One of the city's most creative dining spots, Alinea, was even named the top restaurant in the United States by *Gourmet* magazine in 2007 (take that, New York and San Francisco!). The city's top chefs consistently win national awards and make appearances on the Food Network, while we locals try to keep up with all the new restaurant openings.

What makes eating out in Chicago fun is the variety. We've got it all: stylish see-and-be-seen spots, an amazing array of steakhouses, chef-owned temples to fine dining, and every kind of ethnic cuisine you could possibly crave. Plus—yes—some not-to-be-missed deep-dish pizza places.

I've divided restaurants in this chapter into four price categories: "Very Expensive" means that most entrees cost $25 to $30 (and sometimes more); "Expensive" indicates that most entrees run from $18 to $25; "Moderate" means that most entrees are $20 or less; and at an "Inexpensive" place, they cost $15 or less.

To find out more about restaurants that have opened since this book went to press, check out the *Chicago Tribune*'s entertainment website (**www.metromix.com**), the websites for the monthly magazine *Chicago* (**www.chicagomag.com**) and the weekly *Time Out Chicago* (**www.timeoutchicago.com**), and the entertainment/ nightlife website **http://chicago.citysearch.com**.

1 The Loop

In keeping with their proximity to the towers of power, many of the restaurants in the Loop and its environs feature expense-account-style prices, but it's still possible to dine here for less than the cost of your hotel room.

VERY EXPENSIVE

Everest ★★★ ALSATIAN/FRENCH   Towering high above the Chicago Stock Exchange, Everest is an oasis of fine-dining civility, a place where you can taste the creations of one of Chicago's top chefs

Dining in the Loop, West Loop, Magnificent Mile, Gold Coast & River North

52

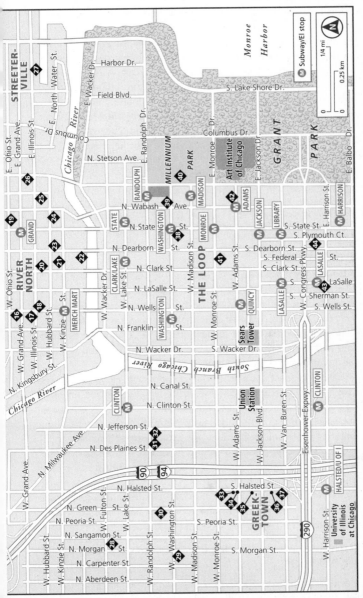

while enjoying one of the city's top views. The space is nothing dramatic (it looks like a high-end corporate dining room), but the focus here is the view, the food, and you (the service team seamlessly anticipates your every need). Chef Jean Joho draws inspiration from the earthy cuisine of his native Alsace, and mixes what he calls "noble" and "simple" ingredients, such as caviar or foie gras with potatoes or turnips. While the menu changes frequently, the salmon soufflé and cream-of-Alsace-cabbage soup with smoked sturgeon and caviar are popular appetizers; signature entrees include roasted Maine lobster in Alsace Gewürztraminer butter and ginger, and poached tenderloin of beef cooked *pot-au-feu* style and served with horseradish cream. Desserts are suitably sumptuous, and the wine list offers some wonderful American and Alsatian selections.

440 S. LaSalle St., 40th floor (at Congress Pkwy.). ℂ 312/663-8920. www.everest restaurant.com. Reservations required. Main courses $27–$46; menu degustation $89; 3-course pretheater dinner $49. AE, DC, DISC, MC, V. Tues–Thurs 5:30–9pm; Fri 5:30–9:30pm; Sat 5–10pm. Complimentary valet parking. Subway/El: Brown Line to LaSalle/Van Buren, or Red Line to Adams.

EXPENSIVE

Atwood Café 𝒦𝒦 *(finds)* AMERICAN   If you're tired of the exotic menus at trendy restaurants, Atwood Café will come as a welcome relief. Located in the historic Hotel Burnham, this place combines a gracious, 1900-era feel with a fresh take on American comfort food. The dining room—one of my favorites in the city—mixes elegance and humor with soaring ceilings; lush velvet curtains; and whimsical, colorful china and silverware.

Executive Chef Heather Terhune dabbles in global influences (most notably Asian and Southwestern) here, but the vast majority of the dishes are straightforward American. Recent entree selections included maple-grilled pork chops with three-cheese macaroni; braised lamb shank with lemon zest–mint pesto; and spinach tagliatelle with bacon, peas, and shrimp in a garlic cream sauce. In the winter, try one of the signature potpies. Terhune began as a pastry chef, so desserts are a high point of Atwood Café's menu. Seasonal fruit is the basis for cobblers, trifles, and pies; for a decadently rich experience, tackle the banana-and-white-chocolate bread pudding.

1 W. Washington St. (at State St.). ℂ 312/368-1900. www.atwoodcafe.com. Main courses $18–$26. AE, DC, DISC, MC, V. Mon–Fri 7–10am; Sat 8–10am; Sun 8am–3pm; Mon–Sat 11:30am–3:45pm; Sun–Thurs 4:30–10pm; Fri–Sat 5–11pm. Subway/El: Red Line to Washington.

Park Grill 𝒦𝒦 AMERICAN   Location, location, location—it's what sets Park Grill apart from all the other upscale comfort-food restaurants in town. Set in the middle of Millennium Park, a hugely popular gathering spot along Michigan Avenue and Randolph Street, Park Grill makes a great stop after a late-afternoon stroll or before a summer concert at the Pritzker Music Pavilion (since this is a popular preshow dinner spot, definitely make a reservation). The menu highlights American favorites, some prepared simply (grilled leg of lamb and rotisserie chicken), others featuring a more international twist, such as pappardelle pasta with littleneck clams, chorizo sausage, leeks, and basil; and braised rabbit. For lighter appetites, there are a number of fish dishes, salads, and some thin-crust pizzas. Lunch selections include a good mix of sandwiches—everything from Cajun chicken breast and barbecue beef to a smoked-salmon club and BLT with truffle mayonnaise. There's also a kids' menu.

11 N. Michigan Ave. (at Madison St.). ℭ 312/521-PARK. Reservations recommended. Main courses $10–$21 lunch, $17–$41 dinner. AE, DC, MC, V. Sun–Thurs 11am–9:30pm; Fri–Sat 11am–10:30pm. Subway/El: Red Line to Washington or Brown, Orange, Purple, or Green line to Madison.

Russian Tea Time *Finds* RUSSIAN/TEA   Russian Tea Time is far from being the simple tea cafe that its name implies. Reading through this family-owned restaurant's extensive menu is like taking a tour through the cuisine of czarist Russia and the former Soviet republics (for Russian neophytes, all the dishes are well described). The atmosphere is old-world and cozy, with lots of woodwork and a friendly staff. Start off a meal with potato pancakes, blini with Russian caviar, or chilled smoked sturgeon; if you can't decide, there are a number of mixed appetizer platters to share. For the best sampling of old Russia, try the beef stroganoff; *kulebiaka* (meat pie with ground beef, cabbage, and onions); or roast pheasant served with a brandy, walnut, pomegranate sauce, and brandied prunes.

77 E. Adams St. (between Michigan and Wabash aves.). ℭ 312/360-0000. www. russianteatime.com. Reservations recommended. Main courses $15–$27. AE, DC, DISC, MC, V. Sun–Thurs 11am–9pm; Fri–Sat 11am–midnight (the restaurant sometimes closes earlier during the summer months). Tea service daily 2:30–4:30pm. Subway/El: Brown, Purple, Green, or Orange line to Adams; or Red Line to Monroe or Jackson.

MODERATE

The Village *Finds* ITALIAN   The Village, complete with a midnight-blue ceiling, twinkling "stars," and banquettes tucked into private corners, is the kind of pan-Chicago place where you might see one man in a tux and another in shorts. This is old-school Italian: eggplant parmigiana, a heavy fettuccine Alfredo that would send your cardiologist into fits, veal scaloppini, and even calves' liver. The

Kids Family-Friendly Restaurants

One of the city's first "theme" restaurants, **Ed Debevic's,** 640 N. Wells St., at Ontario Street (✆ 312/664-1707), is a temple to America's hometown lunch-counter culture. The burgers-and-milkshakes menu is kid-friendly, but it's the staff shtick that makes this place memorable. The wait-resses play the parts of gum-chewing toughies who make wisecracks, toss out good-natured insults, and even sit right down at your table. It's all a performance—but it works.

The Southern-style restaurant **Wishbone** ✪✪ (p. 59) is one of the best all-around options, and a homegrown place as well. Children can be kept busy looking at the large and surrealistic farm-life paintings on the walls or reading a picture book, *Floop the Fly,* loaned to diners (written and illustrated by the parents of the owners). The food is diverse enough that both adults and kids can find something to their liking, but there's also a menu geared just toward children.

At **Gino's East** ✪✪ (p. 71), the famous Chicago pizzeria, long waits can be an issue during the prime summer tourist season. But once you get your table, the kids can let loose: patrons are invited to scrawl all over the graffiti-strewn walls and furniture.

food is good rather than great, but what sets The Village apart is the bordering-on-corny faux-Italian atmosphere. The service is out-standing, from the Italian maitre d' who flirts with all the ladies to the ancient waiters who manage somehow to keep up with the non-stop flow. The staff here are pros at handling pretheater dining.

71 W. Monroe St. (between Clark and Dearborn sts.). ✆ **312/332-7005.** www.italian village-chicago.com. Reservations recommended (accepted for parties of 3 or more). Main courses (including salad) $9–$23 lunch, $13–$24 dinner. AE, DISC, MC, V. Mon–Thurs 11am–1am; Fri–Sat 11am–2am; Sun noon–midnight. Subway/El: Red Line to Monroe.

INEXPENSIVE

Heaven on Seven ✪✪ (Finds) BREAKFAST & BRUNCH/CAJUN & CREOLE/DINER   Hidden on the seventh floor of an office building opposite Macy's, this is truly an insider's spot (you'll find it by following the office workers who line up for lunch during the week). Loud, crowded, and casual, it's a no-frills spot that buzzes with energy. Chef/owner Jimmy Bannos's Cajun and Creole specialties come with a cup of soup and include such Louisiana staples as red beans and rice, a catfish po' boy sandwich, and jambalaya. If you don't have a taste for Tabasco, the extensive coffee-shop-style menu covers all the traditional essentials: grilled-cheese sandwiches, omelets, tuna—the works.

Heaven also has another downtown location just off the Mag Mile at **600 N. Michigan Ave.** (© **312/280-7774**); unlike the original location, they accept reservations and credit cards and are open for dinner. The ambience is more lively than gritty, making it a popular spot for families.

111 N. Wabash Ave. (at Washington St.), 7th floor. © **312/263-6443**. www.heavenonseven.com. Reservations not accepted. Sandwiches $8–$12; main courses $10–$14. No credit cards. Mon–Fri 8:30am–5pm; Sat 10am–3pm; 3rd Fri of each month 5:30–9pm. Subway/El: Red Line to Washington.

2 The West Loop

The stretch of Randolph Street just west of the Chicago River—once known as the Market District—used to be filled with produce trucks and warehouses that shut down tight after nightfall. In the 1990s, in an echo of New York's Meatpacking District, a few bold restaurant pioneers moved in, bringing their super-hip clientele with them.

VERY EXPENSIVE

Blackbird 𝒜𝒜 AMERICAN   Stylishly spare, Chef Paul Kahan's Blackbird exudes a smart urban chic that could blend into the dining scene of any major city. As in many newer restaurants, the noise level can get high (and the tables are crammed much too close together). Nevertheless, Blackbird is fun for people who like a scene (everyone pretends not to be looking around too much), but I'd recommend somewhere else if you're looking for a romantic dinner.

Kahan is a big proponent of local, organic ingredients, so expect top-notch quality—but you'll pay for it (a plate of two melt-in-your-mouth Maine diver scallops goes for $14). Artfully prepared dishes make up the entree list: pan-roasted monkfish with Parmesan, crispy prosciutto, ruby grapefruit and salsify; grilled organic veal rib-eye with cornbread porridge, rapini, bittersweet chocolate, black truffle, and rosemary; and crispy buckwheat crepes with hazelnut "cassoulet," fresh ricotta, pickled baby carrots, and grilled abalone mushrooms. Recent desserts included bittersweet chocolate brioche with smoked banana, Manjari chocolate ice cream, and aged rum.

619 W. Randolph St. ℂ **312/715-0708**. www.blackbirdrestaurant.com. Reservations recommended. Main courses $8–$19 lunch, $25–$36 dinner. AE, DC, DISC, MC, V. Mon–Fri 11:30am–2pm and 5:30–10:30pm; Fri–Sat 5:30–11:30pm.

Moto ⭐⭐⭐ ECLECTIC   If you think food is meant to be experienced with all the senses, book a table at Moto, home to Chicago's most jaw-droppingly original dishes. Chef Homaro Cantu, who worked with Chicago celebrity chef Charlie Trotter for 4 years, calls his cuisine "avant-garde with Asian influences"—but what he's really interested in is taking dining beyond just eating. Dishes here are interactive experiences. For example, he entwines fresh herbs in custom-designed corkscrew-handled spoons, which allows the scent of the herbs to waft toward diners as they eat. For the ultimate made-to-order dish, an insulated box cooks a piece of fish right at the table. Cantu's got a sense of humor, too—during a raw food course, he uses a "virtual aroma device" to emit a subtle smoky scent, and sometimes the menu itself is edible. Dining here is strictly degustation, with a five-course, seven-course, and "gastronomic tasting menu" of up to 18 courses. Courses are creative but not necessarily filling, so be prepared to snack later if you choose the five-course option. The restaurant itself has a minimalist Zen feel—here, all the drama is at your table.

945 W. Fulton Market Ave. (at Sangamon St.). ℂ **312/491-0058**. www.motorestaurant.com. Reservations recommended. Prix-fixe dinners $70–$165. AE, DC, DISC, MC, V. Tues–Sat 5–11pm.

EXPENSIVE

Sushi Wabi ⭐ JAPANESE/SUSHI   Artfully presented sushi and chic crowds are the order of the day at Sushi Wabi, Randolph Street's Japanese jewel. The minimal-chic decor is industrial and raw, and the lighting is dark and seductive—giving the restaurant the feel of a nightclub rather than a casual sushi bar (weekend DJ music adds to the clubby feel).

Choose from dozens of nigiri sushi (fish and various eggs perched on vinegared rice), maki (rolls of seafood, veggies, and rice in seaweed), a chef's selection sashimi plate, and a smattering of appetizers, entrees, and sides. Simple entrees such as seared tuna, grilled salmon, teriyaki beef, and sesame-crusted chicken breast will satisfy landlubbers who are accommodating their sushi-loving companions. An intriguing side is the Japanese whipped potato salad with ginger, cucumber, carrots, and scallions. Make a reservation or expect quite a wait, even on school nights. A selection of teas in cast-iron pots and chilled sakes is offered; or try a martini with a ginger-stuffed olive.

842 W. Randolph St. ℭ **312/563-1224.** www.sushiwabi.com. Reservations recommended. Main courses $12–$30. AE, DC, DISC, MC, V. Mon–Fri 11:30am–2pm; Sun–Tues 5–11pm; Wed–Sat 5pm–midnight.

MODERATE

Avec ℱ MEDITERRANEAN   A casual wine bar owned by Chef Paul Kahan of neighboring Blackbird (p. 57), Avec keeps things simple: top-quality ingredients in simple preparations that take inspiration from Italian, French, and Spanish cuisines. The menu focuses on a variety of "small plates" meant for sharing (although there are always five or six entree-size offerings as well). This focus on communal dining is reflected in the restaurant's design; the long, narrow dining room, with its wood walls and floors, will strike you as either cramped or cozy.

The small plates include salads and upscale appetizer-style dishes such as smoked lamb and quail brochettes; dates stuffed with chorizo sausage; and spicy meatballs with Spanish rice and chickpeas. Large plates feature seasonal ingredients and tend to be heartier (pork shoulder or pappardelle with wild mushrooms, for example). Whether you like the tight quarters or not, Avec has become a late-night hangout for local chefs and sommeliers—so they must be doing something right.

615 W. Randolph St. ℭ **312/377-2002.** Reservations not accepted. Small plates $5–$12; large plates $15–$20. AE, DC, DISC, MC, V. Mon–Thurs 3:30pm–midnight; Fri–Sat 3:30pm–1am; Sun 3:30pm–10pm.

INEXPENSIVE

Wishbone ℱℱ *Kids* BREAKFAST & BRUNCH/CAJUN & CRE-OLE/SOUTHERN   One of my best friends—a transplanted Chicagoan who now lives in New York—always has one request when she comes back to town: dinner at Wishbone. It's that kind of place; a down-home, casual spot that inspires intense loyalty (even if the food is only good rather than outstanding).

Known for Southern food and big-appetite breakfasts, Wishbone's extensive, reasonably priced menu blends hearty, home-style choices with healthy and vegetarian items. Brunch is the 'Bone's claim to fame, when an eclectic crowd of bedheads pack in for the plump and tasty salmon cakes, omelets, and red eggs (a lovely mess of tortillas, black beans, cheese, scallions, chile-ancho sauce, salsa, and sour cream). However, brunch at Wishbone can be a mob scene, so I suggest lunch or dinner; offerings include "yardbird" (charbroiled chicken with sweet red-pepper sauce), blackened catfish, and hoppin'

Finds **Ethnic Dining near the Loop**

CHINATOWN

Chicago's Chinatown is about 20 blocks south of the Loop. The district is strung along two thoroughfares, Cermak Road and Wentworth Avenue as far south as 24th Place.

The spacious, fairly elegant **Phoenix,** 2131 S. Archer Ave. (between Wentworth Ave. and Cermak Rd.; ℂ **312/328-0848**), has plenty of room for big tables of family or friends to enjoy the Cantonese (and some Szechuan) cuisine. A good sign: The place attracts lots of Chinatown locals.

Penang, 2201 S. Wentworth Ave. (at Cermak Rd.; ℂ **312/326-6888**), serves mostly Malaysian dishes, but some lean toward Indian and Chinese (they've even added a sushi bar to complete the Pan-Asian experience). Sink your teeth into the *kambing rendang* (lamb curry in 11 spices) or the barbecued stingray wrapped in a banana leaf.

LITTLE ITALY

Convenient to most downtown locations, a few blocks' stretch of Taylor Street is home to a host of time-honored, traditional, hearty Italian restaurants.

Expect to wait well beyond the time of your reservation at **Rosebud on Taylor** ⊛, 1500 W. Taylor St. (at Laflin St.; ℂ 312/942-1117), but fear not—your hunger will be satisfied. Rosebud is known for enormous helpings of pasta, most of which lean toward heavy Italian-American favorites: deep-dish lasagna and a fettuccine Alfredo that defines the word "rich." I highly recommend any of the pastas served with vodka sauce. Another location is near the Mag Mile at 720 N. Rush St. (ℂ **312/266-6444**).

John, the classic Southern dish of brown rice, black-eyed peas, and ham (there's also a vegetarian version, hoppin' Jack). The tart Key lime pie is one of my favorite desserts in the city. The casual ambience is a good bet for families (plus a children's menu is available).

1001 Washington St. (at Morgan St.). ℂ 312/850-2663. www.wishbonechicago. com. Reservations accepted, except for weekend brunch. Main courses $5–$10 breakfast and lunch, $6–$15 dinner. AE, DC, DISC, MC, V. Mon–Fri 7am–3pm; Tues–Thurs 5–9pm; Fri–Sat 5–10pm; brunch Sat–Sun 8am–3pm.

Tuscany, 1014 W. Taylor St. (between Morgan and Miller sts.; ✆ **312/829-1990**), is one of the most reliable Italian restaurants on Taylor Street. In contrast to the city's more fashionable Italian spots, family-owned Tuscany has the comfortable feel of a neighborhood restaurant.

GREEKTOWN

A short cab ride across the south branch of the Chicago River will take you to the city's Greektown, a row of moderately priced and inexpensive Greek restaurants clustered on Halsted Street between Van Buren and Washington streets.

To be honest, there's not much here to distinguish one restaurant from the other: They're all standard Greek restaurants with similar looks and similar menus. That said, **Santorini,** 800 W. Adams St. (at Halsted St.; ✆ **312/829-8820**); **Parthenon,** 314 S. Halsted St. (between Jackson and Van Buren sts.; ✆ **312/726-2407**); and **Costas,** 340 S. Halsted St. (between Jackson and Van Buren sts.; ✆ **312/263-0767**), are all good bets for gyros, Greek salads, shish kabobs, and the classic moussaka. On warm summer nights, opt for either **Athena** ⭐, 212 S. Halsted St. (between Adams and Jackson sts.; ✆ **312/655-0000**), which has a huge outdoor seating area, or **Pegasus,** 130 S. Halsted St. (between Monroe and Adams sts.; ✆ **312/226-3377**), with its rooftop patio serving drinks, appetizers, and desserts. Both have wonderful views of the Loop's skyline.

3 The Magnificent Mile & the Gold Coast

Many tourists who visit Chicago never stray far from the Magnificent Mile and the adjoining Gold Coast area. From the array of restaurants, shops, and pretty streets, it's not hard to see why.

VERY EXPENSIVE

Gibsons Bar & Steakhouse ⭐⭐ STEAK & CHOPS   Popular with its Gold Coast neighbors, Gibsons is the steakhouse you visit when you want to take in a scene. There are sporty cars idling at the valet stand, photos of celebs and near-celebs who've appeared here, and overdressed denizens mingling and noshing in the bar, which has a life all its own. The dining rooms evoke a more romantic feel, from the sleek Art Deco decor to the bow-tied bartenders. The portions are notoriously enormous, so Gibsons is best for groups who are happy to share dishes (I wouldn't recommend it, however, for a romantic dinner *à deux*). If huge portions aren't your thing, you can also order from the bar menu. The namesake martinis are served in 10-ounce glasses, and the entrees are outlandishly scaled, from the six-piece shrimp cocktail so huge you swore you downed a dozen, to the turtle pie that comes with a steak knife (and could easily serve eight people). Yes, Gibsons has a clubby atmosphere, but considering the crowds who show up nightly, the food deserves some credit.

1028 N. Rush St. (at Bellevue Place). ℃ 312/266-8999. www.gibsonssteakhouse. com. Reservations strongly recommended. Main courses $25–$80. AE, DC, DISC, MC, V. Daily 11am–midnight (bar open later). Subway/El: Red Line to Clark/Division.

Morton's ⭐⭐⭐ STEAK & CHOPS   Morton's is a well-known chain with a couple dozen locations nationwide, but it's Chicago born and bred, and many people still consider it the king of Chicago-style steakhouses. Named for its founding father, renowned Chicago restaurateur Arnie Morton, Morton's is hidden on the lower level of an undistinguished high-rise (look for a discreet sign on the closed door in the lobby). Starters include lobster bisque, Caesar salad, shrimp, or jumbo lump-crabmeat cocktail, but meat is the main event. House specialties include the double filet mignon with béarnaise sauce, and classic cuts of porterhouse, New York strip, and rib-eye, with the usual array of a la carte sides. Overall, Morton's steaks are dependable rather than awe-inspiring, but the place has a relaxed, welcoming ambience that attracts a wide range of customers (I've seen everyone from power-suited businessmen to 20-somethings in jeans chowing down here).

Morton's also has a Loop location at 65 E. Wacker Place, between Michigan and Wabash avenues (℃ **312/201-0410**), with the same menu and a slightly more upscale, clubby decor; unlike the original location, it's open for lunch.

1050 N. State St. (at Rush St.). ℃ 312/266-4820. www.mortons.com. Reservations recommended. Main courses $26–$44. AE, DC, DISC, MC, V. Mon–Sat 5:30–11pm; Sun 5–10pm. Subway/El: Red Line to Chicago.

Spiaggia ⭐⭐⭐ ITALIAN   Spiaggia is widely acknowledged as the best fine-dining Italian restaurant in the city (and maybe the entire U.S.). The dining room is bright, airy, and sophisticated, an atmosphere far removed from your neighborhood trattoria—so dress to impress (gentlemen, wear your jackets).

You can order a la carte or a seven-course degustation menu; entree choices change often and emphasize seasonal ingredients. Recent starters included carpaccio of smoked Sicilian swordfish or pork loin wrapped in pancetta, served with sautéed artichoke hearts in a balsamic vinegar dressing. This ain't your mama's pasta, either: Recent offerings have included pheasant-stuffed ravioli, pumpkin risotto, and gnocchi with black-truffle sauce. Entree examples include products of the restaurant's wood-burning oven, including monkfish; salmon; duck breast with Ligurian black olives, tomatoes, fennel, and baby artichokes; and grilled squab over lentils with foie gras. You're encouraged to order Italian-style (appetizer, pasta, meat), which means the bill can add up pretty quickly. But if you're a cheese lover, this is the place to splurge on a cheese course: They'll roll out a cart filled with rare varieties and give you extensive descriptions of each one.

980 N. Michigan Ave. (at Oak St.). ✆ **312/280-2750**. www.levyrestaurants.com. Reservations strongly suggested on weekends. Main courses $34–$41; menu degustation $95–$135. AE, DC, DISC, MC, V. Sun–Thurs 6–9:30pm; Fri–Sat 5:30–10:30pm. Subway/El: Red Line to Chicago.

Tru ⓡⓡⓡ AMERICAN   Chefs Rick Tramonto and Gale Gand have made Tru a top dining destination, thanks to its sophisticated-but-not-snobbish cuisine and atmosphere. The menu shines with appetizers such as grilled diver sea scallops with red pepper essence, chorizo, and avocado dumplings; and entrees such as Colorado lamb rib-eye with white turnips, grapefruit, and bergamot. The three-course menu is prix fixe ($95), with all items on the menu available a la carte. If your wallet and stomach permit, go for Chef Tramonto's Market Collection ($145), nine courses featuring selections inspired by what was available at that day's markets. Gand is one of the city's best pastry chefs, and her desserts perfectly echo Tramonto's savory menus.

676 N. St. Clair St. (at Huron St.). ✆ **312/202-0001**. www.trurestaurant.com. Reservations required. Prix-fixe menu $80–$150. AE, DC, DISC, MC, V. Mon–Thurs 5:30–10pm; Fri–Sat 5:30–11pm. Subway/El: Red Line to Chicago.

EXPENSIVE

De La Costa ⓡ LATIN AMERICAN   The name means "of the coast," but don't come here expecting shoreline views; Lake Michigan is a few blocks away. Executive chef Douglas Rodriguez (of New York's Patria and Philadelphia's Alma de Cuba) says the menu was inspired by the coastal cuisines of Spain, the Caribbean, and South

Only in Chicago

PIZZA

We have three pizza styles in Chicago: Chicago style, also known as deep-dish, which is thick-crusted and often demands a knife and fork; stuffed, which is similar to a pie, with a crust on both top and bottom; and thin crust. Many pizzerias serve both thick and thin, and some make all three kinds.

Three of Chicago's best gourmet deep-dish restaurants are **Pizzeria Uno** ⭐ (p. 74), **Pizzeria Due** (p. 74), and **Gino's East** ⭐⭐ (p. 71). In River North, **Lou Malnati's Pizzeria** ⭐, 439 N. Wells St. (at Hubbard St.; ℭ **312/828-9800**), bakes both deep-dish and thin-crust pizza, and even has a low-fat-cheese option. **Edwardo's** is a local pizza chain that serves all three varieties, but with a wheat crust and all-natural ingredients (spinach pizza is the specialty here); locations are in the Gold Coast at 1212 N. Dearborn St. (at Division St.; ℭ **312/337-4490**); in the South Loop at 521 S. Dearborn St. (between Congress Pkwy. and Harrison St.; ℭ **312/939-3366**); and in Lincoln Park at 2622 N. Halsted St. (at Wrightwood Ave.; ℭ **773/871-3400**).

America—which means plenty of fresh fish and some bold flavor combinations. The overall vibe (and price tag) is Miami-chic rather than beachcomber casual, with a long, gleaming white bar, artfully draped curtains, and a buzzing, boisterous clientele.

Whether you graze tapas-style or want to fill up with a hearty meat entree, you should definitely start with one of the house specialty ceviches, such as the Fire and Ice (which mixes tuna, calamari, chiles, coconut, and lime for a unique spicy-yet-cool experience). Among the entrees, the Churrasco De La Costa—a tender beef tenderloin topped with a tasty, mildly spicy chimichurri sauce—lives up to its billing as a house signature dish. The Brazilian-inspired Xim Xim (chicken and giant shrimp in a coconut sauce with roasted cashews) is flavorful and ideal for smaller appetites.

465 E. Illinois St. (between McClurg Ct. and Lake Shore Dr.). ℭ **312/464-1700.** http://delacostachicago.com. Reservations recommended. Main courses $21–$38. AE, DC, DISC, MC, V. Mon–Fri 11:30am–2pm; Sun–Thurs 5–10pm; Fri–Sat 5–11pm; bar open until 1am Fri–Sat. Subway/El: Red Line to Grand, then a short cab ride.

HOT DOGS

The classic Chicago hot dog includes a frankfurter by Vienna Beef (a local food processor and hallowed institution), heaps of chopped onions and green relish, a slather of yellow mustard, pickle spears, fresh tomato wedges, a dash of celery salt, and, for good measure, two or three "sport" peppers, those thumb-shaped holy terrors that turn your mouth into its own bonfire.

Chicago is home to many standout hot-dog spots including **Gold Coast Dogs,** 159 N. Wabash Ave., at Randolph Street (© **312/917-1677**), in the Loop just a block from Michigan Avenue. **Fluky's,** in The Shops at North Bridge mall, 520 N. Michigan Ave. (© **312/245-0702**), is part of a local chain that has been serving great hot dogs since the Depression (Dan Aykroyd and Jay Leno are fans). **Portillo's,** 100 W. Ontario St. (at Clark St.; © **312/587-8930**), is another local chain that specializes in hot dogs but also serves tasty pastas and salads.

MODERATE

Le Colonial 🗯🗯 *Finds* FRENCH/VIETNAMESE   Appropriately enough for its tony Oak Street environs, Le Colonial has one of the loveliest dining rooms in the city—and the second-floor lounge is a sultry, seductive cocktail destination. An escapist's paradise, the restaurant is a cleverly crafted re-creation of the civilized yet exotic world of 1920s Saigon: bamboo shutters, rattan chairs, potted palms and banana trees, fringed lampshades and ceiling fans, and evocative period photography.

While the ambience certainly merits a visit, the flavorful cuisine is a draw on its own. Start with the hearty oxtail soup or the light and refreshing beef-and-watercress salad. Entrees include grilled lime-glazed sea scallops with garlic noodle salad, sautéed jumbo shrimp in curried coconut sauce, and roasted chicken with lemon-grass-and-lime dipping sauce. Le Colonial offers outdoor seating in warm weather; try to reserve one of the coveted, romantic mezzanine terrace tables.

937 N. Rush St. (just south of Oak St.). ℭ **312/255-0088.** www.lecolonialchicago. com. Reservations recommended. Main courses $15–$22 lunch, $17–$28 dinner. AE, DC, MC, V. Daily 11:30am–2:30pm; Mon–Wed 5–11pm; Thurs–Sat 5pm–midnight; Sun 5–10pm. Subway/El: Red Line to Chicago.

Shaw's Crab House and Blue Crab Lounge ✿ SEAFOOD Shaw's is a local institution—if you ask average Chicagoans where to go for seafood, chances are they'll point you here. The bright, busy dining room has a lively vibe, and the extensive menu should suit all tastes (the appetizers, for example, run the gamut from popcorn shrimp and fried calamari to crab cakes and exotic sushi combinations). Main courses include Alaskan king crab, sautéed scallops, Texas stone-crab claws, crab cakes, and french-fried shrimp; you can also take advantage of various (expensive) surf-and-turf combinations. Shaw's trademark dessert, Key lime pie, suggests the restaurant's subtle Key West/Papa Hemingway theme, as do the suave strains of such 1930s tunes as "Begin the Beguine" playing in the background. On Sunday, Tuesday, and Thursday nights, there's live jazz and blues in the lounge.

21 E. Hubbard St. (between State St. and Wabash Ave.). ℭ **312/527-2722.** www. shawscrabhouse.com. Reservations accepted only for the main dining room. Main courses $14–$35. AE, DC, DISC, MC, V. Mon–Fri 11:30am–2pm; Mon–Thurs 5:30– 10pm; Fri–Sat 5–11pm; Sun 5–10pm. Subway/El: Red Line to Grand.

INEXPENSIVE

Billy Goat Tavern ✿ *Value* BREAKFAST & BRUNCH/BURG-ERS "Cheezeborger, Cheezeborger—No Coke . . . Pepsi." Viewers of the original *Saturday Night Live* will certainly remember the classic John Belushi routine, a moment in the life of a crabby Greek short-order cook. The comic got his material from the Billy Goat Tavern, located under North Michigan Avenue near the bridge that crosses to the Loop (you'll find it by walking down the steps across the street from the Chicago Tribune building). Just BUTT IN ANY-TIME, says the sign on the red door. The tavern is a classic dive: dark, seedy, and no-frills. The menu is pretty basic (mostly hamburgers and hot dogs), but yes, the cheeseburgers are pretty good. Billy Goat is a hangout for newspaper workers and writers, so you might overhear the latest media buzz. After work this is a good place to watch a game, chitchat at the bar, and down a few beers.

430 N. Michigan Ave. ℭ **312/222-1525.** www.billygoattavern.com. Reservations not accepted. Menu items $4–$7. No credit cards. Mon–Fri 6am–2am; Sat 10am– 2am; Sun 11am–2am. Subway/El: Red Line to Chicago.

foodlife ✿✿ *Finds* ECLECTIC   Taking the standard food court up a few notches, foodlife consists of a dozen or so kiosks offering both ordinary and exotic specialties on the mezzanine of Water Tower Place mall. Seats are spread out cafe style in a pleasant environment under realistic boughs of artificial trees festooned with strings of lights. A hostess will seat you, give you an electronic card, and then it's up to you to stroll around and get whatever food strikes your fancy (each purchase is recorded on your card, and you pay on the way out).

The beauty of a food court, of course, is that it offers something for everybody. At foodlife, diners can choose from burgers; pizza; south-of-the-border dishes; an assortment of Asian fare; and veggie-oriented, low-fat offerings. A lunch or snack is basically inexpensive, but the payment method makes it easy to build up a big tab while holding a personal taste-testing session at each kiosk.

In Water Tower Place, 835 N. Michigan Ave. ✆ **312/335-3663.** Reservations not accepted. Most items $8–$15. AE, DC, DISC, MC, V. Breakfast kiosk daily 7:30–10:30am. All other kiosks Mon–Thurs 11am–8pm; Fri–Sun 11am–9pm. Subway/El: Red Line to Chicago.

4 River North

River North, the area north of the Loop and west of Michigan Avenue, is home to the city's most concentrated cluster of art galleries and a something-for-everyone array of restaurants—from fast food and themed restaurants to chains and some of our trendiest dining destinations.

VERY EXPENSIVE

mk ✦✦✦ AMERICAN   Even though foodies rank it one of the top American restaurants in the city, mk doesn't flaunt its pedigree. The loftlike dining room is as understated as the lowercase initials that give the restaurant its name. Chef Michael Kornick keeps the menu focused on a fairly straightforward seasonal mix of meat and seafood: Menu selections might range from hearty (roasted duck breast with baby turnips and fava beans; rack of lamb with lamb-stuffed cannelloni and fig jam) to lighter offerings, such as grilled salmon with a Chinese mustard glaze and ginger-soy vinaigrette. The presentations are tasteful rather than dazzling; Kornick wants you to concentrate on the food, and that's just what the chic, mixed-age crowd does. Service is disciplined yet agreeable, and fine table appointments signal this restaurant's commitment to quality. As for dessert, The Peanut Gallery (peanut butter mousse, crispy milk chocolate, warm brownies, pretzels, hot fudge and caramel) is worth the calories.

868 N. Franklin St. (1 block north of Chicago Ave.). ℂ **312/482-9179.** www.mk
chicago.com. Reservations recommended. Main courses $27–$46; menu degustation $80 ($90 with cheese course). AE, DC, MC, V. Sun–Thurs 5:30–10pm; Fri–Sat
5:30–10:30pm. Subway/El: Brown Line to Chicago.

EXPENSIVE

Bin 36 👁👁 AMERICAN   In one lofty, airy space, this River North
hot spot combines wine, food, and retail in a successful, wine-cen-
tric concept. The restaurant is certainly serious about wine and
cheese, but you're not expected to be an expert—this is a place where
you're encouraged to experiment. The menu includes two or three
suggested wines for every dish, all of which are available by the
glass—and you won't go wrong by following the menu's suggestions.
"Small plates" include shiitake spring rolls, steamed mussels, and a
selection of homemade pâtés, along with a few basic full-portion
entrees (hamburgers, roast chicken, ahi tuna). You can also have fun
ordering creative "wine flights," small glasses organized around a
theme (Italian, Australian, and so on). The Cellar menu focuses on
upscale American dishes, including a variety of seafood, seared veni-
son, and braised pork shank. The food-wine pairings continue on
the dessert menu; a recommended sherry along with a slice of gin-
gerbread-pear cake here one evening was a delight.

339 N. Dearborn St. ℂ **312/755-9463.** www.bin36.com. Reservations recommended.
Main courses $9–$15 lunch, $17–$24 dinner. AE, DC, DISC, MC, V. Mon–Thurs
11am–midnight; Fri 11am–2am; Sat noon–2am; Sun noon–10pm. Subway/El: Red Line
to Grand.

Brasserie Jo 👁 ALSATIAN/FRENCH   Brasserie Jo showcases
the casual side of chef Jean Joho, whose upscale Everest (p. 51) is one
of the city's longtime gourmet destinations. The high-ceilinged dining room here is open and spacious (as compared to a cozy bistro);
you'll feel as if you're dining in an Art Deco Parisian cafe.

You can order a hearty Alsatian *choucroute* here, but the menu
focuses more on casual French classics: Entrees are divided into
seafood, steak, and a variety of bistro-style specialties (chicken coq au
vin, pork tenderloin ratatouille, rack of lamb), along with tartes, the
Alsatians' version of thin-crust pizza. One house specialty that's worth
a try is the "shrimp bag," a phyllo pastry filled with shrimp, peas, and
herb rice garnished with lobster sauce. Save room for dessert: The
delightfully decadent caramel-banana coupe is served in a tall glass,
and just might be the perfect sundae. I also love the rich chocolate
mousse, which is served tableside from a massive silver bowl, then
topped with fresh cream and shaved chocolate—just like in Paris.

59 W. Hubbard St. (between Dearborn and Clark sts.). ℂ **312/595-0800.** www.
brasseriejo.com. Reservations recommended. Main courses $18–$30. AE, DC, DISC,
MC, V. Mon–Thurs 5–10pm; Fri–Sat 5–11pm; Sun 4–9pm. Subway/El: Brown Line to
Merchandise Mart or Red Line to Grand.

Frontera Grill & Topolobampo ⭒⭒⭒ MEXICAN Owners
Rick and Deann Groen Bayless are widely credited with bringing
authentic Mexican regional cuisine to a wider audience. The building actually houses two restaurants: the casual Frontera Grill (plain
wood tables, terra-cotta tile floor) and the fine-dining Topolobampo
(white linen tablecloths, a more hushed environment). At both
restaurants, the focus is on fresh, organic ingredients supplied by
local artisanal farmers.

At Frontera, the signature appetizer is the *sopes surtidos,* corn-tor-
tilla "boats" with a sampler of fillings (chicken in red mole, black
beans with homemade chorizo, and so on). The ever-changing entree
list might include pork loin in a green mole sauce; smoked chicken
breast smothered in a sauce of chiles, pumpkin seeds, and roasted
garlic; or a classic *sopa de pan* ("bread soup" spiced up with almonds,
raisins, grilled green onions, and zucchini). Yes, you can also get
tacos (with fillings such as portobello mushrooms, duck, and catfish). The Baylesses up the ante at the adjacent Topolobampo, where
both the ingredients and presentation are more upscale.

It can be tough to snag a table at Frontera during prime dining
hours, so do what the locals do: Put your name on the list and order
a few margaritas in the lively, large bar area.

445 N. Clark St. (between Illinois and Hubbard sts.). ℂ **312/661-1434.** www.frontera
kitchens.com. Reservations accepted at Frontera Grill for parties of 5–10; accepted at
Topolobampo for parties of 1–6. Frontera Grill main courses $21–$28. Topolobampo
main courses $32–$38; chef's 5-course tasting menu $75 ($120 with wine pairings).
AE, DC, DISC, MC, V. Frontera Grill Tues–Fri 11:30am–2:30pm; Sat 10:30am–2:30pm;
Tues–Thurs 5–10pm; Fri–Sat 5–11pm. Topolobampo Tues 11:45am–2pm; Wed–Fri
11:30am–2pm; Tues–Thurs 5:30–9:30pm; Fri–Sat 5:30–10:30pm. Subway/El: Red Line
to Grand.

Osteria Via Stato ⭒⭒ (Finds) ITALIAN Like Italian? Like sur-
prises? Then you'll enjoy Osteria Via Stato's twist on traditional Italian dining. A set price of $36 buys you a full, European-style meal: a
range of antipasto plates (which could be anything from house-cured
olives to braised veal meatballs), two pasta dishes (served family style),
and a meat entree (the only dish you actually choose from the menu).
Pastas are usually a mix of hearty and light; pappardelle with free-
range chicken ragu might be served alongside gemelli with sage and
brown butter. Entrees include halibut Milanese with lemon-herb

breadcrumbs; braised pork shank with white beans and bacon; and chicken Mario, a simple chicken breast perfectly seared with butter and olive oil. Lunch follows the same format, but there are fewer antipasti, and the entrees include salads and panini.

620 N. State St. (at Ontario St.). ✆ **312/642-8450.** www.leye.com. Reservations recommended. Set price $20 per person lunch, $36 dinner. AE, DC, DISC, MC, V. Mon–Sat 11:30am–2pm; Mon–Thurs 5–10pm; Fri–Sat 5–11pm; Sun 4–8:30pm (bar open later). Subway/El: Red Line to Grand.

SushiSamba Rio ✮✮ LATIN AMERICAN/SUSHI   In the early 20th century, Japanese immigrants moved to Peru and Brazil in search of work, eventually combining their native cuisine with South American dishes. SushiSamba takes the concept and runs with it, creating a theatrical experience that's backed up by very solid technique.

Designed by David Rockwell (Nobu, Vong, various W hotels), SushiSamba's dramatic dining room has become an "it" scene for fashionable young Chicagoans. There's something here for everyone, making it a good choice for groups (even those who don't eat raw fish). I'd recommend trying at least one of the creative "samba rolls," which combine the traditional sticky-rice-and-seaweed wrapping with unexpected fillings. The El Topo, a mix of salmon, jalapeño pepper, fresh melted mozzarella, and crispy onions, tastes better than it sounds; also worth trying is the Samba Rio roll, with guava-glazed short ribs and sweet pepper. If you'd prefer something more straightforward, Surf & Turf matches seared rare tuna and a tender beef filet on a bed of carrot-and-ginger purée.

504 N. Wells St. (at Illinois St.). ✆ **312/595-2300.** www.sushisamba.com. Reservations recommended. Main courses $8–$17 lunch, $12–$29 dinner. AE, MC, V. Sun–Tues 11:30am–11pm; Wed–Fri 11:30am–1am; Sat 11:30am–2am; Sun brunch 11:30am–3:30pm. Subway/El: Brown Line to Merchandise Mart or Red Line to Grand.

MODERATE

Carson's ✮ AMERICAN/BARBECUE   A true Chicago institution, Carson's calls itself "The Place for Ribs," and, boy, is it ever. The barbecue sauce here is sweet and tangy, and the ribs are meaty. Included in the $22 price for a full slab of baby backs are coleslaw and one of four types of potatoes (the most decadent are au gratin), plus right-out-of-the-oven rolls.

In case you don't eat ribs, Carson's also barbecues chicken, pork chops, and (in a nod to health-consciousness) salmon. But let's be honest, you don't come to a place like this for the seafood, and the waitstaff will be shocked if no one in your group orders the famous ribs. If by some remarkable feat you have room left after dinner, the candybar sundaes are a scrumptious finale to the meal. Carson's popularity has led to something of a factory mentality among management, which evidently feels the need to herd diners in and out, but the servers are responsive to requests not to be hurried through the meal.

612 N. Wells St. (at Ontario St.). © 312/280-9200. www.ribs.com. Reservations accepted for groups of 6 or more. Main courses $13–$34. AE, DC, DISC, MC, V. Mon–Thurs 11:30am–10:30pm; Fri 11:30am–11:30pm; Sat noon–11:30pm; Sun noon–10:30pm. Subway/El: Red Line to Grand.

Cyrano's Bistrot & Wine Bar *Value* BISTRO/FRENCH Warm and welcoming, Cyrano's represents a haven of authentic bistro charm in the congested River North restaurant scene, due in no small part to the friendly presence of chef Didier Durand and his wife, Jamie. The cheery blue-and-red wood exterior, eclectic artwork, and charming personal asides on the menu ("Use of cellular phones may interfere with the stability of our whipped cream") all signal the owners' hands-on touch. The house specialties are the rotisserie duck and chicken served with your choice of sauce and classics such as steak frites, roasted rabbit with mustard sauce, and cassoulet. There are also a variety of salads to choose from (and some vegetarian options), but overall this is a place to eat hearty. The restaurant's lower-level cabaret has live entertainment most nights of the week, and in warmer months, a sidewalk cafe is open all day.

546 N. Wells St. (between Ohio St. and Grand Ave.). © 312/467-0546. www.cyranos bistrot.com. Main courses $14–$28; 3-course prix-fixe dinner $29. AE, DC, DISC, MC, V. Mon–Fri 11:30am–2:30pm; Mon–Sat 5:30–10:30pm. Subway/El: Brown Line to Merchandise Mart.

Gino's East *Kids* PIZZA Many Chicagoans consider Gino's the quintessential deep-dish Chicago-style pizza (I know transplanted Midwesterners who come here for their cheesy fix whenever they're back in town). True to its reputation, the pizza is heavy (a small cheese pizza is enough for two), so work up an appetite before chowing down. Specialty pizzas include the supreme, with layers of cheese, sausage, onions, green pepper, and mushrooms; and the vegetarian, with cheese, onions, peppers, asparagus, summer squash, zucchini, and eggplant. Gino's also offers salads, sandwiches, and pastas—but I've never seen anyone order them. A warning for hungry families: Pizzas are cooked to order, so you'll have to wait about 45 minutes for your food (I highly recommend calling ahead to preorder, which will save you about a half-hour of waiting time, but preorders aren't accepted Fri–Sat).

633 N. Wells St. (at Ontario St.). © 312/943-1124. www.ginoseast.com. Reservations not accepted. Pizza $12–$29. AE, DC, DISC, MC, V. Mon–Thurs 11am–10pm; Fri–Sat 11am–11pm; Sun noon–9pm. Subway/El: Red Line to Grand.

Dining Alfresco

Cocooned for 6 months of the year, with furnaces and electric blankets blazing, Chicagoans revel in the warm months of late spring, summer, and early autumn.

LOOP & VICINITY

Athena ✸   This Greektown mainstay offers a stunning three-level outdoor seating area. It's paved with brick and landscaped with 30-foot trees, flower gardens, and even a waterfall. Best of all: an incredible view of the downtown skyline with the Sears Tower right in the middle. 212 S. Halsted St., between Adams and Jackson sts. ✆ 312/655-0000.

Park Grill ✸✸   Millennium Park's restaurant serves upscale versions of American comfort food with panoramic views of Michigan Avenue. For a review, see p. 54. 11 N. Michigan Ave., at Madison St. ✆ 312/521-PARK.

MAGNIFICENT MILE & GOLD COAST

Le Colonial ✸✸   This lovely French-Vietnamese restaurant, located in a vintage Gold Coast town house and evocative of 1920s Saigon, *does* have a sidewalk cafe, but you'd do better to reserve a table on the tiny second-floor porch, overlooking the street. For a full review, see p. 65. 937 N. Rush St., just south of Oak St. ✆ 312/255-0088.

RIVER NORTH

SushiSamba Rio ✸✸   For stunning nighttime views of the skyline—accompanied by views of some pretty stunning people—head to the rooftop deck of this Latin-Asian fusion spot. Canopied banquettes and flickering tea lights create a sultry atmosphere, along with a menu of specialty cocktails. For more info, see p. 70. 504 N. Wells St., at Illinois St. ✆ 312/595-2300.

LINCOLN PARK

North Pond ✸✸✸   Set on the banks of one of Lincoln Park's beautiful lagoons, the excellent North Pond serves

INEXPENSIVE

Café Iberico ✸✸ SPANISH & TAPAS   This no-frills tapas spot won't win any points for style, but the consistently good food and upscale, fresh-as-can-be American cuisine in a romantic and sylvan setting. Also see p. 78. 2610 N. Cannon Dr., halfway between Diversey Pkwy. and Fullerton Ave. © 773/477-5845.

O'Brien's Restaurant Wells Street in Old Town is lined with several alfresco options, but the best belongs to O'Brien's, the unofficial nucleus of neighborhood life. The outdoor patio has teakwood furniture, a gazebo bar, and a mural of the owners' country club on a brick wall. 1528 N. Wells St., 2 blocks south of North Ave. © 312/787-3131.

WRIGLEYVILLE & VICINITY

Moody's For 30 years, Moody's has been grilling some of the best burgers in Chicago. It's ideal in winter for its dark, cozy dining room (warmed by a fireplace), but it's better still in summer for its awesome outdoor patio, a real hidden treasure. 5910 N. Broadway Ave., between Rosedale and Thorndale aves. © 773/275-2696.

WICKER PARK/BUCKTOWN

Meritage Café and Wine Bar ✹✹ Meritage wins my vote for most romantic outdoor nighttime seating. The food (American cuisine with Pacific Northwest influences) is topnotch, but it's the outdoor patio, twinkling with overhead lights, that makes for a magical experience. Best of all, the patio is covered and heated in the winter, so you can enjoy the illusion of outdoor dining even in February. 2118 N. Damen Ave., at Charleston St. © 773/235-6434.

Northside Café On a sunny summer day, Northside seems like Wicker Park's town square, packed with an eclectic mix of locals catching up and checking out the scene. The entire front of the restaurant opens onto the street, making it relatively easy to get an "outdoor" table. For more info, see p. 85. 1635 N. Damen Ave., just north of North Ave. © 773/384-3555.

festive atmosphere make it a longtime local favorite for singles in their 20s and 30s. Crowds begin pouring in at the end of the workday, so you'll probably have to wait for a table. Not to worry: Order a pitcher of fruit-filled sangria at the bar with everyone else. When you get a table, I'd suggest starting with the *queso de cabra* (baked goat cheese with fresh tomato-basil sauce), then continue ordering rounds of hot and cold tapas as your hunger demands. A few standout dishes are the vegetarian Spanish omelet, spicy potatoes with tomato sauce, chicken brochette with caramelized onions and rice, and grilled octopus with potatoes and olive oil. There are a handful of entrees on the menu, and a few desserts if you're still not sated.

739 N. LaSalle St. (between Chicago Ave. and Superior St.). ℂ **312/573-1510.** www.cafe-iberico.com. Reservations accepted for parties of 6 or more; no reservations for Fri–Sat dinner. Tapas $4–$7; main courses $7–$10. DC, DISC, MC, V. Mon–Thurs 11am–11:30pm; Fri 11am–1:30am; Sat noon–1:30am; Sun noon–11pm. Subway/El: Red Line to Chicago or Brown Line to Chicago.

Pizzeria Uno 𝕲 *(Value* PIZZA   Pizzeria Uno invented Chicago-style pizza, and many deep-dish aficionados still refuse to accept any imitations. Uno's is now a chain of restaurants throughout the country, but this location is the original. You can eat in the restaurant itself on the basement level or, weather permitting, on the outdoor patio right off the sidewalk. Salads, sandwiches, and a house minestrone are also available, but let's be honest—the only reason to come here is for the pizza. As with Gino's East (see above), pizzas take about 45 minutes to make, so if you're starving, order an appetizer or salad.

Uno was so successful that the owners opened **Pizzeria Due** in a lovely gray-brick Victorian town house nearby at 619 N. Wabash Ave., at Ontario Street (ℂ **312/943-2400**). The menu is exactly the same; the atmosphere just a tad nicer (with more outdoor seating).

29 E. Ohio St. (at Wabash Ave.). ℂ **312/321-1000.** www.unos.com. Reservations not accepted Fri–Sat. Pizza $7–$22. AE, DC, DISC, MC, V. Mon–Fri 11am–1am; Sat 11:30am–2am; Sun 11:30am–11:30pm. Subway/El: Red Line to Grand.

5 Lincoln Park & Old Town

Singles and upwardly mobile young families inhabit Lincoln Park, the neighborhood roughly defined by North Avenue on the south, Diversey Parkway on the north, the park on the east, and Clybourn Avenue on the west. In the southeast corner of this area is Old Town, a neighborhood of historic town houses that stretches out from the intersection of North Avenue and Wells Street.

VERY EXPENSIVE

Alinea 𝕲𝕲𝕲 ECLECTIC   Alinea—anointed the best restaurant in the country by *Gourmet* magazine in 2007—is a place no serious foodie should miss. Like Homaro Cantu at Moto (p. 58), Chef Grant

Achatz wants to revolutionize the way we eat, which he does by presenting familiar foods in new contexts and unexpected forms. (He's been known, for example, to serve dishes on lavender-scented pillows, so the floral scent wafts up as you eat). The menu changes constantly, but you're guaranteed to taste something new here, whether it's ravioli with a liquid-truffle filling or bites of bison tenderloin wrapped in crispy potatoes and seasoned with cinnamon. Achatz, who has worked with Spain's Ferran Adrià (the master of food deconstruction), as well as French Laundry's Thomas Keller, says he wants diners to feel like they're taking a journey, "zigzagging between challenge and comfort." The restaurant itself is certainly comfortable, with shoulder-high chairs you can sink into and soft, flattering lighting sparkling off the sharp angles of the grand staircase. But you'll only be comfortable dining here if you're willing to go along for the ride. Eat with an open mind (and a full wallet), and you'll be well rewarded.

1723 N. Halsted St. (between North Ave. and Willow St.). ② **312/867-0110.** www.alinea-restaurant.com. Reservations strongly recommended. Fixed-price menus $135 and $175. AE, DC, DISC, MC, V. Wed–Sun 5:30–9:30pm. Subway/El: Red Line to North/Clybourn.

Charlie Trotter's ✿✿✿ ECLECTIC   Foodies flock to the namesake restaurant of chef Charlie Trotter, Chicago's first celebrity chef. Yes, he's done TV shows and authored a series of cookbooks (with almost impossible-to-follow recipes), but Trotter's focus is this restaurant, a shrine to creative fine dining.

There is no a la carte menu, so this is not the place to come if you're a picky eater. Your only choice is to decide between the vegetable ($135) or grand ($155) degustation menu. Trotter delights in presenting diners with unfamiliar ingredients and presentations, and prides himself on using only organic or free-range products (so you can feel good about indulging). The entree descriptions signal Trotter's attention to detail; sample dishes from a recent menu include steamed Casco Bay cod with cockles, picholine olives, artichokes, and stinging nettles; and roasted saddle of rabbit with fingerling potatoes, turnips, and mustard greens. Be prepared to linger: dinner here can take up to 3 hours. The dining room may be formal, but the overall attitude is not intimidating. The wine list is extensive, and a sommelier is on hand to help match wines with each course.

816 W. Armitage Ave. (at Halsted St.). ② **773/248-6228.** www.charlietrotters.com. Reservations required. Jackets required, ties requested. Fixed-price menus $135 and $155. AE, DC, DISC, MC, V. Tues–Thurs at 6 and 9pm; Fri–Sat at 5:30 and 9pm. Subway/El: Brown Line to Armitage.

Dining in Lincoln Park, Old Town & Wrigleyville

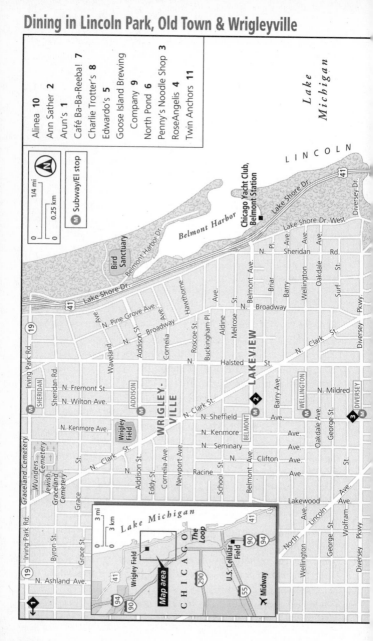

Alinea **10**
Ann Sather **2**
Arun's **1**
Café Ba-Ba-Reeba! **7**
Charlie Trotter's **8**
Edwardo's **5**
Goose Island Brewing
    Company **9**
North Pond **6**
Penny's Noodle Shop **3**
RoseAngelis **4**
Twin Anchors **11**

1/4 mi
0.25 km

Ⓜ Subway/El stop

Lake Michigan

LINCOLN

Bird Sanctuary

Belmont Harbor

Chicago Yacht Club,
Belmont Station

Lake Shore Dr.

Lake Shore Dr. West

N. Pl. Sheridan Rd.

Belmont Ave.

Briar Ave.
Barry Ave.
Wellington Ave.
Oakdale Ave.
Surf St.

Diversey Pkwy.
Diversey Dr.

Waveland Ave.
N. Pine Grove Ave.
Broadway
Addison
Hawthorne Ave.
Roscoe St.
Cornelia
Buckingham Pl.
Aldine
Melrose
N.
Halsted St.
N. Broadway

LAKEVIEW

N. Clark St.

Barry Ave.
Wellington Ave.
N. Mildred
Oakdale Ave.
George St.
Diversey

WRIGLEY-VILLE

N. Fremont St.
N. Wilton Ave.
N. Kenmore Ave.

Sheridan Rd.
Irving Park Rd.

SHERIDAN

ADDISON

Wrigley Field

BELMONT

WELLINGTON

DIVERSEY

N. Clark St.
N. Sheffield Ave.
N. Kenmore Ave.
N. Seminary Ave.
Clifton Ave.
Racine Ave.
School St.
Belmont Ave.
Lakewood Ave.
Lincoln Ave.
Wellington
George St.
Wolfram St.
Diversey Pkwy.

Graceland Cemetery
Wunders Cemetery
Jewish Graceland Cemetery

Addison St.
Eddy St.
Cornelia Ave.
Newport Ave.
N. Clark St.

Grace St.
Byron St.
N. Ashland Ave.
Irving Park Rd.

Lake Michigan

3 mi
3 km

CHICAGO

Wrigley Field

Map area

The Loop

U.S. Cellular Field

✈ Midway

North Ave.

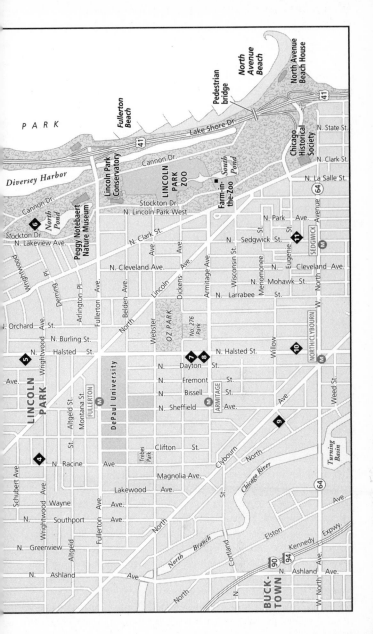

North Pond ⭐⭐⭐ *Finds* AMERICAN   Tucked away in Lincoln Park, North Pond truly is a hidden treasure. You can't drive up to the restaurant's front door: You must stroll along a path to reach the building, which was formerly a warming hut for ice skaters. The building's Arts and Crafts–inspired interior blends perfectly with the park outside, and a glass-enclosed addition lets you dine "outside" all year long.

In keeping with the natural setting, chef Bruce Sherman emphasizes organic, locally grown ingredients and favors simple preparations—although the overall result is definitely upscale (at these prices, it better be). Examples of seasonal menu items include herbed Parmesan gnocchi with braised rabbit, fava beans, asparagus, Wisconsin ramps (wild leeks), and lovage (a celerylike green); poached farm-fresh egg with wilted baby spinach and lemon-caviar butter sauce; and grilled sea scallops with orange-Parmesan grain salad, glazed organic baby carrots, and spiced lobster sauce. For dessert, try a plate of artisanal cheeses or dark chocolate mousse with roasted apricots and a hazelnut biscuit.

2610 N. Cannon Dr. (south of Diversey Pkwy.). ✆ **773/477-5845.** www.northpond restaurant.com. Reservations recommended. Main courses $29–$34. AE, DC, MC, V. Tues–Sat 5:30–10pm; Sun 11am–2pm and 5:30–10pm. Lunch served June–Sept Tues–Sat 11:30am–2pm. Bus: 151.

MODERATE

Café Ba-Ba-Reeba! ⭐ SPANISH & TAPAS   One of the city's first tapas restaurants, Café Ba-Ba-Reeba! is still going strong, thanks to its location on bustling Halsted Street, near the Armitage Avenue shopping strip. The clientele tends to be young and comes to the restaurant in groups, so be prepared: Loud conversations and tipsy toasts over pitchers of sangria may surround you.

Café Ba-Ba-Reeba! isn't breaking any new ground with its menu, but tapas lovers will see plenty of favorites, including garlic potato salad, roasted eggplant salad with goat cheese, beef and chicken empanadas, and roasted dates wrapped in bacon (which have been a popular menu item for years). The menu has also been updated with miniversions of more upscale fare, including a spicy devil's lobster tail dish, a cured pork *lomo* with frisée salad, and a flavorful plate of seared Spanish sausages. Some dishes are available in both tapas and full-portion size, and there's a range of paellas for those who don't want to go the tapas route. The vibrantly decorated cafe makes an excellent, efficient choice for pre- or posttheater dining if you're headed to Steppenwolf Theatre, a few blocks south, for a play.

2024 N. Halsted St. (at Armitage Ave.). ☎ 773/935-5000. www.cafebabareeba. com. Reservations recommended on weekends. Tapas $4–$13; main courses $9–$30. AE, DC, DISC, MC, V. Mon–Thurs 5–10pm; Fri 5pm–midnight; Sat 11am–midnight; Sun 11am–10pm. Subway/El: Red or Brown line to Fullerton, or Brown Line to Armitage.

Twin Anchors ⚓ BARBECUE   A landmark in Old Town since the end of Prohibition, Twin Anchors manages to maintain the flavor of old Chicago. It's a friendly, family-owned pub with Frank Sinatra songs on the jukebox and pictures of Ol' Blue Eyes on the walls (he apparently hung out here on swings through town in the 1960s). But rather than striking a self-consciously retro pose, this feels like the real deal, with a long mahogany bar up front and a modest dining room in back with red Formica-topped tables crowded close. Of course, you don't need anything fancy when the ribs—the fall-off-the-bone variety—come this good. Even non–meat eaters may be swayed if they allow themselves one bite of the enormous slabs of tender baby back pork ribs. (Go for the zesty sauce.) All of this means that you should prepare for a long wait on weekends.

1655 N. Sedgwick St. (1 block north of North Ave.). ☎ 312/266-1616. www. twinanchorsribs.com. Reservations not accepted. Sandwiches $6–$9; main courses $11–$24. AE, DC, DISC, MC, V. Mon–Thurs 5–11pm; Fri 5pm–midnight; Sat noon–midnight; Sun noon–10:30pm. Subway/El: Brown Line to Sedgwick.

INEXPENSIVE

Goose Island Brewing Company AMERICAN   Some of the best beer in Chicago is manufactured at this comfy, award-winning microbrewery on the western edge of Old Town (an impressive cast of professional beer critics agrees). In the course of a year, Goose Island produces about 100 varieties of lagers, ales, stouts, pilsners, and porters that change with the seasons.

The food here is far more than an afterthought. If you prefer to chow down in a restaurant atmosphere (rather than sitting at the large bar), there's a separate, casual dining area that attracts plenty of families on the weekends. Cut-above bar food includes burgers (including a killer, dragon-breath-inducing Stilton burger with roasted garlic), sandwiches (pulled pork, blackened catfish po' boy, chicken Caesar), and some serious salads. Goose Island is also known for its addictive homemade potato chips, doughy Bavarian pretzels, fresh-brewed root beer, and orange cream soda. The zero-attitude, come-as-you-are ambience is very refreshing for a lazy afternoon pit stop or a casual lunch or dinner. A second location at 3535 N. Clark

St. (near W. Eddy St.) in Wrigleyville (© **773/832-9040**) has an enclosed beer garden.

1800 N. Clybourn Ave. (at Sheffield Ave.). © **312/915-0071**. www.gooseisland. com. Reservations accepted. Sandwiches $7.50–$10; main courses $11–$17. AE, DC, DISC, MC, V. Sun–Thurs 11am–1am; Fri–Sat 11am–2am; main dining room closes at 10pm daily, but a late-night menu is available in the bar. Subway/El: Red Line to North/Clybourn.

RoseAngelis ★★ (Value) ITALIAN   What keeps me coming back to RoseAngelis when there's not exactly a shortage of Italian restaurants in this city? The reliably good food, cozy ambience, and very reasonable prices—this is neighborhood dining at its best. Hidden on a residential side street in Lincoln Park, the restaurant fills the ground floor of a former private home with a charming series of cozy rooms and a garden patio. The menu emphasizes pasta (my favorites are the rich lasagna and the ravioli al Luigi, filled with ricotta and served with a sun-dried-tomato cream sauce). Finish with the deliciously decadent bread pudding with warm caramel sauce, one of my favorite desserts in the city (and big enough to share). I suggest stopping by on a weeknight to avoid fighting crowds of locals on Friday and Saturday nights (when you'll wait up to 2 hr. for a table).

1314 W. Wrightwood Ave. (at Lakewood Ave.). © **773/296-0081**. www.roseangelis. com. Reservations accepted for parties of 8 or more. Main courses $10–$16. DISC, MC, V. Tues–Thurs 5–10pm; Fri–Sat 5–11pm; Sun 4:30–9pm. Subway/El: Brown or Red line to Fullerton.

6 Wrigleyville & the North Side

The area surrounding Wrigley Field has a long history as a working-class neighborhood, and although housing prices have shot up recently (as they have everywhere else), the neighborhood still attracts hordes of recent college grads who prefer chicken wings to truffles. Overall, restaurants here are more affordable and low-key than downtown.

VERY EXPENSIVE

Arun's ★★★ THAI   This is the best Thai restaurant in the city—possibly the country. The only downside is its out-of-the-way location. You can get here by public transportation, but I recommend a taxi at night when the bus schedules are less reliable.

The 12-course chef's menu is your only option here, and different tables receive different dishes on a given night. This sequential banquet begins with degustation-style appetizers followed by four family-style entrees and two desserts. You might see courses of various delicate dumplings accented with edible, carved dough flowers; an alchemist's Thai salad of bitter greens and peanuts with green papaya, tomatoes, chiles, and sticky rice; and a medley of clever curries, including a surprisingly delightful sea-bass-and-cabbage sour curry. When classic dishes appear, such as pad thai, they're always above the norm. What really sets Arun's apart is the extremely personal service; dishes are customized for each group's preferences, and if members of a party have different tolerances for spicy food, the staff will provide variations for all taste buds. The menu is paired with an award-winning wine list.

4156 N. Kedzie Ave. (at Irving Park Rd.). ℂ 773/539-1909. www.arunsthai.com. Reservations required with credit card. 12-course chef's menu $85. AE, DC, DISC, MC, V. Tues–Thurs 5–10pm; Fri–Sat 5–10:30pm. Subway/El and bus: Brown Line to Irving Park, and then transfer to westbound bus no. 80, or take a cab.

INEXPENSIVE

Ann Sather 🐾🐾 AMERICAN/BREAKFAST & BRUNCH/ SWEDISH   This is a real Chicago institution, where you can enjoy Swedish meatballs with buttered noodles and brown gravy, or the Swedish sampler of duck breast with lingonberry glaze, meatball, potato-sausage dumpling, sauerkraut, and brown beans. All meals are full dinners, including appetizer, main course, vegetable, potato, and dessert. Sticky cinnamon rolls are a highlight of Sather's popular (and very affordable) weekend brunch menu (it can get frenzied, but you should be okay if you get here before 11am). The people-watching is priceless: a cross section of gay and straight, young and old, from club kids to elderly couples and families with toddlers.

929 W. Belmont Ave. (between Clark St. and Sheffield Ave.). ℂ 773/348-2378. www.annsather.com. Reservations accepted for parties of 6 or more. Main courses $6–$12. AE, DC, MC, V. Mon–Fri 7am–3pm; Sat–Sun 7am–4pm. Free parking with validation. Subway/El: Brown or Red line to Belmont.

Penny's Noodle Shop 🐾 *Value* ASIAN/THAI   Penny Chiamopoulous, a Thai native, has assembled a concise menu of delectable dishes, all of them fresh and made to order—and all at prices that will make you do a double take. The two dining rooms are clean and spare; single diners can usually find a seat along the bar that wraps around the grill. The Thai spring roll, filled with seasoned tofu, cucumber, bean sprouts, and strips of cooked egg, makes a refreshing starter. Of course, noodles unite everything on the menu, so your main decision is choosing among the options (crispy wide rice, rice vermicelli, Japanese udon, and so on) served in a soup or spread out on a plate. There are several barbecued pork and beef entrees, and plenty of options for vegetarians as well.

950 W. Diversey Ave. (at Sheffield St.). ℂ **773/281-8448.** Reservations not accepted. Main courses $5–$8. MC, V. Sun–Thurs 11am–10pm; Fri–Sat 11am–10:30pm. Subway/El: Brown Line to Diversey.

7 Wicker Park/Bucktown

The booming Wicker Park/Bucktown area followed closely on the heels of Lincoln Park and Wrigleyville in the race to gentrification. First came the artists and musicians, followed by armies of yuppies and young families—all attracted by cheap rents and real estate. The result is a well-established, happening scene, which includes some of the city's hippest restaurants and clubs.

EXPENSIVE

Mas 𝕽𝕽 LATIN AMERICAN   Cozy, dimly lit Mas is almost always packed with faithful regulars who come for the Latin cocktails and modern takes on traditional Central and South American cuisine. If you haven't sampled the *nuevo latino* dining trend yet, this is a good place to try it.

The "primero" list includes spicy lime-marinated tuna tacos with papaya, rosemary, and Dijon salsa; and a succulent ceviche of the day (such as yellowtail snapper with smoked poblano chile or blue marlin with rum and vanilla). Star entrees include chile-cured pork tenderloin over smoky white beans; achiote-roasted mako shark with crawfish-lentil salsa and avocado salad; and a traditional Honduran seafood stew of shrimp, mussels, and scallops.

1670 W. Division St. (at Paulina St.). ℂ **773/276-8700.** www.masrestaurant.com. Reservations recommended. Main courses $18–$28. AE, MC, V. Mon–Thurs 5:30–10pm; Fri–Sat 5:30–11:30pm; Sun 11am–3pm and 5:30–10pm. Subway/El: Blue Line to Division.

Spring 𝕽𝕽𝕽 AMERICAN   Chef Shawn McClain is one of Chicago's culinary celebrities, and Spring—his first restaurant—attracted national attention when it opened in 2001. Located in a former Russian bathhouse, the space is now an oasis of Zen tranquillity in soothing, neutral colors. Unlike other chefs who feel pressured to keep outdoing themselves, McClain sticks to a focused menu with a heavy emphasis on seafood and Pan-Asian preparations. Appetizers include an aromatic lemon-grass red-curry broth with rice noodles, and sea-scallop-and-potato ravioli with sautéed mushrooms and truffle essence. Most of the entrees are seafood-based: New Zealand snapper with lemon couscous and fennel salad, or the braised baby monkfish and escargots with roasted eggplant in smoked tomato

Dining & Nightlife in Wicker Park/Bucktown

DINING ◆

Hot Chocolate **6**
Jane's **5**
Le Bouchon **2**
Mas **10**
Northside Café **7**
Spring **8**

NIGHTLIFE ●

The Bucktown Pub **4**
Davenport's Piano Bar
& Cabaret **9**
The Map Room **1**
Marie's Riptide
Lounge **3**

bouillon, for example. Among the nonfish options, beef short-rib pot stickers spiced up with Korean seasonings stand out.

2039 W. North Ave. (at Milwaukee Ave.). © 773/395-7100. www.springrestaurant. net. Reservations recommended. Main courses $22–$31. AE, DC, DISC, MC, V. Tues–Thurs 5:30–10pm; Fri–Sat 5:30–10:30pm; Sun 5:30–9pm. Subway/El: Blue Line to Damen.

MODERATE

Jane's *Finds* ECLECTIC   This is a hugely popular destination among Wicker Park/Bucktown habitués, who'd prefer to keep it a secret. (Wait for your table at the friendly Bucktown Pub across the street.)

More than anything else, it may be the cozy ambience that attracts diners. Jane's is ensconced in an old house that has been gutted and rehabbed to create an open, two-story space with just 16 tables. (In summer, seven more are set up on an outside patio.) The menu offers piquant, upscale comfort food prepared simply and with loving care, including both meat (duck breast pan-seared with turnips and peaches; seared sea bass with mashed potatoes, arugula, caramelized pearl onions, and mushroom coulis) and vegetarian options, such as a goat cheese, tofu, and veggie burrito. The salads are standouts, especially the mesclun greens with pear, blue cheese, pecans, and balsamic vinaigrette.

1655 W. Cortland St. (1 block west of Ashland Ave.). © 773/862-5263. www.janes restaurant.com. Reservations recommended, but only a small number are accepted for each evening. Main courses $15–$25. MC, V. Sun–Thurs 5–10pm; Fri–Sat 5–11pm; Sat–Sun 10am–2:30pm. Subway/El: Blue Line to Damen.

Le Bouchon *Finds* BISTRO/FRENCH   Jean-Claude Poilevey's tiny storefront restaurant, Le Bouchon, is popular for both its intimate yet boisterous atmosphere and affordable authentic bistro fare. Whatever the season, the food here is fairly heavy, although specials are lighter in warmer months. Poilevey could pack this place every night just with regulars addicted to the house specialty of roast duck for two, bathed in Grand Marnier–orange marmalade sauce. The authenticity continues in the entree department, with steak frites, sautéed rabbit in white wine, veal kidneys in mustard sauce, and bouillabaisse. The sounds of prominent music and voices from closely packed tables create an atmosphere that some perceive as cozy and romantic, and others as claustrophobic and noisy. There's a small bar where you can wait—something you might have to do even if you have a reservation.

1958 N. Damen Ave. (at Armitage Ave.). © **773/862-6600.** www.lebouchonof
chicago.com. Reservations recommended. Main courses $16–$20. AE, DC, DISC, MC,
V. Mon–Thurs 5:30–11pm; Fri–Sat 5pm–midnight. Subway/El: Blue Line to Damen,
and then a short cab ride.

INEXPENSIVE

Hot Chocolate ⍟ AMERICAN   Mindy Segal's desserts got raves
when she worked at the restaurant mk (p. 67), so when she opened
her own place in early 2005—with a dessert theme, no less—there
were lines almost immediately. Although Segal knows her way
around high-end kitchens, she's designed Hot Chocolate to be more
of a casual neighborhood spot, the kind of place you can stop in for
a brioche and coffee in the morning, a Kobe beef steak sandwich at
lunch, or a plate of glazed pork tenderloin in the evening. However,
desserts are the main event here; many use seasonal fruit (apple-cider
potpie, or the banana napoleon, with layers of caramelized bananas,
banana coffee cake, graham crackers, and a topping of banana ice
cream), but chocoholics can get their fill, too, with dishes such as the
rich chocolate soufflé with caramel ice cream. Or you can finish up
with a flight of mini hot chocolates served with homemade marsh-
mallows.

1747 N. Damen Ave. (at Willow St.). © **773/489-1747.** Reservations not accepted.
Main courses $10–$13 lunch, $12–$23 dinner. AE, MC, V. Tues–Fri 11am–3pm;
Sat–Sun 10am–2pm; Tues–Wed and Sun 5:30–10pm; Thurs 5:30–11pm; Fri–Sat
5:30–midnight. Subway/El: Blue Line to Damen.

Northside Café AMERICAN/BURGERS   Among the best cheap
eats in the neighborhood, Northside cooks up great burgers, sandwiches, and salads—all for about $15 or less. This is strictly neigh-
borhood dining, without attitude and little in the way of decor; the
back dining room looks like a rec room circa 1973, complete with a
fireplace, pinball machines, and a pool table. In nice weather, Northside opens up its large front patio for dining, and a sky-lit cover
keeps it in use during the winter. You're always sure to be entertained
by people-watching here, as Northside attracts all sorts. During the
week, the cafe is more of a neighborhood hangout, while on weekends a touristy crowd from Lincoln Park and the suburbs piles in. A
limited late-night menu is available from 10pm to 1am.

1635 N. Damen Ave. (at North and Milwaukee aves.). © **773/384-3555.** Reservations not accepted. Menu items $6–$15. AE, DC, DISC, MC, V. Sun–Fri
11:30am–2am; Sat 11am–3am. Subway/El: Blue Line to Damen.

6

Exploring Chicago

Chicago may still be stereotyped as the home of sausage-loving, overweight guys who babble on endlessly about "da Bears" or "da Cubs," but in reality the city offers some of the most sophisticated cultural and entertainment options in the country. You'll have trouble fitting in all of Chicago's museums, which offer everything from action (the virtual-reality visit to the Milky Way galaxy at the Adler Planetarium) to quiet contemplation (the Impressionist masterpieces at the Art Institute of Chicago). Check out Sue, the biggest *T. rex* fossil ever discovered, at the Field Museum of Natural History, or be entranced by the colorful world of the Butterfly Haven at the Peggy Notebaert Nature Museum. Stroll through picture-perfect Lincoln Park Zoo on the Near North Side, and then enjoy the view from the top of the Ferris wheel on historic Navy Pier.

Best of all, the majority of the places you'll want to visit are in or near downtown, making it easy to plan your day and get from place to place.

1 In & Around the Loop: The Art Institute, the Sears Tower & Grant Park

The heart of the Loop is Chicago's business center, where you'll find the Chicago Board of Trade (the world's largest commodities, futures, and options exchange), Sears Tower, and some of the city's most famous early skyscrapers. If you're looking for an authentic big-city experience, wander the area on a weekday, when commuters are rushing to catch trains and businesspeople are hustling to get to work.

THE TOP ATTRACTIONS IN THE LOOP

Art Institute of Chicago ✮✮✮ *(Kids)*   You can't—and shouldn't—miss the Art Institute. (You really have no excuse, since it's conveniently located right on Michigan Ave. in the heart of downtown.) No matter what medium or century interests you, the Art Institute has something in its collection to fit the bill. Japanese *ukiyo-e* prints, ancient Egyptian bronzes, Greek vases, 19th-century British photography, masterpieces by most of the greatest names in 20th-century

Tips Insider Tips for Touring the Art Institute

If you want to enjoy your favorite masterpieces in something resembling peace and quiet, put some thought into the timing of your visit to the Art Institute, a museum so popular that it draws as much traffic as our jammed expressways.

Some tips for avoiding the rush hour: Many people don't realize the museum is open on Monday; keep this secret to yourself, and visit when the galleries are relatively subdued. Also, many visitors aren't aware that the museum stays open late on Thursdays, so consider stopping by after an early dinner (another bonus: free admission).

sculpture, and modern American textiles are just some of the works on display, but for a general overview of the museum's collection, take the free "Highlights of the Art Institute" tour, offered at 2pm on Tuesday, Saturday, and Sunday.

If time is limited, head straight to the museum's renowned anthology of **Impressionist art** 🌟🌟🌟, which includes one of the world's largest collections of Monet paintings; this is one of the most popular areas of the museum, so arriving early pays off. Among the treasures, you'll find Seurat's pointillist masterpiece *Sunday Afternoon on the Island of La Grande Jatte.* The galleries of **European and American contemporary art** 🌟🌟 include paintings, sculptures, and mixed-media works by Pablo Picasso, Henri Matisse, Salvador Dalí, Willem de Kooning, Jackson Pollock, and Andy Warhol. Visitors are sometimes surprised when they discover many of the icons that hang here. (Grant Wood's *American Gothic* and Edward Hopper's *Nighthawks* are two that often get double takes.)

Other recommended exhibits are the collection of delicate mid–19th-century **glass paperweights** in the famous Arthur Rubloff collection, and the great hall of **European arms and armor** 🌟 dating from the 15th to 19th centuries. Composed of more than 1,500 objects, including armor, horse equipment, swords and daggers, polearms, and maces, the collection is one of the most important assemblages of its kind in the country. (If you do head down here, don't miss Marc Chagall's stunning stained-glass windows at the end of the gallery.)

Chicago Attractions

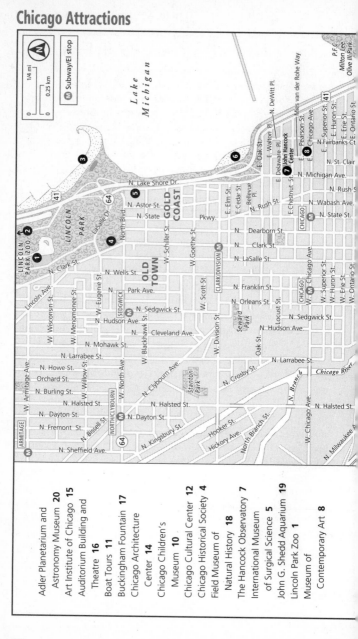

M Subway/El stop

Lake Michigan

LINCOLN PARK

GOLD COAST

OLD TOWN

Adler Planetarium and
Astronomy Museum **20**

Art Institute of Chicago **15**

Auditorium Building and
Theatre **16**

Boat Tours **11**

Buckingham Fountain **17**

Chicago Architecture
Center **14**

Chicago Children's
Museum **10**

Chicago Cultural Center **12**

Chicago Historical Society **4**

Field Museum of
Natural History **18**

The Hancock Observatory **7**

International Museum
of Surgical Science **5**

John G. Shedd Aquarium **19**

Lincoln Park Zoo **1**

Museum of
Contemporary Art **8**

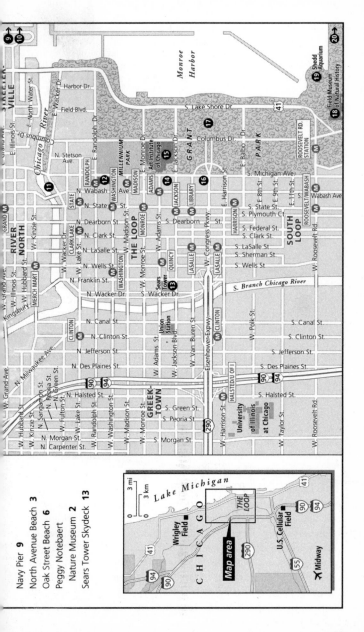

Navy Pier **9**
North Avenue Beach **3**
Oak Street Beach **6**
Peggy Notebaert
Nature Museum **2**
Sears Tower Skydeck **13**

111 S. Michigan Ave. (at Adams St.). ✆ 312/443-3600. www.artic.edu. Admission $12 adults; $7 seniors and students with ID; free for children 11 and under. Additional cost for special exhibitions. Free admission Thurs 5–8pm. Mon–Fri 10:30am–5pm (Thurs until 8pm, until 9pm Thurs–Fri Memorial Day–Labor Day); Sat–Sun 10am–5pm. Closed Jan. 1, Thanksgiving, and Dec 25. Bus: 3, 4, 60, 145, 147, or 151. Subway/El: Green, Brown, Purple, or Orange line to Adams, or Red Line to Monroe/State or Jackson/State.

Sears Tower Skydeck *(Overrated* First Sears sold the building and moved to cheaper suburban offices in 1992. Then the skyscraper got an ego blow when the Petronas Towers in Kuala Lumpur, Malaysia, went up and laid claim to the title of world's tallest building. (The Sears Tower has since put up a 22-ft. antenna in an attempt to win back the title.) Tallest-building posturing aside, this is still a great place to orient yourself to the city, but I wouldn't put it on the top of must-see sights for anyone with limited time (and limited patience for crowds).

The view from the 103rd-floor Skydeck is everything you'd expect it to be—once you get there. Unfortunately, you're often stuck in a very long, very noisy line, so by the time you make it to the top, your patience could be as thin as the atmosphere up there. (Come in the late afternoon or early evening to avoid most of the crowds.) On a clear day, visibility extends up to 50 miles, and you can catch glimpses of four surrounding states. Despite the fact that it's called a "skydeck," you can't actually walk outside. Multimedia exhibits on Chicago history and *Knee High Chicago,* an exhibit for kids, are additional attractions. The 70-second, high-speed elevator trip will feel like a thrill ride for some, but it's a nightmare for anyone with even mild claustrophobia. Allow 1 hour, more if there's a long line.

233 S. Wacker Dr. (enter on Jackson Blvd.). ✆ 312/875-9696. www.the-skydeck. com. Admission $13 adults; $9.50 seniors and children 3–12; free for children 2 and under. Apr–Sept daily 10am–10pm; Oct–Mar daily 10am–8pm. Bus: 1, 7, 126, 146, 151, or 156. Subway/El: Brown, Purple, or Orange line to Quincy, or Red or Blue line to Jackson; and then walk a few blocks west.

THE LOOP SCULPTURE TOUR

Monuments, statues, and contemporary sculptures are on view throughout Chicago, but the concentration of public art within the Loop and nearby Grant Park is worth noting. The best known of these works are by 20th-century artists including Picasso, Chagall, Miró, Calder, Moore, and Oldenburg. The newest addition is the massive elliptical sculpture **Cloud Gate** (known as "The Bean" because it looks like a giant silver kidney bean) by British artist Anish Kapoor. The sculpture, in Millennium Park, was Kapoor's first public commission in the U.S.

The Loop Sculpture Tour

1 *Untitled ("The Picasso")*,
  Pablo Picasso (1967)
2 *Chicago*, Joan Miró (1981)
3 *Monument with Standing Beast*,
  Jean Dubuffet (1984)
4 *Freeform*, Richard Hunt (1993)
5 *Flight of Daedalus and Icarus*,
  120 N. LaSalle St.,
  Roger Brown (1990)
6 *Dawn Shadows*, Louise Nevelson (1983)
7 *Loomings* and *Knights and Squires*,
  Frank Stella
8 *Batcolumn*, Claes Oldenburg (1977)
9 *The Universe*, Alexander Calder (1974)
10 *Gem of the Lakes*,
   Raymond Kaskey (1990)
11 *San Marco II*, Ludovico de Luigi (1986)
12 *The Town-Ho's Story*, Frank Stella (1993)
13 *Ruins III*, Nita K. Sutherland (1978)
14 *Flamingo*, Alexander Calder (1974)
15 *Lines in Four Directions*,
   Sol Lewitt (1985)
16 *The Four Seasons*, Marc Chagall (1974)
17 *Untitled Sounding Sculpture*,
   Harry Bertoia (1975)
18 *Cloud Gate*, Anish Kapoor (2004)
19 *Large Interior Form*, Henry Moore (1983)
20 *Celebration of the 200th Anniversary
   of the Founding of the Republic*,
   Isamu Noguchi (1976)
21 *The Fountain of the Great Lakes*,
   Lorado Taft (1913)

Oprah in Person

Oprah Winfrey tapes her phenomenally successful talk show at Harpo Studios, 1058 W. Washington Blvd., just west of the Loop. If you'd like to be in her studio audience, you'll have to plan ahead: Reservations are taken by phone only (② **312/591-9222**), at least 1 month in advance. For information on upcoming shows, check the website (www.oprah.com); if you've got a great personal story that relates to a show being planned, you can submit it online and just might get booked as a guest.

A free brochure, *The Chicago Public Art Guide* (available at the Chicago Cultural Center, 78 E. Washington St.), can help steer you toward the best examples of monumental public art. You can also conduct a self-guided tour of the city's best public sculptures by following "The Loop Sculpture Tour" map (p. 91).

The single most famous sculpture is **Pablo Picasso's** *Untitled,* located in Daley Plaza and constructed out of Cor-Ten steel, the same gracefully rusting material used on the exterior of the Daley Center behind it. Viewed from various perspectives, its enigmatic shape suggests a woman, bird, or dog. Perhaps because it was the button-down Loop's first monumental modern sculpture, its installation in 1967 was met with hoots and heckles, but today "The Picasso" enjoys semiofficial status as the logo of modern Chicago. It is by far the city's most popular photo opportunity among visiting tourists. At noon on weekdays during warm weather, you'll likely find a dance troupe, musical group, or visual-arts exhibition here as part of the city's long-running "Under the Picasso" multicultural program. Call ② **312/346-3278** for event information.

GRANT PARK & MILLENNIUM PARK

Thanks to architect Daniel Burnham and his coterie of visionary civic planners—who drafted the revolutionary 1909 Plan of Chicago—the city boasts a wide-open lakefront park system unrivaled by most major metropolises. Modeled after the gardens at Versailles, **Grant Park** (② **312/742-PLAY;** www.chicagopark district.com) is Chicago's front yard, composed of giant lawns segmented by *allées* of trees, plantings, and paths, and pieced together by major roadways and a network of railroad tracks. Incredibly, the entire expanse was created from sandbars, landfill, and Chicago Fire debris; the original shoreline extended all the way to Michigan Avenue. A few museums are spread out inside the park, but most of the space is wide open (a legacy of mail-order magnate Aaron Montgomery Ward's *fin de siècle* campaign to limit municipal buildings).

The northwest corner of Grant Park (bordered by Michigan Ave. and Randolph St.) is the site of **Millennium Park** 🏖🏖🏖, one of the city's grandest public-works projects. The park's centerpiece is the dramatic Frank Gehry–designed **Pritzker Music Pavilion,** featuring massive curved ribbons of steel. The Grant Park Symphony Orchestra and Chorus stages a popular series of free outdoor classical music concerts here most Wednesday through Sunday evenings in the summer. For a schedule of concert times and dates, contact the **Grant Park Music Festival** (ⓒ **312/742-7638;** www.grantparkmusic festival.com). Two public artworks well worth checking out are the kidney bean–shaped sculpture *Cloud Gate* and the **Crown Fountain,** where children splash in the shallow water between giant faces projected on video screens. Free walking tours of the park are offered daily from Memorial Day through October at 11:30am and 1pm, starting at the park's Welcome Center, 201 E. Randolph St. (ⓒ **312/ 742-1168**).

Head south to the lake via Congress Parkway, and you'll find **Buckingham Fountain** 🏖, the baroque centerpiece of the park, composed of pink Georgia marble and patterned after—but twice the size of—the Latona Fountain at Versailles, with adjoining esplanades beautified by rose gardens in season. From April through October, the fountain spurts columns of water up to 150 feet in the air every hour on the hour, and beginning at 4pm, a whirl of colored lights and dramatic music amps up the drama. The fountain shuts down at 11pm; concession areas and bathrooms are available on the plaza.

To get to Grant Park, take bus no. 3, 4, 6, 146, or 151. If you want to take the subway or the El, get off at any stop in the Loop along State or Wabash, and walk east.

ALONG SOUTH MICHIGAN AVENUE

Fashion and glamour might have moved north to the Magnificent Mile, but Chicago's grandest stretch of boulevard is still Michigan Avenue, south of the river. Particularly impressive is the great wall of buildings from Randolph Street south to Congress Parkway (beginning with the Chicago Cultural Center and terminating at the Auditorium Building) that architecture buffs refer to as the "Michigan Avenue Cliff."

⌒Moments **Photo Op**

For a great photo op, walk on Randolph Street toward the lake in the morning when the sun, rising in the east over the lake, hits the cliff of buildings along South Michigan Avenue, giving you the perfect backdrop for an only-in-Chicago picture.

The following attractions are listed from north to south.

Chicago Cultural Center ⍟ *Finds*   The Chicago Cultural Center was built in 1897 as the city's public library, and in 1991 it was transformed into a showplace for visual and performing arts. Today, it's an overlooked civic treasure with a basic Beaux Arts exterior and a sumptuous interior of rare marble, fine hardwood, stained glass, and mosaics of Favrile glass, colored stone, and mother-of-pearl inlaid in white marble. The crowning centerpiece is Preston Bradley Hall's majestic **Tiffany dome** ⍟, said to be the largest of its kind in the world.

The building also houses one of the **Chicago Office of Tourism** visitor centers, which makes it an ideal place to kick-start your visit. If you stop in to pick up tourist information and take a quick look around, your visit won't take longer than 15 minutes, but the Cultural Center also schedules an array of art exhibitions, concerts, films, lectures, and other special events (many free), which might convince you to extend your time here. A long-standing tradition is the 12:15pm Dame Myra Hess Memorial classical concert every Wednesday in the Preston Bradley Hall.

Guided architectural tours of the Cultural Center run at 1:15pm on Wednesday, Friday, and Saturday.

78 E. Washington St. ✆ **312/744-6630,** or 312/FINE-ART for weekly events. www.cityofchicago.org/exploringchicago. Free admission. Mon–Thurs 10am–7pm; Fri 10am–6pm; Sat 10am–5pm; Sun 11am–5pm. Closed major holidays. Bus: 3, 4, 20, 56, 145, 146, 147, 151, or 157. Subway/El: Brown, Green, Orange, or Purple line to Randolph, or Red Line to Washington/State.

Chicago ArchiCenter   Chicago's architecture is one of the city's main claims to fame, and a quick swing through this center, run by the well-regarded **Chicago Architecture Foundation** (conveniently located across the street from the Art Institute), will help you understand why. Exhibits include a scale model of downtown Chicago, profiles of the people and buildings that shaped the city's look, and a searchable database with pictures of and information on many of

Chicago's best-known skyscrapers. "Architecture ambassadors" are on hand to provide information on tours run by the foundation (see "Sightseeing Tours" on p. 117). Two galleries feature changing exhibits about ongoing Chicago design projects, so you can see first-hand how local architecture continues to evolve. There's also an excellent gift shop filled with architecture-focused books, decorative accessories, and gifts. Allow a half-hour, more if you want to browse in the store.

224 S. Michigan Ave. ⓒ **312/922-3432,** ext. 241. www.architecture.org. Free admission. Exhibits Mon–Sat 9:30am–4pm. Shop and tour desk Mon–Sat 9am–6:30pm; Sun 9am–6pm. Bus: 3, 4, 145, 147, or 151. Subway/El: Brown, Green, Purple, or Orange line to Adams, or Red Line to Jackson.

Auditorium Building and Theatre 𝕽𝕽   A truly grand theater with historic-landmark status, the Auditorium is worth a visit to experience late–19th-century Chicago opulence. Because it's still a working theater—not a museum—it's not always open to the public during the day; to make sure you'll get in, schedule a guided tour, which are offered on Mondays at 10am and 1pm (call ⓒ **312/431-2389** to confirm the date and time; reservations aren't necessary). Tours cost $8 per person.

Designed and built in 1889 by Louis Sullivan and Dankmar Adler, the 4,000-seat Auditorium was a wonder of the world: the heaviest (110,000 tons) and most massive modern edifice on earth, the most fireproof building ever constructed, and the tallest building in Chicago. Don't miss the lobby fronting Michigan Avenue, with its faux-marble ornamental columns, molded ceilings, mosaic floors, and Mexican onyx walls. Allow 1 hour for the guided tour.

50 E. Congress Pkwy. ⓒ **312/922-2110.** www.auditoriumtheatre.org. For tickets to a performance at the Auditorium, call Ticketmaster at ⓒ **312/902-1500.** Bus: 145, 147, or 151. Subway/El: Brown, Green, Orange, or Purple line to Library/Van Buren, or Red Line to Jackson.

2 The Earth, the Sky & the Sea: The Big Three in the Grant Park Museum Campus

With terraced gardens and broad walkways, the Museum Campus at the southern end of Grant Park makes it easy for pedestrians to visit three of the city's most beloved institutions: the natural history museum, aquarium, and planetarium. The campus is about a 15- to 20-minute walk from the Loop and is easy to reach by bus or subway (a free trolley runs from the Roosevelt Rd. El stop). To get to the Museum Campus from the Loop, head east across Grant Park on East Balbo Drive from South Michigan Avenue, and then trek south along the lakeshore path to the museums. Or, approach on the path that begins at 11th Street from South Michigan Avenue. Follow 11th to the walkway that spans the Metra tracks, cross Columbus Drive, and then pick up the path that will take you under Lake Shore Drive and into the Museum Campus. The CTA no. 146 bus will take you from downtown to all three of these attractions. Call ℂ **836-7000** (from any city or suburban area code) for the stop locations and schedule.

A large indoor parking lot is accessible from Lake Shore Drive southbound; you can park there all day for $15. Be aware that there is no public parking during Chicago Bears games in the fall; Soldier Field is next to the Museum Campus, and football fans get first dibs on all the surrounding parking spaces.

Adler Planetarium and Astronomy Museum 𝕶𝕶   The building may be historic, but some of the attractions here will captivate the most jaded video-game addict. Your first stop should be the modern Sky Pavilion, where the don't-miss experience is the **Star-Rider Theater** 𝕶𝕶. Settle down under the massive dome, and you'll take a half-hour interactive virtual-reality trip through the Milky Way and into deep space, featuring a computer-generated 3-D-graphics projection system and controls in the armrest of each seat. Six high-resolution video projectors form a seamless image above your head—you'll feel as if you're literally floating in space. If you're looking for more entertainment, the **Sky Theater** shows movies with an astronomical bent. Recent shows have included *Secrets of Saturn* and *Mars Now!*, both of which are updated as new discoveries are made.

The planetarium's exhibition galleries feature a variety of displays and interactive activities. If you're only going to see one exhibit (and have kids in tow), check out ***Shoot For the Moon*** 𝕶𝕶, an exhibit on lunar exploration that's full of interactive stations (it also showcases the personal collection of astronaut Jim Lovell, captain of the infamous Apollo 13 mission, who now lives in the Chicago suburbs). Other exhibits include ***Bringing the Heavens to Earth*** 𝕶, which traces the ways different cultures have tried to make sense of astronomical phenomena, and ***From the Night Sky to the Big Bang,*** which includes artifacts from the planetarium's extensive collection of astronomical instruments (although suitable for older children, these can get a bit boring for little ones unless they're real astronomy nuts). Allow 2 hours, more if you want to see more than one show.

1300 S. Lake Shore Dr. ℂ **312/922-STAR.** www.adlerplanetarium.org. Admission $10 adults, $8 seniors, $6 children 4–17, free for children 3 and under; admission including 1 show and audiotour $19 adults, $17 seniors, $15 children. Free admission Mon–Tues Oct–Nov and Jan–Feb. Memorial Day–Labor Day daily 9:30am–6pm; early Sept–late May daily 9:30am–4:30pm; 1st Fri of every month until 10pm. Star-Rider Theater and Sky Shows run throughout the day; call main number for current times. Bus: 12 or 146.

Field Museum of Natural History 𝒦𝒦𝒦 *Kids*   Is it any wonder that Steven Spielberg thought the Field Museum of Natural History was a suitable home turf for the intrepid archaeologist and adventurer hero of his Indiana Jones movies? Spread over the museum's 9 acres of floor space are scores of permanent and temporary exhibitions—some interactive but most requiring the old-fashion skills of observation and imagination.

Navigating all the disparate exhibits can be daunting, so start out in the grand Stanley Field Hall, which you enter from the north or south end. Standing proudly at the north side is the largest, most complete *Tyrannosaurus rex* fossil ever unearthed. The museum acquired the specimen—named **Sue** 𝒦𝒦𝒦 for the paleontologist who discovered it in South Dakota in 1990—for a cool $8.4 million after a high-stakes bidding war. The real skull is so heavy that a lighter copy had to be mounted on the skeleton; the actual one is on display nearby.

Families should head downstairs for two of the most popular kid-friendly exhibits. The pieces on display in ***Inside Ancient Egypt*** 𝒦𝒦 came to the museum in the early 1900s, after researchers in Saqqara, Egypt, excavated two of the original chambers from the tomb of Unis-ankh, son of the Fifth Dynasty ruler Pharaoh Unis. The mastaba (tomb) of Unis-ankh forms the core of a spellbinding exhibit that realistically depicts scenes from Egyptian funeral, religious, and other social practices.

Next to the Egypt exhibit, you'll find ***Underground Adventure*** 𝒦𝒦, a "total immersion environment" populated by giant robotic earwigs, centipedes, wolf spiders, and other subterranean critters. The Disneyesque exhibit is a big hit with kids, but—annoyingly—carries an extra admission charge ($7 on top of regular admission).

You might be tempted to skip the "peoples of the world" exhibits, but trust me, some are not only mind-opening but also great fun. ***Traveling the Pacific*** 𝒦, hidden up on the second floor, is definitely worth a stop. Hundreds of artifacts from the museum's oceanic collection re-create scenes of island life in the South Pacific (there's even a full-scale model of a Maori meetinghouse). *Africa* 🐾, an assemblage of African artifacts and provocative interactive multimedia presentations, takes viewers to Senegal, a Cameroon palace, the wildlife-rich savanna, and on a "virtual" journey aboard a slave ship to the Americas. Allow 3 hours.

Roosevelt Rd. and Lake Shore Dr. ⓒ 312/922-9410. www.fieldmuseum.org. Admission $12 adults; $7 seniors, students with ID and children 4–11; free for children 3 and under. Discounted admission Mon–Tues mid-Sept through Nov and Jan–Feb. Daily 9am–5pm. Closed Dec 25. Bus: 6, 10, 12, 130, or 146.

John G. Shedd Aquarium 🐾🐾🐾 The Shedd is one of the world's largest indoor aquariums, and houses thousands of river, lake, and sea denizens in standard aquarium tanks and elaborate new habitats within its octagon-shaped marble building. The only problem with the Shedd is its steep admission price ($23 for adults). You can keep your costs down by buying the "Aquarium Only" admission, but you'll miss some of the most stunning exhibits. A CityPass can also save you money if you visit enough of the other included attractions.

The first thing you'll see as you enter is the **Caribbean Coral Reef** 🐾. This 90,000-gallon circular tank occupies the Beaux Arts–style central rotunda, entertaining spectators who press up against the glass to ogle divers feeding nurse sharks, barracudas, stingrays, and a hawksbill sea turtle. A roving camera connected to video monitors on the tank's periphery gives visitors close-ups of the animals inside, but I'd recommend sticking around to catch one of the daily feedings, when a diver swims around the tank and (thanks to a microphone) talks about the species and their eating habits.

The exhibits surrounding the Caribbean coral reef re-create marine habitats around the world. The best is *Amazon Rising: Seasons of the River* 🐾, a rendering of the Amazon basin that showcases frogs and other animals as well as fish (although the sharp-toothed piranhas are pretty cool).

You'll pay extra to see the other Shedd highlights, but they're quite impressive, so I'd suggest shelling out for them if you plan to spend more than an hour here. The *Oceanarium* 🐾🐾🐾, with a wall of windows revealing the lake outside, replicates a Pacific Northwest coastal environment and creates the illusion of one uninterrupted expanse of sea. On a fixed performance schedule in a large pool flanked by an amphitheater, a crew of friendly trainers puts dolphins through their paces of leaping dives, breaches, and tail walking. If you're visiting during a summer weekend, you may also want to buy your Oceanarium ticket in advance to make sure you can catch a show that day. *Wild Reef—Sharks at Shedd* 🐾🐾 is a series of 26 connected habitats that house a Philippine coral reef patrolled by sharks and other predators. The floor-to-ceiling windows bring the toothy swimmers up close and personal (they even swim over your head at certain spots). Allow 2 to 3 hours.

1200 S. Lake Shore Dr. (C) 312/939-2438. www.sheddaquarium.org. All-Access Pass (to all exhibits) $23 adults, $16 seniors and children 3–11, free for children 2 and under; admission to aquarium and Wild Reef $18 adults, $14 seniors and children; aquarium only $8 adults, $6 seniors and children. Free admission to aquarium only Mon–Tues Oct–Nov and Jan–Feb. Memorial Day–Labor Day daily 9am–6pm; early Sept–late May Mon–Fri 9am–5pm, Sat–Sun 9am–6pm. Bus: 6 or 146.

3 North of the Loop: The Magnificent Mile & Beyond

Most of these sights are either on the Magnificent Mile (North Michigan Ave.) and its surrounding blocks or close by on the Near North Side.

The Hancock Observatory 𝒶𝒶   The Hancock isn't as famous as the Sears Tower, but for many locals, its bold tapered shape and steel cross-bracing exterior design represent the archetypal Chicago skyscraper. The Hancock Observatory delivers an excellent panorama of the city and an intimate view of nearby Lake Michigan and various shoreline residential areas. While the view from the top of Chicago's third-tallest building is enough to satisfy, high-tech additions have enhanced the experience. "Talking telescopes" have sound effects and narration in four languages, history walls illustrate the growth of the city, and the Skywalk open-air viewing deck allows visitors to feel the rush of the wind at 1,000 feet through a "screened porch." On a clear day, you can see portions of the three states surrounding this corner of Illinois (Michigan, Indiana, and Wisconsin), for a radius of 40 to 50 miles.

94th floor, John Hancock Center, 875 N. Michigan Ave. (enter on Delaware St.). (C) 888/875-VIEW or 312/751-3681. www.hancock-observatory.com. Admission $11 adults, $8 seniors, $7 children 5–12, free for children 4 and under. Daily 9am–11pm. Bus: 145, 146, 147, or 151. Subway/El: Red Line to Chicago/State.

Museum of Contemporary Art 𝒶𝒶   Although the MCA is one of the largest contemporary art museums in the country, theaters and hallways seem to take up much of the space, so seeing the actual art won't take you long. The museum exhibits emphasize experimentation in a variety of media, including painting, sculpture, photography, video and film, dance, music, and performance. The gloomy, imposing building, designed by Berlin's Josef Paul Kleihues, is a bit out of place between the lake and the historic Water Tower, but the interior spaces are more vibrant, with a sun-drenched two-story central corridor, elliptical staircases, and three floors of exhibition space.

You can see the MCA's highlights in about an hour, although art lovers will want more time to wander (especially if a high-profile exhibit is in town). Your first stop should be the handsome barrel-vaulted galleries on the top floor, dedicated to pieces from the permanent collection. Visitors who'd like a little guidance with making sense of the rather challenging works can rent an audio tour or take a free tour (1 and 6pm Tues; 1pm Wed–Fri; noon, 1, 2, and 3pm Sat–Sun). Allow 1 to 2 hours.

220 E. Chicago Ave. (1 block east of Michigan Ave.). ℂ **312/280-2660.** www.mcachicago.org. Admission $10 adults, $6 seniors and students with ID, free for children 12 and under. Free admission Tues. Tues 10am–8pm; Wed–Sun 10am–5pm. Closed Jan 1, Thanksgiving, and Dec 25. Bus: 3, 10, 66, 145, 146, or 151. Subway/El: Red Line to Chicago/State.

Navy Pier ☂ (Kids)   Built during World War I, this 3,000-foot-long pier was a Navy training center for pilots during World War II. The military aura is long gone and replaced with a combination of carnival attractions, a food court, and boat dock, making it a bustling tourist mecca and a place for a fun stroll (if you don't mind the crowds). To get the best views back to the city, walk all the way down to the end.

Midway down the pier are the **Crystal Gardens** ☂, with 70 full-size palm trees, dancing fountains, and other flora in a glass-enclosed atrium; a carousel and kiddie carnival rides; and a 15-story Ferris wheel, a replica of the original that made its debut at Chicago's 1893 World's Fair. The 50 acres of pier and lakefront property are also home to the **Chicago Children's Museum** (p. 116), a **3-D IMAX theater** (ℂ **312/595-5629**), a small ice-skating rink, and the **Chicago Shakespeare Theatre** (p. 152). The shops tend to be bland and touristy, and dining options include a food court, an outpost of Lincoln Park's popular Charlie's Ale House, and the white-tablecloth seafood restaurant Riva.

Take the half-mile stroll to the end of the pier, east of the ballroom, where you can find a little respite and enjoy the wind, the waves, and the city view, which is the real delight of a place like this. Or, unwind in **Olive Park,** a small sylvan haven with a sliver of beach just north of Navy Pier. Allow 1 hour.

600 E. Grand Ave. (at Lake Michigan). ℂ **800/595-PIER** (outside 312 area code) or 312/595-PIER. www.navypier.com. Free admission. Summer Sun–Thurs 10am–10pm, Fri–Sat 10am–midnight; fall–spring Mon–Thurs 10am–8pm, Fri–Sat

10am–10pm, Sun 10am–7pm. Parking: $19/day weekdays; $23/day weekends. Lots fill quickly. Bus: 29, 65, 66, 120, or 121. Subway/El: Red Line to Grand/State; transfer to city bus or board a free pier trolley bus.

4 Lincoln Park Attractions

Lincoln Park is the city's largest park, and certainly one of the longest. Straight and narrow, the park begins at North Avenue and follows the shoreline of Lake Michigan north for several miles. Within its 1,200 acres are a world-class zoo, half a dozen beaches, a botanical conservatory, two excellent museums, a golf course, and the meadows, formal gardens, sporting fields, and tennis courts typical of urban parks. To get to the park, take bus no. 22, 145, 146, 147, 151, or 156.

Chicago History Museum ℱ The Chicago History Museum at the southwestern tip of Lincoln Park is one of the city's oldest cultural institutions (founded in 1856), but it's reinvented itself for the 21st century. The main, must-see exhibit is ***Chicago: Crossroads of America*** ℱℱ, which fills the museum's second floor. A survey of the city's history—from its founding as a frontier trading post to the riots at the 1968 Democratic Convention—it's filled with photos, artifacts, and newsreels that make the past come alive; surrounding galleries track the development of local sports teams, architecture, music, and art. Although the exhibit is geared toward families with older children (you can even download an mp3 audio tour for teenagers from the museum's website), little ones love the re-creation of an 1890s El station, where they can run inside the city's first elevated train. Another museum highlight is the hall of dioramas that re-create scenes from Chicago's past. Although they've been around for decades (and are decidedly low-tech), they're a fun way to trace the city's progression from a few small cabins to the grand World's Columbian Exposition of 1893. The museum's Costume and Textile Gallery showcases pieces from the museum's renowned collection of historic clothing. The Children's Gallery on the ground floor has interactive exhibits for kids, including a giant table where you can experience the "Smells of Chicago" (my personal favorite). Allow 1 to 2 hours.

1601 N. Clark St. (at North Ave.). ℂ **312/642-4600.** www.chicagohistory.org. Admission $12 adults, $10 seniors and students, free for children 12 and under. Free admission Mon. Mon–Sat 9:30am–4:30pm (until 8pm Thurs); Sun noon–5pm. Research center Tues–Thurs 1–4pm; Fri 10am–4:30pm. Bus: 11, 22, 36, 72, 151, or 156.

Lincoln Park Zoo 🐾🐾🐾 *Value* One of the city's treasures, this family-friendly attraction is not only open 365 days a year, it's also free. Even if you don't have time for a complete tour of the various habitats, it's worth at least a quick stop during a stroll through Lincoln Park.

My favorite exhibit is the **Regenstein African Journey** 🐾🐾🐾, a series of linked indoor and outdoor habitats that's home to elephants, giraffes, rhinos, and other large mammals; large glass-enclosed tanks allow visitors to go face-to-face with swimming pygmy hippos and (not for the faint of heart) a rocky ledge filled with Madagascar hissing cockroaches.

Your second stop should be the **Regenstein Center for African Apes** 🐾🐾. Lincoln Park Zoo has had remarkable success breeding gorillas and chimpanzees, and watching these ape families interact can be mesmerizing (and touching). *One caveat:* I've found the building incredibly noisy during weekend visits, so be prepared.

Other exhibits worth a visit are the **Small Mammal–Reptile House,** which features a glass-enclosed walk-through ecosystem simulating river, savanna, and forest habitats, and the popular **Sea Lion Pool** in the center of the zoo, which is home to harbor seals, gray seals, and California sea lions (walk down the ramp and take a look at the underwater viewing area). Allow 3 hours. For the adjoining children's zoo, see "Kid Stuff" on p. 116.

2200 N. Cannon Dr. (at Fullerton Pkwy.). ☏ 312/742-2000. www.lpzoo.com. Free admission. Buildings daily 10am–5pm (Memorial Day–Labor Day until 6:30pm Sat–Sun). Grounds Memorial Day–Labor Day daily 9am–7pm; Apr–late May and early Sept–Oct daily 9am–6pm; Nov–Mar daily 9am–5pm. Parking $14 for up to 3 hours in on-site lot. Bus: 151 or 156.

Peggy Notebaert Nature Museum 🐾 *Kids* Built into the rise of an ancient sand dune—once the shoreline of Lake Michigan—this museum bills itself as "an environmental museum for the 21st century." While that sounds pretty dull, most of the exhibits are very hands-on, making this a good stop for active kids (most exhibits are designed for children rather than adults).

Rooftop-level walkways give strollers a view of birds and other urban wildlife below, and paths wind through gardens planted with native Midwestern wildflowers and grasses. Inside, large windows create a dialogue between the outdoor environment and the indoor exhibits designed to illuminate it. My favorite exhibit by far is the ***Butterfly Haven*** 🐾🐾, a greenhouse habitat where about 25 Midwestern species of butterflies and moths carry on their complex life cycles (wander through as a riot of color flutters all around you). If you're traveling with little ones, I'd also recommend the **Extreme Green House** *(K*, a bungalow where kids can play while learning about environmentally friendly habits, and **RiverWorks,** a water play exhibit that gives children an excuse to splash around while building dams and maneuvering boats along a mini river. Allow 1 to 2 hours.

Fullerton Ave. and Cannon Dr. *C* **773/755-5100**. www.chias.org. Admission $7 adults, $5 seniors and students, $4 children 3–12, free for children 2 and under. Free admission Thurs. Mon–Fri 9am–4:30pm; Sat–Sun 10am–5pm. Closed Jan 1, Thanksgiving, and Dec 25. Bus: 151 or 156. Free trolley service from area CTA stations and parking garages Sat–Sun and holidays 10am–6pm Memorial Day–Labor Day. Visit the museum website for route information and schedule.

5 Exploring Hyde Park: The Museum of Science & Industry & More

Hyde Park, south of the loop, is the birthplace of atomic fission, home to the University of Chicago and the popular Museum of Science and Industry, and definitely worth a trip. You should allow at least half a day to explore the campus and neighborhood (one of Chicago's most successfully integrated) and a full day if you want to explore museums as well.

GETTING THERE   From the Loop, the ride to Hyde Park on the **no. 6 Jeffrey Express bus** takes about 30 minutes. The southbound express bus fare adds a surcharge of 25¢ to the normal fare of $2 (there's no surcharge if you use a CTA transit card). The **no. 1 local bus** originates at Union Station on Jackson Boulevard and Canal Street and takes about an hour.

For a faster trip, take the **Metra Electric train** on the South Chicago line, which goes from downtown to Hyde Park in about 15 minutes. Downtown stations are at Randolph Street and Michigan Avenue, Van Buren Street and Michigan Avenue, and Roosevelt Road and Michigan Avenue (near the Museum Campus in Grant Park). Printed schedules are available at the stations. The fare is approximately $2 each way.

For CTA bus and Metra train information, call *C* **836-7000** (from any city or suburban area code), or visit **www.transitchicago. com** or **www.metrarail.com**.

For taxis, dial *C* **312/TAXI-CAB** (312/829-4222) for **Yellow Cab** or *C* **312/CHECKER** (312/243-2537) for **Checker.** The one-way fare from downtown is around $15 to $20.

A SUGGESTED ITINERARY   A long 1-day itinerary for Hyde Park should include the following: a walk through the University of

Chicago campus (including a stroll along the Midway Plaisance); a visit to the Museum of Science and Industry (for families), Frank Lloyd Wright's Robie House or one of the other local museums; and lunch or dinner in the neighborhood's commercial center.

THE TOP ATTRACTIONS

DuSable Museum of African-American History   The DuSable Museum is a repository of the history, art, and artifacts pertaining to the African-American experience and culture. Named for Chicago's first permanent settler, Jean Baptiste Point du Sable, a French-Canadian of Haitian descent, it has managed to accumulate a respectable collection of more than 13,000 artifacts, books, photographs, art objects, and memorabilia. Its collection of paintings, drawings, and sculpture by African American and African artists is excellent.

In 1993, the DuSable Museum added a 25,000-square-foot wing named in honor of the city's first and only African-American mayor, Harold Washington. The permanent exhibit on Washington contains memorabilia and personal effects, and surveys important episodes in his political career. The museum also has a gift shop, a research library, and an extensive program of community-related events. Allow 1 to 2 hours.

740 E. 56th Place. (✆ 773/947-0600. www.dusablemuseum.org. Admission $3 adults, $2 students and seniors, $1 children 6–13, free for children 5 and under. Free admission Sun. Tues–Sat 10am–5pm; Sun noon–5pm. Closed major holidays. Bus: 6 or Metra Electric train to 57th St. and Lake Park Ave., and then a short cab ride.

Museum of Science and Industry ⟨⟨⟨ *Kids*   Even if you don't plan on spending the day in Hyde Park, you'll pass through the neighborhood on your way to one of Chicago's most popular tourist attractions. The massive Museum of Science and Industry is the granddaddy of interactive museums, with some 2,000 exhibits. Schedule at least 3 hours here; a comprehensive visit can take all day, especially if you catch an OMNIMAX movie.

While the museum is constantly adding new displays to cover the latest scientific breakthroughs, you shouldn't miss certain tried-and-true exhibits that have been here for years and epitomize the museum for Chicagoans. The **U-505** ⟨⟨⟨, a German submarine that was captured in 1944 and arrived at the museum 10 years later, brings home the claustrophobic reality of underwater naval life. The sub is displayed in a dramatic indoor arena with exhibits and newsreel footage that put the U-boat in historical context (a guided tour of the sub's interior costs $5 extra, but the exhibit is worth visiting even if you don't go inside). The full-scale **Coal Mine** 🏆🏆, which dates back to 1934, incorporates modern mining techniques into the exhibit—but the best part is the simulated trip down into a dark, mysterious mine. Get to these exhibits quickly after the museum opens because they attract amusement-park-length lines during the day.

Kids who love planes, trains, and automobiles shouldn't miss *All Aboard the Silver Streak,* a refurbished Burlington Pioneer Zephyr train with onboard interactive exhibits; the massive model-train exhibit that makes up *The Great Train Story* 🏆🏆; or *Take Flight,* an aviation exhibit featuring a full-size 727 airplane that revs up its engines and replays the voice recordings from a San Francisco–Chicago flight periodically throughout the day. *Networld* 🏆, which offers a flashy immersion in the Internet (with plenty of interactive screens), will entrance computer addicts. More low-tech—but fun for kids—are *The Farm* (where children can sit at the wheel of a giant combine) and the **chick hatchery** inside the exhibit *Genetics: Decoding Life,* where you can watch as tiny newborn chicks poke their way out of eggs.

I hate to indulge in gender stereotypes, but girls (myself included) love **Colleen Moore's Fairy Castle** 🏆🏆, a lavishly decorated miniature palace filled with priceless treasures (yes, those are real diamonds and pearls in the chandeliers). The castle is hidden on the lower level. Also tucked away in an inconspicuous spot—along the Blue stairwell between the Main Floor and the Balcony—are the *Human Body Slices,* actual slivers of human cadavers that are guaranteed to impress teenagers in search of something truly gross.

A major addition to the museum is the **Henry Crown Space Center** 🏆🏆, which documents the story of space exploration in copious detail, highlighted by a simulated space-shuttle experience through sight and sound at the center's five-story OMNIMAX Theater. The theater offers double features on the weekends; call for show times.

Although it's quite a distance from the rest of Chicago's tourist attractions, the museum is easy enough to reach without a car; your best options are the no. 6 Jeffery Express bus and the Metra Electric train from downtown (the no. 10 bus runs from downtown to the museum's front entrance during the summer).

57th St. and Lake Shore Dr. ☎ **800/468-6674** outside the Chicago area, 773/ 684-1414, or TTY 773/684-3323. www.msichicago.org. Admission to museum only: $11 adults, $9 seniors, $7 children 3–11, free for children 2 and under. Free admission Mon–Tues mid-Sept through Nov and Jan–Feb. Combination museum and OMNIMAX Theater: $17 adults, $15 seniors, $12 children 3–11, free for children 2 and under on an adult's lap. Memorial Day–Labor Day Mon–Sat 9:30am–5:30pm, Sun 11am–5:30pm; early Sept–late May Mon–Sat 9:30am–4pm, Sun 11am–4pm. Closed Dec 25. Bus: 6 or Metra Electric train to 57th St. and Lake Park Ave.

Oriental Institute Museum 🕊🕊   Near the midpoint of the campus is the Oriental Institute, which houses one of the world's major collections of Near Eastern art. It won't take you long to see the highlights here, and a few impressive pieces make it worth a stop for history and art buffs.

Your first stop should be the **Egyptian Gallery** 🕊🕊, which showcases the finest objects among the museum's 35,000 Egyptian artifacts. At the center stands a monumental, 17-foot solid-quartzite statue of the boy king Tutankhamen; the largest Egyptian sculpture in the Western Hemisphere, it tips the scales at 6 tons. The Oriental Institute also houses important collections of artifacts from civilizations that once flourished in what are now Iran and Iraq. The highlight of the **Mesopotamian Gallery** 🕊 is a massive 16-foot-tall sculpture of a winged bull with a human head, which once stood in the palace of Assyrian king Sargon II. Artifacts from Persia, ancient Palestine, Israel, Anatolia, and Nubia fill other galleries. Allow 1 hour.

1155 E. 58th St. (at University Ave.). ☎ **773/702-9514.** http://oi.uchicago.edu. Free admission; suggested donation $5 adults, $2 children. Tues–Sat 10am–6pm (Wed until 8:30pm); Sun noon–6pm. Bus: 6 or Metra Electric train to 57th St. and Lake Park Ave.

Robie House 🕊🕊   Frank Lloyd Wright designed this 20th-century American architectural masterpiece for Frederick Robie, a bicycle and motorcycle manufacturer. The home, which was completed in 1909, bears signs of Wright's Prairie School of design (an open layout and linear geometry of form), as well as exquisite leaded- and stained-glass doors and windows. It's also among the last of Wright's Prairie School–style homes: During its construction, he abandoned both his family and his Oak Park practice to follow other pursuits, most prominently the realization of his Taliesin home and studio in Spring Green, Wisconsin. Docents from Oak Park's Frank Lloyd Wright Home and Studio Foundation lead tours here, even though the house is undergoing a massive, 10-year restoration (the house is open throughout the process, but your photos may include some scaffolding). A Wright specialty bookshop is in the building's former three-car garage—which was highly unusual for the time in which it was built. Allow 1 hour per tour, plus time to browse the gift shop.

5757 S. Woodlawn Ave. (at 58th St.). © **773/834-1847.** www.wrightplus.org. Admission $12 adults, $10 seniors and children 7–18, free for children 6 and under. Mon–Fri tours at 11am, 1, and 3pm; Sat–Sun every half-hour 11am–3:30pm. Bookshop daily 10am–5pm. Bus: 6 or Metra Electric train to 57th St. and Lake Park Ave.

EXPLORING THE UNIVERSITY OF CHICAGO

Walking around the Gothic spires of the University of Chicago campus is bound to conjure up images of the cloistered academic life. Allow about an hour to stroll through the grassy quads and dramatic stone buildings (if the weather's nice, do as the students do, and vegetate for a while on the grass). If you're visiting on a weekday, your first stop should be the university's **Visitors Information Desk** (© 773/702-9739) on the first floor of Ida Noyes Hall, 1212 E. 59th St., where you can pick up campus maps and get information on university events. The center is open Monday through Friday from 10am to 7pm. If you stop by on a weekend when the Visitors Information Desk is closed, you can get the scoop on campus events at the **Reynolds Clubhouse** student center (© 773/702-8787).

Start your tour at the **Henry Moore statue,** *Nuclear Energy,* on South Ellis Avenue between 56th and 57th streets. It's next to the Regenstein Library, which marks the site of the old Stagg Field where, on December 2, 1942, the world's first sustained nuclear reaction was achieved in a basement laboratory below the field. Then turn left and follow 57th Street until you reach the grand stone Hull Gate; walk straight to reach the main quad, or turn left through the column-lined arcade to reach **Hutchinson Court** (designed by John Olmsted, son of revered landscape designer Frederick Law Olmsted). The Reynolds Clubhouse, the university's main student center, is here; you can take a break at the C-Shop cafe or settle down at a table at Hutchinson Commons. The dining room and hangout right next to the cafe will bring to mind the grand dining halls of Oxford and Cambridge.

Other worthy spots on campus include the charming, intimate **Bond Chapel,** behind Swift Hall on the main quad, and the blocks-long **Midway Plaisance,** a wide stretch of green that was the site of carnival sideshow attractions during the World's Columbian Exposition in 1893 (ever since, the term "midway" has referred to carnivals in general).

6 More Museums

International Museum of Surgical Science 𝕽 *Finds*   This unintentionally macabre shrine to medicine is my pick for the weirdest tourist attraction in town. Not for the faint of stomach, it occupies a historic 1917 Gold Coast mansion designed by the noted architect Howard Van Doren Shaw, who modeled it after Le Petit Trianon at Versailles. Displayed throughout its four floors are surgical instruments, paintings, and sculptures depicting the history of surgery and healing practices in Eastern and Western civilizations (it's run by the International College of Surgeons). The exhibits are old-fashioned (no interactive computer displays here), but that's part of the museum's odd appeal.

You'll look at your doctor in a whole new way after viewing the trephined skulls excavated from an ancient tomb in Peru. The accompanying tools bored holes in patients' skulls, a horrific practice thought to release the evil spirits causing their illness (some skulls show signs of new bone growth, meaning that some lucky headache-sufferers actually survived the low-tech surgery). There are also battlefield amputation kits, a working iron-lung machine in the polio exhibit, and oddities such as a stethoscope designed to be transported inside a top hat. Allow 1 hour.

1524 N. Lake Shore Dr. (between Burton Place and North Ave.). ℂ **312/642-6502.** www.imss.org. Admission $8 adults, $4 seniors and students. Tues–Sat 10am–4pm; May–Sept Sun 10am–4pm. Closed major holidays. Bus: 151.

Jane Addams Hull-House Museum   Three years after the 1886 Haymarket Riot, a young woman named Jane Addams bought a mansion on Halsted Street that had been built in 1856 as a "country home" but was surrounded by the shanties of poor immigrants. Here, Addams and her co-worker, Ellen Gates Starr, launched the American settlement-house movement with the establishment of Hull House, an institution that endured on this site in Chicago until 1963. Of the original settlement, what remain today are the Hull-House Museum, the mansion itself, and the residents' dining hall, snuggled among the ultramodern, poured-concrete buildings of the university campus. Inside are the original furnishings, Jane Addams' office, and numerous settlement maps and photographs. Rotating exhibits re-create the history of the settlement and the work of its residents, showing how Addams was able to help transform the dismal streets around her into stable inner-city environments worth fighting over. Allow a half-hour.

University of Illinois at Chicago, 800 S. Halsted St. (at Polk St.). © 312/413-5353. www.uic.edu/jaddams/hull. Free admission. Tues–Fri 10am–4pm; Sun noon–4pm. Closed university holidays. Bus: 8. Subway/El: Blue Line to Halsted/University of Illinois.

McCormick Tribune Freedom Museum _Kids_

As you might guess from the name, the *Chicago Tribune* newspaper is the guiding force behind this celebration of the First Amendment. Thankfully, though, this is no corporate-PR stunt, but rather a thought-provoking overview of how freedom of speech impacts our daily life. Aimed predominantly at junior-high and high-school students, it includes the requisite high-tech bells and whistles aimed at jaded young attention spans (such as computer kiosks where you can listen to once-banned songs or take sides in a free speech debate), and during the week, you might be surrounded by loud school groups. But some of the exhibits—such as the stories of reporters who were jailed for telling the truth—are emotionally affecting, and it makes an easy stop during a walk along Michigan Avenue. Allow 1 hour.

445 N. Michigan Ave. (between Illinois St. and the Chicago River). © 312/222-4860. www.freedommuseum.us. Admission $5, children 5 and under free. Wed–Mon 10am–6pm. Closed Thanksgiving, Christmas, and New Year's Day. Subway/El: Red Line to Grand. Bus: 145, 146, 147, or 151.

National Museum of Mexican Art _Kids_

Chicago's vibrant Pilsen neighborhood, just southwest of the Loop, is home to one of the nation's largest Mexican-American communities. This institution— the only Latino museum accredited by the American Association of Museums—may be the neighborhood's most prized possession. That's quite an accomplishment, given that it was founded in 1987 by a passel of public-school teachers who pooled $900 to get it started.

Exhibits showcase Mexican and Mexican-American visual and performing artists, often drawing on the permanent collection of more than 5,000 works, but the visiting artists, festival programming, and community participation make the museum really shine. Its Day of the Dead celebration, which runs for about 8 weeks beginning in September, is one of the most ambitious in the country. The Del Corazon Mexican Performing Arts Festival, held in the spring, features programs by local and international artists here and around town, and the Sor Juana Festival, presented in the fall, honors Mexican writer and pioneering feminist Sor Juana Inés de la Cruz with photography and painting exhibits, music and theater performances, and poetry readings by Latina women. Allow 1 hour.

1852 W. 19th St. (a few blocks west of Ashland Ave.). ℂ **312/738-1503**. www. nationalmuseumofmexicanart.org. Free admission. Tues–Sun 10am–5pm. Closed major holidays. Bus: 9. Subway/El: Blue Line to 18th St.

National Vietnam Veterans Art Museum ⟨⟨ *Finds*   This museum houses a stirring collection of art by Vietnam veterans, and is the only one of its kind in the world. After the war, many veterans made art as personal therapy, never expecting to show it to anyone, but in 1981 a small group began showing their work together in Chicago and in touring exhibitions. The collection has grown to more than 1,500 paintings, drawings, photographs, and sculptures from all over the world, including Vietnam. (Recently, the museum has also started hosting exhibits of work by veterans who have returned from Iraq.) Titles such as *We Regret to Inform You, Blood Spots on a Rice Paddy,* and *The Wound* give you an idea of the power of the images. Housed in a former warehouse in the Prairie Avenue district south of the Loop, the museum is modern and well organized. An installation suspended from the ceiling, *Above & Beyond* ⟨, comprises more than 58,000 dog tags with the names of the men and women who died in the war—it creates an emotional effect similar to that of the Wall in Washington, D.C. Allow 1 hour.

1801 S. Indiana Ave. (at 18th St.). ℂ **312/326-0270**. www.nvvam.org. Admission $10 adults, $7 seniors and students with ID. Tues–Fri 11am–6pm; Sat 10am–5pm. Closed major holidays. Bus: 3 or 4.

7 Exploring the 'Burbs
OAK PARK
Architecture and literary buffs alike make pilgrimages to Oak Park, a nearby suburb on the western border of the city that is easily accessible by car or train. Bookworms flock here to see the town where Ernest Hemingway was born and grew up, while others come to catch a glimpse of the Frank Lloyd Wright–designed homes that line the well-maintained streets.

GETTING THERE
BY CAR   Oak Park is 10 miles due west of downtown Chicago. By car, take the Eisenhower Expressway (I-290) west to Harlem Avenue (Ill. 43) and exit north. Continue on Harlem north to Lake Street. Take a right on Lake Street and continue to Forest Avenue. Turn left here, and immediately on your right you'll see the **Oak Park Visitor Center** (see below).

BY PUBLIC TRANSPORTATION   Take the Green Line west to the Harlem stop, roughly a 25-minute ride from downtown. Exit the station onto Harlem Avenue, and proceed north to Lake Street. Take a right on Lake Street, follow it to Forest Avenue, and then turn left to the **Oak Park Visitor Center** (see below).

BY TOUR   The **Chicago Architecture Foundation** regularly runs guided tours from downtown Chicago to Oak Park. For details, see "Sightseeing Tours" on p. 117.

VISITOR INFORMATION

The **Oak Park Visitor Center,** 158 Forest Ave. (© **888/OAK-PARK;** www.visitoakpark.com), is open daily from 10am to 5pm April through October, and from 10am to 4pm November through March. Stop here for orientation, maps, and guidebooks. There's a city-operated parking lot next door. The heart of the historic district and the Frank Lloyd Wright Home and Studio are only a few blocks away.

An extensive tour of Oak Park's historic district leaves from the **Ginkgo Tree Bookshop,** 951 Chicago Ave., on weekends from 11am to 4pm on the hour (tour times are noon, 1, and 2pm Nov–Feb). The tour lasts 1 hour and costs $12 for adults, $10 for seniors and students ages 11 to 18, and $5 for children 4 to 10. If you can't make it to Oak Park on the weekend, you can follow a self-guided map and audiocassette tour of the historic district for the same price; the audio tour is available at the Ginkgo Tree Bookshop from 10am to 3:30pm.

THE WRIGHT STUFF

Frank Lloyd Wright Home and Studio 𝔊𝔊𝔊   For the first 20 years of Wright's career, this remarkable complex served first and foremost as the sanctuary where he designed and executed more than 130 of an extraordinary output of 430 completed buildings. The home began as a simple shingled cottage that the 22-year-old Wright built for his bride in 1889, but it became a living laboratory for his revolutionary reinvention of interior spaces. Wright remodeled the house constantly until 1911, when he moved out permanently (in 1909, he left his wife and six children and went off to Europe with the wife of one of his clients). With many add-ons—including a barrel-vaulted children's playroom and a studio with an octagonal balcony suspended by chains—the place has a certain whimsy that others might have found less livable. This was not an architect's masterpiece but rather the master's home, and visitors can savor every room in it for the view it reflects of the workings of a remarkable mind.

Tours cannot be booked in advance by phone, but a select number of tickets for each day can be reserved online. Allow 1 hour for the tour, more time if you want to browse in the bookshop.

951 Chicago Ave. © 708/848-1976. www.wrightplus.org. Admission $12 adults, $10 seniors and students 11–18, $5 children 4–10; combined admission for Home and Studio tour and guided or self-guided historic district tour $20 adults, $10 seniors and students 11–18, $5 children 4–10. Admission to home and studio is by guided tour only; tours depart from bookshop Mon–Fri 11am, 1, and 3pm; Sat–Sun every 20 min. 11am–3:30pm. Closed Jan 1, last week in Jan, Thanksgiving, and Dec 25. Facilities for people with disabilities are limited; please call in advance.

Unity Temple 𝒜   After a fire destroyed its church around 1900, a Unitarian Universalist congregation asked one of its members, Frank Lloyd Wright, to design an affordable replacement. Using poured concrete with metal reinforcements—a necessity due to a small $40,000 budget—Wright created a building that on the outside seems as forbidding as a mausoleum but inside contains all the elements of the Prairie School that has made Wright's name immortal. He wanted Unity Temple to be "democratic," but perhaps Wright was unable to subdue his own personal hubris and hauteur in the creative process, for the ultimate effect of his chapel, and much of the building's interior, is grand and imperial. This is no simple meetinghouse; instead, its principal chapel looks like the chamber of the Roman Senate. Even so, the interior, with its unpredictable geometric arrangements and its decor reminiscent of Native American art, is no less beautiful.

Wright was a true hands-on, can-do person; he knew the materials he chose to use as intimately as the artisans who carried out his plans. He added pigment to the plaster (rather than the paint) to achieve a pale, natural effect. His use of wood trim and other decorative touches is still exciting to behold; his sensitivity to grain, tone, and placement was akin to that of an exceptionally gifted woodworker. His stunning, almost-minimalist use of form is what still sets him apart as a relevant and brilliant artist. Unity Temple still feels groundbreaking 100 years later—which Wright would consider the ultimate compliment. Allow a half-hour.

875 Lake St. © 708/383-8873. http://unitytemple-utrf.org. Self-guided tours $8 adults; $6 seniors, children 6–12, and students with ID; free for children 5 and under. Free guided tours weekends at 1, 2 and 3pm. Mon–Fri 10:30am–4:30pm; Sat–Sun 1–4pm. Church events can alter schedule; call in advance.

ON THE TRAIL OF HEMINGWAY
Hemingway Museum   Frank Lloyd Wright might be Oak Park's favorite son, but the town's most famous native son is Ernest

Hemingway. Hemingway had no great love for Oak Park; he moved away right after high school and later referred to his hometown as a place of "wide lawns and narrow minds." But that hasn't stopped Oak Park from laying claim to the great American writer. A portion of the ground floor of this former church, now the Oak Park Arts Center, holds a small but interesting display of Hemingway memorabilia. A 6-minute video sheds considerable light on Hemingway's time in Oak Park, where he spent the first 18 years of his life, and covers his high school experiences particularly well.

The **Ernest Hemingway Birthplace Home** is 2 blocks north, at 339 N. Oak Park Ave. The lovely Queen Anne house—complete with wraparound porch and turret—was the home of Hemingway's maternal grandparents, and it's where the writer was born on July 21, 1899. Its connection to Hemingway is actually pretty tenuous— he spent most of his boyhood and high school years at 600 N. Kenilworth Ave., a few blocks away (that house is still privately owned)—but the birthplace has been carefully restored to replicate its appearance at the end of the 19th century, making this an appealing stop for fans of historic house tours (whether they're Hemingway fans or not). The hours are the same as the Hemingway Museum's. Allow 1 hour.

200 N. Oak Park Ave. ⓒ 708/848-2222. www.ehfop.org. Combined admission to Hemingway Museum and Ernest Hemingway Birthplace Home $7 adults, $5.50 seniors and children 5–12, free for children 4 and under. Sun–Fri 1–5pm; Sat 10am–5pm.

THE NORTH SHORE

Between Chicago and the state border of Wisconsin is one of the nation's most affluent residential areas, a swath of suburbia known as the North Shore. Although towns farther west like to co-opt the name for its prestige, the North Shore proper extends from Evanston, Chicago's nearest neighbor to the north, along the lakefront to tony Lake Forest, originally built as a resort for Chicago's aristocracy.

Although a Metra train line extends to Lake Forest and neighboring Lake Bluff, I highly recommend that you rent a car and drive north along **Sheridan Road,** which wends its leisurely way through many of these communities, past palatial homes and mansions designed in a startling array of architectural styles. Aside from Lake Shore Drive in Chicago, you won't find a more impressive stretch of roadway in the entire metropolitan area.

EXPLORING EVANSTON

Despite being frequented by Chicagoans, Evanston, the city's oldest suburb, retains an identity all its own. A unique hybrid of sensibilities, it manages to combine the tranquillity of suburban life with a highly cultured, urban charm. It's great fun to wander amid the shops and cafes in its downtown area or along funky Dempster Street at its southern end. The beautiful lakefront campus of **Northwestern University** (© **847/491-3741;** www.northwestern.edu) is here, and many of its buildings—such as Alice Millar Chapel, with its sublime stained-glass facade, and the Mary and Leigh Block Gallery, a fine-arts haven that offers a top-notch collection and intriguing temporary exhibitions—are well worth several hours of exploration.

For a bit of serenity, head to **Grosse Point Lighthouse and Maritime Museum,** 2601 Sheridan Rd. (© **847/328-6961;** www.grossepointlighthouse.net), a historic lighthouse built in 1873, when Lake Michigan still teemed with cargo-laden ships. Tours of the lighthouse, situated in a nature center, take place on weekends from June to September at 2, 3, and 4pm ($6 adults, $3 children 8–12; children under 8 not admitted for safety reasons). The adjacent Lighthouse Beach is a favorite spot for local families during the summer. If you're here between Memorial Day and Labor Day, you'll have to pay to frolic on the sand ($7 adults, $5 children 1–11), but it's a great place for a (free) stroll on a sunny spring or fall day.

OTHER AREA ATTRACTIONS

Chicago Botanic Garden ☆☆ *Value*   Despite its name, the world-class Chicago Botanic Garden is 25 miles north of the city in the suburb of Glencoe. This 385-acre living preserve includes eight large lagoons and a variety of distinct botanical environments including the Illinois prairie, an English walled garden, and a three-island Japanese garden. Also on the grounds are a large fruit-and-vegetable garden, an "enabling garden" (which shows how gardening can be adapted for people with disabilities), and a 100-acre old-growth oak woodland. If you're here in the summer, don't miss the extensive rose gardens (just follow the bridal parties who flock here to get their pictures taken). Carillon concerts take place at 7pm Monday evenings from late June through August; tours of the carillon are offered beforehand. Allow 3 hours.

1000 Lake-Cook Rd. (just east of Edens Expwy./I-94), Glencoe. © 847/835-5440. www.chicago-botanic.org. Free admission. Daily 8am–sunset. Tram tours Apr–Oct. Closed Dec 25. From Chicago, take Sheridan Rd. north along Lake Michigan or the Edens Expwy. (I-94) to Lake-Cook Rd. Parking $15/day.

Ravinia Festival 𝘒𝘒 *Finds* Want to know where the natives get away from it all? Come summertime, you'll find us chilling on the lawn at Ravinia, the summer home of the highly regarded Chicago Symphony Orchestra in suburban Highland Park. The season runs from mid-June to Labor Day and includes far more than classical concerts: You can also catch pop acts, dance performances, operatic arias, and blues concerts. Tickets are available for the lawn and the covered pavilion, where you get a reserved seat and a view of the stage. The lawn is the real joy of Ravinia: sitting under the stars and a canopy of leafy branches while listening to music and indulging in an elaborate picnic (it's a local tradition to try to outdo everyone else by bringing candelabras and fine china).

On concert nights, a special Ravinia Metra commuter train leaves at 5:50pm from the North Western train station at Madison and Canal streets (just west of the Loop). After the concert, trains wait right outside the gates to take commuters back to the city. The round-trip train fare is $5, a real bargain considering that traffic around the park can be brutal.

Green Bay and Lake-Cook roads, Highland Park. © **847/266-5100** or 312/RAVINIA. www.ravinia.org. Tickets: Pavilion $20–$75; lawn $10–$20. Most concerts are in the evening.

THE WESTERN SUBURBS

Brookfield Zoo 𝘒𝘒 *Kids* Brookfield is the Chicago area's largest zoo. In contrast to Lincoln Park Zoo, Brookfield is spacious, spreading out over 216 acres and housing thousands of animals—camels, dolphins, giraffes, baboons, wolves, tigers, green sea turtles, Siberian tigers, snow leopards, and more—in naturalistic environments that put them side by side with other inhabitants of their regions. These creative indoor and outdoor settings, filled with activities to keep kids interested, are what set Brookfield apart.

Start out at ***Habitat Africa!*** 𝘒𝘒, a multiple-ecosystem exhibit that encompasses 30 acres—about the size of the entire Lincoln Park Zoo. Then wander through some of the buildings that allow you to see animals close up; my personal favorites are ***Tropic World*** 𝘒, where you hang out at treetop level with monkeys, and ***Australia House,*** where fruit bats flit around your head. ***The Living Coast*** 𝘒𝘒 explores the west coast of Chile and Peru, and includes everything from a tank of plate-size moon jellies to a rocky shore where Humboldt penguins swim and nest as Inca terns and gray gulls fly freely overhead. The dolphins at the ***Seven Seas Panorama*** 𝘒𝘒 put on an amazing show that has been a Brookfield Zoo fixture for years. If you go on a weekend, buy tickets to the dolphin show at least a couple of hours before the one you plan to attend, because they tend to sell out quickly.

The **Hamill Family Play Zoo** is a wonderful stop for kids. They not only get to pet animals but can also build habitats, learn how to plant a garden, and even play animal dress-up. The only catch: the separate admission fee ($3.50 adults, $2.50 children). Allow 3 hours.

First Ave. and 31st St., Brookfield. © **708/485-0263.** www.brookfieldzoo.org. Admission $10 adults, $6 seniors and children 3–11, free for children 2 and under. Parking $8. Free admission Tues and Thurs Oct–Feb. Memorial Day–Labor Day daily 9:30am–6pm (Sun until 7:30pm); fall–spring daily 10am–5pm. Bus: 304 or 311. Take the Stevenson (I-55) and Eisenhower (I-290) expressways 14 miles west of the Loop.

8 Kid Stuff

Chicago Children's Museum *Kids*   Located on tourist-filled Navy Pier, this museum is one of the most popular family attractions in the city. The building has areas especially for preschoolers as well as for children up to age 10, and several permanent exhibits allow kids a maximum of hands-on fun. *Dinosaur Expedition* re-creates an expedition to the Sahara, allowing kids to experience camp life, conduct scientific research, and dig for the bones of *Suchomimus,* a Saharan dinosaur discovered by Chicago paleontologist Paul Sereno (a full-scale model stands nearby). There's also a **three-level schooner** that children can board for a little climbing, from the crow's nest to the gangplank; *PlayMaze,* a toddler-scale cityscape with everything from a gas station to a city bus that children under 5 can touch and explore; and an **arts-and-crafts area** where visitors can create original artwork to take home. Allow 2 to 3 hours.

Navy Pier, 700 E. Grand Ave. © **312/527-1000.** www.chichildrensmuseum.org. Admission $8 adults and children, $7 seniors. Free admission Thurs 5–8pm. Mon–Fri 10am–5pm (Thurs until 8pm); Sat 10am–8pm; Sun 10am–5pm. Closed Thanksgiving and Dec 25. Bus: 29, 65, or 66. Subway/El: Red Line to Grand; transfer to city bus or Navy Pier's free trolley bus.

Lincoln Park Pritzker Children's Zoo & Farm-in-the-Zoo *Value Kids*   After hours of looking at animals from afar in the rest of Lincoln Park Zoo, kids can come here to get up close and personal. Unlike many other children's zoos, there are no baby animals at the **Pritzker Children's Zoo;** instead, the outdoor habitats feature wildlife of the North American woods, including wolves, beavers, and otters. Although there are a few interactive displays outside, most kids head inside to the Treetop Canopy Climbing Adventure, a 20-foot high wood-and-fabric tree (encased in soft safety netting) that kids can scramble up and down. There are also a few small padded play areas for little ones.

The **Farm-in-the-Zoo** ⊕ is a working reproduction of a Midwestern farm, complete with a white-picket-fenced barnyard, chicken coops, and demonstrations of butter churning and weaving. You'll also spot plenty of livestock, including cows, sheep, and pigs. Inside the Main Barn (filled with interactive exhibits), the main attraction is the huge John Deere tractor that kids can climb up into and pretend to drive. (Can you say "photo opportunity"?) Allow 1 hour.

2200 N. Cannon Dr. ✆ 312/742-2000. www.lpzoo.com. Free admission. Daily 9am–5pm. Bus: 151 or 156.

9 Sightseeing Tours

If you're in town for a limited time, an organized tour may be the best way to get a quick overview of the city's highlights.

CARRIAGE RIDES

Noble Horse (✆ 312/266-7878) maintains the largest fleet of antique horse carriages in Chicago, stationed around the old Water Tower Square at the northwest corner of Chicago and Michigan avenues. Each of the drivers, outfitted in a black tie and top hat, has his or her own variation on the basic Magnificent Mile itinerary (you can also do tours of the lakefront, river, Lincoln Park, and Buckingham Fountain). The charge is $35 for each half-hour for up to four people. The coaches run year-round, with convertible coaches in the warm months and enclosed carriages furnished with wool blankets on bone-chilling nights. There are several other carriage operators, all of whom pick up riders in the vicinity.

ORIENTATION TOURS

Chicago Trolley Company   Chicago Trolley Company offers guided tours on a fleet of rubber-wheeled "San Francisco–style" trolleys that stop at a number of popular spots around the city, including Navy Pier, the Grant Park museums, the historic Water Tower, and the Sears Tower. You can stay on for the full 2-hour ride, or get on and off at each stop. The same company also operates the **Chicago Double Decker Company,** which has a fleet of London-style red buses. The two-level buses follow the same route as the trolleys; if you buy an all-day pass, you can hop from bus to trolley at any point.

ⓒ **773/648-5000.** www.chicagotrolley.com. All-day hop-on, hop-off pass $25 adults, $20 seniors, $10 children 3–11; family package (2 adults, 2 children) $64. Apr–Oct daily 9am–6:30pm; Nov–Mar daily 9am–5pm.

LAKE & RIVER CRUISES

Chicago from the Lake   This company runs two types of 90-minute cruises: a tour of architecture along the Chicago River, and excursions that travel on the lake and river to explore the development of the city. The price includes coffee (Starbucks, no less), lemonade, cookies, and muffins. For tickets, call or stop by the company's ticket office on the lower level on the east end of River East Plaza. Advance reservations are recommended.

465 N. McClurg Ct., at the end of E. Illinois St. ⓒ **312/527-1977.** www.chicagoline. com. Tickets $32 adults, $30 seniors, $18 children 7–18, free for children 6 and under. May–Oct daily. Tours depart hourly 9am–4pm Memorial Day to Labor Day; every 2 hr. 10am–4pm May, Sept, and Oct.

Mystic Blue Cruises   A more casual alternative to fancy dinner cruises, this is promoted as more of a "fun" ship (that means DJs at night, although you'll have to put up with some kind of "live entertainment" no matter when you sail). Daily lunch and dinner excursions are available, as are midnight voyages on weekends. The same company offers more formal (and expensive) cruises aboard the *Odyssey* (www.odysseycruises.com) and motorboat rides on the 70-passenger *Seadog* (www.seadogcruises.com), if you really want to feel the water in your face.

Departing from Navy Pier. ⓒ **877/299-7783.** www.mysticbluecruises.com. Lunch cruise $32–$37; dinner cruise $60–$80; midday cruise $25; moonlight cruise $30. Cruises run year-round.

Shoreline Sightseeing ⓡ   Shoreline launches 30-minute lake cruises every half-hour from its two dock locations at the Shedd Aquarium and Navy Pier. Shoreline has also gotten in on the popularity of architecture tours. Narrated by architectural guides, they cost more than regular tours. A **water taxi** also runs every half-hour between Navy Pier and the Sears Tower, Michigan Avenue, and the Shedd Aquarium. Tickets for the water taxi cost $3 to $13, depending how far you travel.

Departing from Navy Pier, Shedd Aquarium, and Buckingham Fountain in Grant Park. ⓒ **312/222-9328.** www.shorelinesightseeing.com. Tickets weekdays $14 adults, $13 seniors, $6 children 11 and under ($1 more per ticket on weekends); architectural tours $24 adults, $21 seniors, $12 children 11 and under ($2 more per ticket on weekends). May–Sept daily. Tours depart hourly 10am–5:30pm Memorial Day to Labor Day; every 30 min. 10am–4pm May and Sept.

Wendella Sightseeing Boats ☞ Wendella is the granddaddy of Chicago sightseeing operators. Started in 1935, it's run by the original owner's son, Bob Borgstrom, whose own two sons serve as captains. You won't find a more authoritative source on the Chicago River than Borgstrom.

Wendella operates a 1-hour tour along the Chicago River and a 1½-hour tour along the river and out onto Lake Michigan. (One of the most dramatic events during the boat tours is passing through the locks that separate the river from the lake.) Boats run from late April to early October. The 2-hour sunset tour runs Memorial Day to Labor Day starting at 7:45pm. Scheduling depends on the season and the weather, but cruises usually leave every hour during the summer.

Departing from Michigan Ave. and Wacker Dr. (north side of the river, at the Wrigley Building). ☎ 312/337-1446. www.wendellaboats.com. Tickets $22 adults, $20 seniors, $11 children 3–11, free for children 2 and under. Apr–Oct daily.

SPECIAL-INTEREST TOURS

Chicago Architecture Foundation ☞☞☞ Chicago's architecture is world famous. Luckily, the Chicago Architecture Foundation offers first-rate guided tours to help visitors understand what makes this city's skyline so special.

One of the CAF's most popular tours is the 1½-hour **Architecture River Cruise,** which glides along both the north and the south branches of the Chicago River. Although you can see the same 50 or so buildings by foot, traveling by water lets you enjoy the buildings from a unique perspective. The docents generally do a good job of making the cruise enjoyable for visitors with all levels of architectural knowledge.

Tours are $26 per person weekdays, $28 on weekends and holidays, and begin hourly every day June through October from 11am to 3pm (with more limited schedules in May and Nov). The trips are extremely popular, so purchase tickets in advance through **Ticketmaster** (☎ 312/902-1500; www.ticketmaster.com), or avoid the service charge and buy tickets at one of the foundation's tour centers or from the boat launch on the southeast corner of Michigan Avenue and Wacker Drive.

If you want to squeeze a lot of sightseeing into a limited time, try **Highlights by Bus,** a 3½-hour overview tour that covers the Loop, Hyde Park—including a visit to the interior of Frank Lloyd Wright's Robie House—and the Gold Coast, plus several other historic districts. Tours start at 9:30am on Wednesday, Friday, Saturday, and Sunday April through November (Sat only Dec–Mar). Tickets are $38 per person.

If you prefer exploring on your own, the CAF offers a variety of guided walking tours. For first-time visitors, I highly recommend two tours for an excellent introduction to the dramatic architecture of the Loop. **Historic Skyscrapers** (daily 10am) covers buildings built between 1880 and 1940, including the Rookery and the Chicago Board of Trade; **Modern Skyscrapers** (daily 1pm) includes modern masterpieces by Mies van der Rohe and postmodern works by contemporary architects. The 2-hour tours cost $15 each for adults and $12 each for seniors and students.

Departing from the Chicago ArchiCenter, 224 S. Michigan Ave.; a few tours leave from the John Hancock Center, 875 N. Michigan Ave. ⓒ 312/922-3432, or 312/922-TOUR for recorded information. www.architecture.org. Tickets for most walking tours $10–$15. Subway/El: Brown, Green, Purple, or Orange line to Adams, or Red Line to Jackson.

Untouchable Tours   The days of Al Capone are long gone, but Chicago's notorious past is still good for business, it seems, given the popularity of these "Gangster Tours." The 2-hour bus trip takes you to all of the city's old hoodlum hangouts from the Prohibition era, including O'Banion's flower shop, the site of the St. Valentine's Day massacre. The focus is definitely more on entertainment than history (guides with names such as "Al Dente" and "Ice Pick" appear in costume and role-play their way through the tour), but the trip does give you a pretty thorough overview of the city.

Departs from the southeast corner of Clark and Ohio sts. ⓒ 773/881-1195. www.gangstertour.com. $25 adults, $19 children. Tours depart Mon–Wed 10am; Thurs 10am and 1pm; Fri 10am, 1 and 7:30pm; Sat 10am, 1 and 5pm; Sun 10am and 1pm.

NEIGHBORHOOD TOURS

It's a bit of a cliché to say that Chicago is a city of neighborhoods, but if you want to see what really makes the place special, that's where you have to go.

Sponsored by the city's Department of Cultural Affairs, **Chicago Neighborhood Tours** ⓡ (ⓒ 312/742-1190; www.chgocitytours.com) are 4- to 5-hour narrated bus excursions to about a dozen diverse communities throughout the city. Departing at 10am from the Chicago Cultural Center, 77 E. Randolph St., every Saturday, the tours visit different neighborhoods, from Chinatown and historic Bronzeville on the South Side to the ethnic enclaves of Devon Avenue and Uptown on the North Side. Tickets (including a light snack) are $25 for adults and $20 for seniors, students, and children 8 to 18. Regularly available specialty tours include Literary Chicago; the Great Chicago Fire; Roots of Blues, Gospel & Jazz; Threads of

Ireland; Jewish Legacy; and an Ethnic Cemetery tour. These tours, which generally run about 4 to 6 hours and include lunch, are more expensive ($50 adults, $45 seniors and children).

On Saturday mornings in the summer, the **Chicago History Museum** offers 2-hour walking tours of the neighborhoods surrounding the museum: the **Gold Coast, Old Town,** and **Lincoln Park.** Led by museum docents, they average about four per month June through August. Day and evening tours are available, and a few specialty walking tours are usually offered as well. Tours are $10 per person, and registration is recommended but not required.

Groups can arrange tours of Chicago's **"Black Metropolis,"** the name given to a South Side area of Bronzeville where African Americans created a flourishing business-and-artistic community after World War II. Contact **Tour Black Chicago** (© **773/684-9034;** www.tourblackchicago.com) for more information.

10 Staying Active

Perhaps because winters can be brutal, Chicagoans take their summers seriously. In the warmer months, with the wide blue lake and the ample green parks, it's easy to think that the city is one big grown-up playground. Whether you prefer your activity in the water or on dry ground, you'll probably find it here. For information, contact the city's park district (© **312/742-PLAY;** www.chicagopark district.com); for questions about the 29 miles of beaches and parks along Lake Michigan, call the park district's lakefront region office at © **312/747-2474.**

BEACHES

Public beaches line Lake Michigan all the way up north into the suburbs and Wisconsin, and southeast through Indiana and into Michigan. The best known is **Oak Street Beach.** Its location, at the northern tip of the Magnificent Mile, creates some interesting sights as sun worshippers sporting swimsuits and carting coolers make their way down Michigan Avenue. The most popular is **North Avenue Beach,** about 6 blocks farther north, which has developed into a volleyball hot spot and recently rebuilt its landmark steamship-shaped beach house and added a Venice Beach–style outdoor gym; this is where the Lincoln Park singles come to play, check each other out, and fly by on bikes and in-line skates. For more seclusion, try **Ohio Street Beach,** an intimate sliver of sand in tiny Olive Park, just north of Navy Pier, which, incredibly enough, remains largely ignored despite its central location.

Beaches officially open with a full retinue of lifeguards on duty around June 20, though swimmers can wade into the chilly water from Memorial Day to Labor Day. Only the bravest souls venture into the water before July, when the temperature creeps up enough to make swimming an attractive proposition. Please take note that the entire lakefront is not beach, and don't go do anything stupid such as dive off the rocks.

BIKING

Biking is a great way to see the city, particularly along the lakefront bike path that extends for more than 18 miles.

To rent bikes, try **Bike Chicago** (www.bikechicago.com), which has locations at Navy Pier (© **312/595-9600**), North Avenue Beach (© **773/327-2706**), and Millennium Park (© **888/BIKE-WAY**). Open from 8am to 8pm May through October (weather permitting), Bike Chicago stocks mountain and touring bikes, kids' bikes, strollers, and—most fun of all—quadcycles, which are four-wheel contraptions equipped with a steering wheel and canopy that can accommodate four or five people. Rates for bikes start at $8.75 an hour, $34 a day, with helmets, pads, and locks included. If you'd like to cycle your way past some Chicago landmarks, guided tours are also available.

GOLFING

For a major metropolis, Chicago has an impressive number of golf options within the city limits (not to mention many plush and pricey suburban courses). The closest you'll get to golfing downtown is **The Green at Grant Park** (© **312/642-7888;** www.thegreen online.com), an 18-hole putting course on Monroe Street between Columbus Avenue and Lake Shore Drive, just east of Millennium Park. It's not exactly tournament-level play, but it's more challenging than miniature golf—and the setting can't be beat. The course is open daily from 10am to 10pm, and putters and golf balls are provided. Rates are $9 per round for adults, $6 for children under 13.

11 In the Grandstand: Watching Chicago's Athletic Events

BASEBALL

Baseball is imprinted on the national consciousness as part of Chicago, not because of victorious dynasties but because of the opposite—the Black Sox scandal of 1919 and the perennially losing Cubs.

The **Chicago Cubs** haven't made a World Series appearance since 1945 and haven't been world champs since 1908, but that doesn't stop people from catching games at **Wrigley Field** 𝒶𝒶, with its ivy-covered outfield walls, its hand-operated scoreboard, its view of the shimmering lake from the upper deck, and its "W" or "L" flag announcing the outcome of the game to the unfortunates who couldn't attend.

No matter how the Cubs are doing, tickets ($15–$50) go fast; most weekend and night games sell out by Memorial Day. Your best bet is to hit a weekday game, or try your luck buying a ticket on game day outside the park (you'll often find some season-ticket holders looking to unload a few seats).

Wrigley Field, 1060 W. Addison St. (© **773/404-CUBS;** www. cubs.mlb.com), is easy to reach. Take the Red Line to the Addison stop, and you're there. Or take the no. 22 bus, which runs up Clark Street. To buy tickets in person, stop by the ticket windows at Wrigley Field, Monday through Friday from 9am to 6pm, Saturday from 9am to 4pm, and on game days. Call © **800/THE-CUBS** for tickets through **Tickets.com** (© **866/652-2827** outside of Illinois); you can also order online through the team website.

Despite their stunning World Series win in 2005, the **Chicago White Sox** still struggle to attract the same kind of loyalty (despite the fact that they regularly win more games than the Cubs). Long-time fans rue the day owner Jerry Reinsdorf (who is also majority owner of the Bulls) replaced admittedly dilapidated Comiskey Park with a concrete behemoth that lacks the yesteryear charm of its predecessor. That said, sightlines at the new stadium, **U.S. Cellular Field,** are spectacular from every seat (if you avoid the vertigo-inducing upper deck), and the park has every conceivable amenity, including above-average food concessions, shops, and plentiful restrooms. The White Sox' endearing quality is the blue-collar aura with which so many Cubs-loathing Southsiders identify. Games rarely sell out—an effect, presumably, of Reinsdorf's sterile stadium and the blighted neighborhood that surrounds it. All of this makes it a bargain for bona fide baseball fans. Tickets cost $12 to $45 and are half-price on Monday.

U.S. Cellular Field is at 333 W. 35th St. (© **312/674-1000;** www.whitesox.mlb.com), in the South Side neighborhood of Bridgeport. To get Sox tickets, call **Ticketmaster** (© **866/SOX-GAME**), or visit the ticket office, open Monday through Friday from 10am to 6pm, Saturday and Sunday from 10am to 4pm, with extended hours on game days. To get to the ballpark by subway/El, take the Red Line to Sox/35th Street.

BASKETBALL

When it comes to basketball, Chicagoans still live in the past, associating the **Chicago Bulls** (✆ **312/455-4000**) with the glory days of Michael Jordan and the never-ending championships of the 1990s. Although the team has rebounded somewhat from the dismal seasons following the departure of Jordan et al., the current players don't inspire the same city-wide excitement. The upside for visitors? The Bulls don't consistently sell out, which means you might be able to catch a game at the cavernous **United Center,** 1901 W. Madison St. (✆ **312/455-4500;** www.chicagosports.com). Most tickets run $20 to $100 through **Ticketmaster** ✆ **312/559-1212**).

FOOTBALL

The **Chicago Bears** play at **Soldier Field,** Lake Shore Drive and 16th Street (✆ **847/295-6600;** www.chicagobears.com), site of a controversial renovation that added what looks like a giant space ship on top of the original stadium's elegant colonnade. Architecturally, it's a disaster, but from a comfort perspective, the place is much improved—although that doesn't impress longtime fans who prided themselves on surviving blistering-cold game days and horrifying bathrooms. The Bears themselves have been inspiring high hopes—most recently, winning a trip to the Superbowl in 2007. But even during losing seasons, tickets are hard to come by (most are snapped up by season-ticket holders long before the season starts). If you plan ahead, individual tickets run $45 to $300; expensive seats are usually available through ticket brokers or online sites.

The **Northwestern Wildcats** play Big Ten college ball at **Ryan Field,** 1501 Central St., in nearby Evanston (✆ **847/491-CATS**).

7

Shopping

Forget Rodeo Drive or Fifth Avenue—Chicago is the country's original shopping center. As the United States expanded westward, catalogs from Chicago-based Sears and Montgomery Ward made clothes, books, and housewares accessible to even the most remote frontier towns. Department store magnate Marshall Field operated his namesake department store here, which opened in 1852, under the motto "Give the lady what she wants." Field pioneered many customer-service policies that are now standard, such as hassle-free returns.

Today Montgomery Ward is no more (and Marshall Field's has been taken over by Macy's), but downtown Chicago still draws hordes of shoppers (as anyone who's tried to walk quickly down Michigan Ave. on a busy summer Saturday can attest to). From the fine furniture showrooms at the imposing Merchandise Mart to the who's who of designer boutiques lining Oak Street and Michigan Avenue, the quality of stores in Chicago is top-notch. Because so many of the best are concentrated in one easy-to-walk area, the convenience of shopping in Chicago is unmatched.

1 Shopping the Magnificent Mile

The nickname "Magnificent Mile"—hyperbole to some, an understatement to others—refers to the roughly mile-long stretch of North Michigan Avenue between Oak Street and the Chicago River.

Even jaded shoppers from other worldly capitals are delighted at the ease and convenience of the stores concentrated here. Even if you're not the shop-till-you-drop type, it's worth a stroll because this stretch is, in many ways, the heart of the city, a place that bustles with life year-round (although it's especially crowded around Christmas and during the summer).

For the ultimate Mag Mile shopping adventure, start at one end of North Michigan Avenue and try to work your way to the other. Below I've listed some of the best-known shops on the avenue and nearby side streets.

A NORTH MICHIGAN AVENUE SHOPPER'S STROLL

This shopper's stroll begins at Oak Street at the northern end of the avenue and heads south toward the river. It just hits the highlights; you'll find much more to tempt your wallet as you meander from designer landmarks to well-known chain stores. (In general, this is not the place to pick up distinctive, one-of-a-kind items—other neighborhoods described later in this chapter cater more to shoppers searching for something unique). North Michigan Avenue's four vertical malls—each a major shopping destination in its own right—are discussed below under "The Magnificent Malls."

The parade of designer names begins at the intersection of Michigan Avenue and Oak Street, including a couple housed in The Drake Hotel, such as the legendary Danish silversmith **Georg Jensen,** 959 N. Michigan Ave. (© **312/642-9160**), known for outstanding craftsmanship in sterling silver and gold, including earrings, brooches, watches, tie clips, and flatware; and **Chanel,** 935 N. Michigan Ave. (© **312/787-5500**). One block south is another luxury emporium, the spacious **Louis Vuitton** store at 919 N. Michigan Ave. (© **312/944-2010**), where you'll find trendy handbags and the company's distinctive monogrammed luggage.

On the other side of the street, opposite the dark, soaring Hancock Building, you'll find a quiet oasis that's worth a quick peek. The **Fourth Presbyterian Church,** 126 E. Chestnut St. (© **312/787-4570**), looks like something out of an English country village, with a Gothic stone exterior and a peaceful, flower-filled courtyard (perfect for escaping the Mag Mile crowds for a few moments).

Giorgio Armani's sleek boutique, 800 N. Michigan Ave., in the Park Hyatt Hotel (© **312/573-4220**), faces the small park next to the historic Water Tower. Across the street, a few doors west of Michigan Avenue, is one of Chicago's hottest family destinations: **American Girl Place,** at 111 E. Chicago Ave. (© **877/AG-PLACE**). The three-story doll emporium attracts hordes of young girls (and parents) hooked on the popular mail-order company's line of historic character dolls. A stage show brings stories from the American Girl books to life, and the store's cafe is a nice spot for a special mother-daughter lunch or afternoon tea.

The next block of Michigan Avenue has a New York vibe, thanks to the world's largest **Polo Ralph Lauren,** 750 N. Michigan Ave. (© **312/280-1655**), a four-floor, wood-paneled minimansion, and **Tiffany & Co.,** 730 N. Michigan Ave. (© **312/944-7500**), with its signature clock, jewels, and tabletop accessories (if you want to get your hands on one of the coveted robin's-egg blue shopping bags without spending a fortune, the $80 sterling-silver key chains are the least expensive items in the store).

A few doors south are **Neiman Marcus,** 737 N. Michigan Ave. (© **312/642-5900**), and at 669 N. Michigan Ave. (© **312/642-6363**), the hugely popular **Niketown,** a multilevel complex that helped pioneer the concept of retail as entertainment. Across the street, you'll probably see a line of people trailing out from the **Garrett Popcorn Shop,** 670 N. Michigan Ave. (© **312/944-2630**), a 50-year-old landmark. Join the locals in line and pick up some caramel corn for a quick sugar rush.

At the intersection of Michigan Avenue and Erie Street is the appropriately barrel-shaped **Crate & Barrel,** 646 N. Michigan Ave. (© **312/787-5900**). Crate & Barrel was started in Chicago, so this is the company's flagship location. Countless varieties of glassware, dishes, cookware, and kitchen gadgets for everyday use line the shelves. The top two floors are devoted to furniture.

Continuing south, you'll find **Burberry,** 633 N. Michigan Ave. (© **312/787-2500**), where the classic beige plaid shows up on chic purses, shoes, and bathing suits (if you're looking for luxury souvenirs, check out the collection of baby clothes and dog accessories).

THE MAGNIFICENT MALLS

Many of the Magnificent Mile's shops are hidden inside high-rise malls, most of which take up a whole city block. Here's a quick guide to what you'll find inside.

Chicago Place This mall's main claim to fame is as the home of upscale retailer **Saks Fifth Avenue** (p. 141). The rest of the stores here are not as exclusive; in fact, the mall as a whole lacks a clear identity. You'll find a few home-decor and clothing stores here—but the main draw is the food court on the top floor. 700 N. Michigan Ave. (between Superior and Huron sts.). © **312/642-4811.** Subway/El: Red Line to Chicago.

900 North Michigan Shops The most upscale of the Magnificent Mile's four vertical malls, 900 North Michigan (often called the Bloomingdale's building, for its most prominent tenant), avoids the tumult of Water Tower Place by appealing to a more well-heeled shopper. In addition to about 70 stores, there are a few good restaurants and a movie theater on the lower level.

The Chicago outpost of **Gucci** (ground floor; © **312/664-5504**) has the same hip attitude as the label's sexy clothing and much-in-demand purses. Also on the ground floor is **MaxMara** (© **312/475-9500**), the Italian women's fashion house known for elegantly constructed coats and separates (some of which will cost you about as much as a flight to Italy). Other goodies worth checking out include funky European footwear at **Charles David** (second floor; ✆ 312/944-9013), amazingly intricate French glassware at **Lalique** (ground floor; ✆ 312/867-1787), and an eclectic selection of hats, mittens, scarves, and other accessories at **Glove Me Tender** (fifth floor; ✆ 312/664-4022), which should be your first stop if you're caught here during an unexpected cold spell. 900 N. Michigan Ave. (between Walton St. and Delaware Place). ✆ 312/915-3916. Subway/El: Red Line to Chicago.

Water Tower Place   Water Tower was the first big indoor mall to open downtown (in 1975), and 30 years ago its glass elevators and shiny gold trim gave the place a glamorous air. These days the mall remains popular, but doesn't have much to distinguish it from any other upscale shopping center. Water Tower is a magnet for suburban teenagers (just like your mall back home) and can get quite crowded during prime summer tourist season. Most of its stores are part of national chains (Ann Taylor, Victoria's Secret, and so on). The department stores anchoring the mall are the Mag Mile outpost of **Macy's** and a **Lord & Taylor** (see "Department Stores," in "Shopping A to Z," later in this chapter). One of Water Tower's best features is its funky food court, **foodlife** (p. 66). 835 N. Michigan Ave. (between Pearson and Chestnut sts.). ✆ 312/440-3166. Subway/El: Red Line to Chicago.

Westfield North Bridge   The anchor of this development is a four-story **Nordstrom** (p. 140). The rest of the mall is bright and open, thanks to high ceilings and a wide central walkway—but it can also feel somewhat deserted compared to the bustling street outside. The stores are a mix of clothing, jewelry, and bath-and-body shops (in a midrange to upscale price bracket). Distinctive stores that are worth checking out include the high-style chocolatier **Vosges Haut-Chocolat** on the second floor (p. 137) and the **LEGO** store on the third floor (✆ 312/494-0760), which features a mini re-creation of the Chicago skyline. The third-floor food court is a good stop for lunch, with a food station run by Tuscany, a local Italian restaurant, and other stands that offer Japanese tempura, grilled wraps, and Chicago-style hot dogs. 520 N. Michigan Ave. (between Grand Ave. and Illinois St.). ✆ 312/327-2300. Subway/El: Red Line to Grand.

CHIC SHOPPING ON NEARBY OAK STREET

Oak Street has long been a symbol of designer-label shopping; if a store has an Oak Street address, you can count on it being expensive.

It's well worth a stroll for people-watching: this is Main Street for Chicago socialites. Most of Oak Street is closed on Sunday, except during the holiday season.

Chicago's most high-profile clothing boutique, **Ultimo,** is right around the corner from Michigan Avenue; upscale and exclusive, it caters to the seriously fashionable (p. 138). Footwear fans can browse Italian shoemaker **Tod's,** best known for its luxuriously soft (and pricey) driving shoes. Shoes, stationery, and handbags are available at **kate spade,** 101 E. Oak St. (𝄬 312/654-8853), along with the Jack Spade line of men's accessories. The priciest accessories on this very pricey block can likely be found at French luxury house **Hermès of Paris,** 110 E. Oak St. (𝄬 312/787-8175). Thread-count fanatics swear by the sheets from **Pratesi,** 67 E. Oak St. (𝄬 312/943-8422), and **Frette,** 41 E. Oak St. (𝄬 312/649-3744), both of which supply linens to top hotels (and where sheet sets cost more than what some people pay in rent).

Anchoring the western end of the block are two haute heavyweights, hip Italian designer **Prada,** 30 E. Oak St. (𝄬 312/951-1113), which offers three floors of sleek, postmodern fashions for men and women and plenty of the designer's signature handbags; and equally style-conscious **Barneys New York** (p. 139).

2 More Shopping Neighborhoods

STATE STREET & THE LOOP

Shopping in the Loop is mostly concentrated along State Street, from Randolph Street south to Congress Parkway (although there are stores sprinkled elsewhere, they're mostly places that cater to office workers: drugstores, sandwich shops, and chain clothing stores). One grand old department store makes it worth a visit: **Macy's at State Street** (formerly Marshall Field's), 111 N. State St., at Randolph Street (𝄬 312/781-1000). A city landmark and one of the largest department stores in the world, it occupies an entire city block and features the largest Tiffany glass mosaic dome in the U.S. If you're in Chicago between Thanksgiving and New Year's, Macy's has maintained a long-time Marshall Field's tradition: lavishly decorated holiday windows and lunch under the Great Tree in the store's restaurant, The Walnut Room.

RIVER NORTH

Since the 1960s, when the Chicago Imagists (painters Ed Paschke, Jim Nutt, and Roger Brown among them) attracted international attention with their shows at the Hyde Park Art Center, the city has been a fertile breeding ground for emerging artists and innovative art dealers. Today, the primary gallery district is concentrated in the River North neighborhood, where century-old, redbrick warehouses have been converted into lofty exhibition spaces. More recently, a new generation of gallery owners has set up shop in the rapidly gentrifying West Loop neighborhood, where you'll tend to find more cutting-edge work. The River North gallery district is an easy walk from many hotels; the West Loop may seem a little farther afield, but it's only a short cab ride from downtown (you can also take the bus, but I'd recommend a taxi at night).

The River North gallery season officially gets underway on the first Friday after Labor Day in September. Besides fall, another great time to visit the district is from mid-July through August, when the Chicago Art Dealers Association presents **Vision,** an annual lineup of programs tailored to the public. The *Chicago Reader,* a free weekly newspaper available at many stores, taverns, and cafes on the North Side, publishes a very comprehensive listing of current gallery exhibitions, as does the quarterly *Chicago Gallery News* (www.chicago gallerynews.com), which is available free at the city's three visitor information centers. Another good resource is the Chicago Art Dealers Association (© **312/649-0065;** www.chicagoartdealers.org); the group's website has descriptions of all member galleries. For descriptions of the city's top galleries, see "Art Galleries" under "Shopping A to Z," below.

Along with its status as Chicago's primary art-gallery district, River North—the area west of the Magnificent Mile and north of the Chicago River—has attracted many interesting home-design shops concentrated on Wells Street from Kinzie Street to Chicago Avenue. My favorites include **Manifesto,** 755 N. Wells St., at Chicago Avenue (© **312/664-0733**), which offers custom-designed furniture, as well as imports from Italy and elsewhere in Europe; **Mig & Tig,** 540 N. Wells St., at Ohio Street (© **312/644-8277**), a charming furniture and decorative-accessories shop; and **Lightology,** 215 W. Chicago Ave., at Wells St. (© **312/944-1000**), a massive lighting store that carries a mind-boggling array of funky lamps, chandeliers, and glowing orbs from more than 400 manufacturers (even if you have no intention of flying home with a stack of lamps in your luggage, it's fun to browse).

Looming above the Chicago River at the southern end of River North is the **Merchandise Mart,** the world's largest commercial building. The massive complex was built in 1930 by Marshall Field & Company and was bought in 1945 by Joseph P. Kennedy (JFK's dad); the Kennedy family ran the Mart until the late 1990s. Now the building houses mostly interior-design showrooms, which are open only to professional designers. One exception is Luxe Home, a collection of kitchen and bath showrooms on the first floor, all of which are open to the public (and worth a look for interior-design junkies). Public tours of the whole complex are offered once a week, usually on Fridays ($12 adults; © **312/527-7762** for dates and reservations).

ARMITAGE AVENUE

Hovering between the North Side neighborhoods of Old Town and Lincoln Park, Armitage Avenue has emerged as a shopping destination in its own right, thanks to an influx of wealthy young professionals who have settled into historic town homes on the neighboring tree-lined streets. The main shopping district is concentrated between Halsted Street and Racine Avenue; I'd suggest starting at the Armitage El stop (Brown Line), working your way east to Halsted Street, and then wandering a few blocks north to Webster Street. As you stroll around, you'll get a good sense of the area's strong community spirit, with neighbors greeting each other and catching up on the street corners.

The shops and boutiques here are geared toward a sophisticated, well-heeled shopper and make for great browsing. (Most are suited for female shoppers—sorry, guys). You'll find trendy clothing boutiques, including that of local-gal-made-good **Cynthia Rowley** (808 W. Armitage Ave.; © **773/528-6160**); jaw-droppingly beautiful home-decor stores; beauty emporiums; and one of my favorite impossible-to-classify gift shops, **Art Effect** (p. 141). Despite the area's upscale feel, you can snag bargains at some top-notch discount and consignment shops, including **Lori's Designer Shoes, McShane's Exchange,** and **Fox's** (see "Vintage Fashion/Resale Shops" under "Shopping A to Z," below).

LINCOLN PARK & LAKEVIEW

A few major north-south thoroughfares—Lincoln Avenue, Clark Street, and Broadway—are the main shopping streets in both Lincoln Park (south of Diversey Pkwy.) and Lakeview (north of Diversey). Most of the shops cater to young singles who live in the surrounding apartment buildings; you'll find plenty of minimart groceries, some clothing and shoe boutiques, and the occasional used-book store, but not much that's worth a special trip.

Radiating from the intersection of Belmont Avenue and Clark Street is a string of shops catering to rebellious kids on tour from their homes in the 'burbs (the Dunkin' Donuts on the corner is often referred to as "Punkin' Donuts" in their honor). One constant in the ever-changing youth culture has been the **Alley,** 3228 N. Clark St., at Belmont Avenue (✆ **773/883-1800**), an "alternative shopping complex" selling everything from plaster gargoyles to racks of leather jackets. It has separate shops specializing in condoms, cigars, and bondage wear. **Tragically Hip,** a storefront women's boutique, 931 W. Belmont Ave. (✆ **773/549-1500**), next to the Belmont El train stop, has outlasted many other similar purveyors of cutting-edge women's apparel.

SOUTHPORT AVENUE

West of Lakeview, a few blocks from Wrigley Field, this residential area was considered up-and-coming about 10 years ago; now it's definitely arrived. The mix of restaurants, cool (but not *too* cool) clothing boutiques, and cafes appeals to the upscale urban families who have flocked to the area (watch out for strollers hogging the sidewalk). It's worth a look if you want to hang out in a neighborhood that's a little more laid-back than the Gold Coast or Wicker Park. Start at the Southport El stop on the Brown Line, and work your way north to Grace Street (round-trip, the walk will take you about half an hour—but allow more if you're doing some serious shopping or want to stop for lunch). Along the way you'll pass the historic **Music Box Theater** at 3733 N. Southport Ave. (✆ **773/871-6604**), north of Addison Street, which shows independent films from around the world. Two clothing shops catering to hip young women with plenty of disposable income are **Krista K,** 3458 N. Southport Ave. (✆ **773/248-1967**), and **Red Head Boutique,** 3450 N. Southport Ave. (✆ **773/325-9898**), which both stock hot new designers that aren't widely available in Chicago. **Shane,** 3657 N. Southport Ave. (✆ **773/549-0179**), and **Jake,** 3740 N. Southport Ave. (✆ **773/929-5253**), carry more casual clothes for both men and women (think trendy T-shirts and specialty-label denim).

WICKER PARK/BUCKTOWN

The go-go gentrification of the Wicker Park/Bucktown area has been followed by not only a rash of restaurants and bars but also retailers with an artsy bent that reflect the neighborhood's bohemian spirit. Mixed in with old neighborhood businesses, such as discount furniture stores and religious-icon purveyors, is a proliferation of antique-furniture shops, too-cool-for-school clothing boutiques, and eclectic galleries and gift emporiums. Despite the hefty price tags in many of these shops, the neighborhood still feels gritty—so come here if you want to feel like you've gotten a real urban fix.

Start at the Damen El stop on the Blue Line, and walk north along Damen to Armitage Avenue to scope out the trendiest shops. If you've got time, some stores are also scattered along Milwaukee Avenue south of North Avenue.

The friendly modern-day Marco Polos at **Pagoda Red,** 1714 N. Damen Ave., second floor (© 773/235-1188), have imported beautiful (and expensive) antique furniture and art objects, including Chinese concubine beds, painted Tibetan cabinets, Burmese rolling water vessels, cast-iron lotus bowls, bronze Buddhas, and Chinese inspiration stones. The upscale bazaar **Embelezar,** 1639 N. Damen Ave. (© 773/645-9705), carries exotic merchandise from around the world, both old and new, including the famous Fortuny silk lamps—hand-painted in Venice at the only studio allowed to reproduce the original Fortuny designs.

WEST DIVISION STREET

Once home to just a few pioneering restaurants, Division Street is quickly being transformed from a desolate urban landscape to a hot shopping destination. It's a work in progress (you'll still find some boarded-up buildings among the cool boutiques), but for now this is what Wicker Park used to be: a place where rents are still cheap enough for eager young entrepreneurs. Start at the Division El stop on the Blue Line, and head west along Division; most stores are concentrated between Milwaukee Avenue and Damen Avenue (a round-trip walk will take about half-an-hour). Along the way, you'll stroll past eclectic clothing and shoe boutiques, bath-and-beauty shops, and home-decor stores such as **Porte Rouge,** 1911 W. Division St. (© 773/269-2800), which is filled with French antiques and housewares (they'll even offer you a complimentary cup of tea). The mix of people living here—from working-class Latino families to self-consciously edgy young singles—makes the local cafes great for people-watching.

3 Shopping A to Z

Chicago has shops selling just about anything you could want or need, be it functional or ornamental, whimsical or exotic.

ANTIQUES

The greatest concentration of antiques businesses, from packed-to-the-rafters malls to idiosyncratic individual shops, can be found on Belmont Avenue west of Southport Avenue, or stretching north and south of Belmont Avenue along intersecting Lincoln Avenue. Here are a few others:

Architectural Artifacts, Inc. ⟨★★⟩ *(Finds)*   Chicago has a handful of salvage specialists who cater to the design trades and retail customers seeking an unusual architectural piece for their homes. This one is the best and is well worth seeking out at its location next to the Metra train line in the far-northwest corner of the city's Lakeview neighborhood. Its brightly lit, well-organized, cavernous showroom features everything from original mantels and garden ornaments to vintage bathroom hardware and American and French Art Deco lighting fixtures. 4325 N. Ravenswood Ave. (east of Damen Ave. and south of Montrose Ave.). ⟨℘⟩ **773/348-0622.** www.architecturalartifacts.com. Subway/El: Brown Line to Montrose.

Broadway Antique Market ⟨★⟩   Visiting Hollywood prop stylists and local interior designers flock here to find 20th-century antiques in near-perfect condition. 6130 N. Broadway (half-mile north of Hollywood Ave. and Lake Shore Dr.). ⟨℘⟩ **773/743-5444.** www.bamchicago.com. Subway/El: Red Line to Granville.

Jay Robert's Antique Warehouse   This mammoth River North space is within walking distance of downtown hotels, but you'll need comfortable shoes to explore all 50,000 square feet. The selection is wildly eclectic: fine furniture that includes fireplaces, stained glass, statues, tapestries, and an impressive selection of antique clocks in a variety of styles ranging from elaborate Victorian to sophisticated Art Deco. 149 W. Kinzie St. (at LaSalle St.). ⟨℘⟩ **312/222-0167.** www.jayroberts.com. Subway/El: Brown Line to Merchandise Mart.

ART GALLERIES

Ann Nathan Gallery ⟨★★⟩   Ann Nathan, who started out as a collector, shows exciting (and sometimes outrageous) pieces in clay, wood, and metal—along with paintings, photographs, and "functional art" (pieces that blur the line between furniture and sculpture). Nathan's space in the center of the River North district is one of the most beautiful in the city. 212 W. Superior St. (at Wells St.). ⟨℘⟩ **312/ 664-6622.** www.annnathangallery.com. Subway/El: Brown or Red line to Chicago.

Carl Hammer Gallery   A former schoolteacher and one of the most venerated dealers in Chicago, Carl Hammer touts his wares as "contemporary art and selected historical masterworks by American and European self-taught artists"—but it's the "self-taught" part that warrants emphasis. Hammer helped pioneer the field known as "outsider art," which has since become a white-hot commodity in the international art world. 740 N. Wells St. (at Superior St.). ⟨℘⟩ **312/266-8512.** www.hammergallery.com. Subway/El: Brown or Red line to Chicago.

Donald Young Gallery 𝕽   This dramatic West Loop gallery is a haven for critically acclaimed artists working in video, sculpture, photography, painting, and installation, including Anne Chu, Gary Hill, Martin Puryear, Bruce Nauman, Cristina Iglesias, Robert Mangold, and Charles Ray. 933 W. Washington St. (at Sangamon St.). ℂ 312/455-0100. www.donaldyoung.com. Bus: 20 (Madison).

Kavi Gupta Gallery   Owner Kavi Gupta is widely credited with kicking off the West Loop art scene when he developed this property as a home for new galleries. Gupta specializes in contemporary art by national and international emerging artists, so you never quite know what you're going to see here. Also worth checking out in the same building are the **Carrie Secrist Gallery** (ℂ 312/491-0917) and **Thomas McCormick Gallery** (ℂ 312/226-6800). 835 W. Washington St. (at Green St.). ℂ 312/432-0708. www.kavigupta.com. Bus: 20 (Madison).

Rhona Hoffman Gallery   The New York–born Rhona Hoffman maintains a high profile on the international contemporary-art scene. She launched her gallery in 1983 and, from the start, sought national and international artists, typically young and cutting-edge artists who weren't represented elsewhere in Chicago. Today she is the purveyor of such blue-chip players as Sol LeWitt and Jenny Holzer; she has also added young up-and-comers such as Dawoud Bey. 118 N. Peoria St. (between Randolph and Washington sts.). ℂ 312/455-1990. www.rhoffmangallery.com. Bus: 20 (Madison).

Richard Gray Gallery 𝕽   Richard Gray—whose gallery opened in 1963—is widely considered the dean of art dealers in Chicago. The gallery specializes in paintings, sculpture, and drawings by leading artists from the major movements in 20th-century American and European art (he also has a second location in New York). John Hancock Center, 875 N. Michigan Ave., Suite 2503 (between Delaware and Chestnut sts.). ℂ 312/642-8877. www.richardgraygallery.com. Subway/El: Red Line to Chicago.

Zolla/Lieberman Gallery 𝕽𝕽   Bob Zolla and Roberta Lieberman kicked off the River North revival when they opened their gallery (considered the grande dame of the area) here in 1976. Today, Zolla/Lieberman, directed by Roberta's son William Lieberman, represents a wide range of artists, including sculptor Deborah Butterfield, installation artist Vernon Fisher, and painter Terence LaNoue. 325 W. Huron St. (at Orleans St.). ℂ 312/944-1990. www.zollaliebermangallery.com. Subway/El: Brown Line to Chicago.

BOOKS

Abraham Lincoln Book Shop ✿ This bookstore houses one of the country's most outstanding collections of Lincolniana, from rare and antique books about the 16th president to collectible signatures, letters, and other documents illuminating the lives of other U.S. presidents and historical figures. 357 W. Chicago Ave. (between Orleans and Sedgwick sts.). ✆ 312/944-3085. Subway/El: Brown Line to Chicago.

Barnes & Noble This two-level Gold Coast store comes complete with a cafe in case you get the munchies while perusing the miles of books. There's another store in Lincoln Park, at 659 W. Diversey Ave., 1 block west of Clark Street (✆ 773/871-9004), and one at 1441 W. Webster Ave., at Clybourn Avenue (✆ 773/871-3610). 1130 N. State St. (at Elm St.). ✆ 312/280-8155. Subway/El: Red Line to Clark/Division.

Borders You couldn't ask for a better location, right across from Water Tower Place. This place is like a mini department store, with books, magazines, CDs, and computer software spread over four floors, and a cafe with a view overlooking the Mag Mile. There's also a Borders in the Loop at 150 N. State St., at Randolph Street (✆ 312/606-0750), and one in Lincoln Park at 2817 N. Clark St., at Diversey Avenue (✆ 773/935-3909). 830 N. Michigan Ave. (at Pearson St.). ✆ 312/573-0564. Subway/El: Red Line to Chicago.

Prairie Avenue Bookshop ✿✿ This South Loop store does Chicago's architectural tradition proud with the city's finest stock of architecture, design, and technical books. 418 S. Wabash Ave. (between Congress Pkwy. and Van Buren St.). ✆ 312/922-8311. Subway/El: Red Line to Jackson.

Unabridged Books This quintessential neighborhood bookseller in the area known as Boys Town has strong sections in gay and lesbian literature, travel, film, and sci-fi. 3251 N. Broadway (between Belmont Ave. and Addison St.). ✆ 773/883-9119. Subway/El: Red Line to Addison.

CANDY, CHOCOLATES & PASTRIES

Bittersweet ✿✿ Run by Judy Contino, one of the city's top pastry chefs and bakers, this Lakeview cafe and shop is sought out by brides-to-be and trained palates who have a yen for gourmet cakes, cookies, tarts, and ladyfingers. The rich chocolate mousse cake, a specialty of the house, is out of this world. 1114 W. Belmont Ave. (between Seminary and Clifton aves.). ✆ 773/929-1100. Subway/El: Red Line to Belmont.

Ethel's Chocolate Lounge A celebration of all things chocolate, this bright, candy-colored cafe has a distinctly feminine vibe; I have yet to see a group of guys huddling on one of the hot-pink couches. But what better way to catch up with a girlfriend than over a selection of gourmet truffles or a pot of hot chocolate? Ethel's also has locations inside the 900 N. Michigan Avenue mall (© **312/440-9747**) and along the Armitage Avenue shopping strip, 819 W. Armitage Ave. (© **773/281-0029**). 520 N. Michigan Ave. (inside the Westfield North Bridge mall). © **312/464-9330**. www.ethelschocolate.com. Subway/El: Red Line to Grand.

Vosges Haut-Chocolat ⚜ *(Finds)* Chocolatier Katrina Markoff's exotic gourmet truffles—with fabulous names such as absinthe, mint julep, wink of the rabbit, Woolloomooloo, and ambrosia—are made from premium Belgian chocolate and infused with rare spices, seasonings, and flowers from around the world. The store—which looks more like a modern art gallery than a chocolatier—includes a gourmet hot-chocolate bar, where you're welcome to sit and sip. Vosges also has a small store on trendy Armitage Avenue (951 W. Armitage Ave.; © **773/296-9866**). 520 N. Michigan Ave. (in the Westfield North Bridge shopping center). © **312/644-9450**. Subway/El: Red Line to Grand.

CLOTHING BOUTIQUES

Chasalla More low-key than many of its Oak Street neighbors, this cozy, minimalist boutique specializes in men's and women's clothing from designers' younger, slightly more affordable labels, including Versace's Versus, D&G, Hugo Red Label, and Cinque. 70 E. Oak St. (between Rush St. and Michigan Ave.). © **312/640-1940**. Subway/El: Red Line to Chicago.

Ikram ⚜⚜⚜ Run by Ikram Goldman, a former saleswoman at well-known women's clothing store Ultimo (see below), this shop stocks all the big names, from Valentino to Yves St. Laurent—and whatever else *Vogue* has declared "hot" for the season. Tucked among the high-priced pieces are jewelry, stationery, and decorative accessories that give the place a personal touch. 873 Rush St. (between Delaware and Chestnut sts.). © **312/587-1000**. www.ikram.com. Subway/El: Red Line to Chicago.

p45 ⚜ You'll find a number of cool boutiques aimed at the younger crowd clustered along Damen Avenue in Bucktown, but this is the most cutting-edge, with a vibe that's funky rather than girly. A gold mine of urbane women's fashion, the dark, spare space is filled with a unique mix of hip national labels (Michelle Mason, Susana Monaco, Lauren Moffat) and local designers you've never heard of. If you're looking for something no one else at home will be wearing, this is the place to shop. 1643 N. Damen Ave. (between North and Wabansia aves.). ✆ 773/862-4523. www.p45.com. Subway/El: Blue Line to Damen.

Scoop NYC The newest hot spot for trendy young things with plenty of spending money is this loft-life space in Bucktown, the first Midwest outpost of the popular New York clothing boutique Scoop NYC. You'll find a mix of major fashion names (Marc Jacobs bags, Jimmy Choo shoes) along with the requisite selection of designer denim, flirty dresses, and seemingly simple T-shirts that will make you do a double-take when you check out the price tag. (The store stocks men's and kids' clothing, too.) 1702 N. Milwaukee Ave. (at Wabansia Ave.). ✆ 773/227-9930. www.scoopnyc.com. Subway/El: Blue Line to Damen.

Shopgirl ✦ Lincoln Park 20- and 30-somethings flock to Shopgirl for the latest looks from trendy lines such as Blue Cult and Free People. It's a girly gathering place (pink walls, glittery chandeliers) with three-digit price tags, but it still has the feel of a neighborhood hangout, thanks to the friendly staff. The same owner runs a maternity store and kids' clothing shop across the street. 1206 W. Webster Ave. (at Racine Ave.). ✆ 773/935-7467. Subway/El: Red or Brown line to Fullerton.

Tangerine You can't help but smile when you enter this cheery Bucktown shop. Huge windows fill the place with light, and the colorful clothing selection—from designers such as Tocca, Nanette Lepore, and Trina Turk—is feminine and fun. (You will, however, pay a fair amount for these cute looks—most pieces start at $100 and up.) The sales staff has an upbeat attitude to match. 1719 N. Damen Ave. (at Wabansia Ave.). ✆ 773/772-0505. Subway/El: Blue Line to Damen.

The T-Shirt Deli ✦✦ *Finds* For a new twist on custom clothing, stop by this cozy Bucktown storefront, where you can order up your own personalized T-shirt creation. Browse through the entertaining books of vintage iron-on patches, and you'll find everything from '80s icons such as Mr. T to '70s-style "Foxy Lady" logos. Choose a design (or create your own message), and your shirt will be printed up while you wait. When it's done, the shirt is packaged in a paper bag with a side of potato chips—just like a real deli. 1739 N. Damen Ave. (between Willow St. and St. Paul Ave.). ✆ 773/276-6266. www.tshirtdeli.com. Subway/El: Blue Line to Damen.

Ultimo ✦✦ The grande dame of local boutiques, Ultimo is known for carrying high-profile (and high-priced) designers, as well as up-and-coming names that have yet to show up in department stores. The store's warren of rooms, decked out in luxurious dark wood and red velvet, feels more like a spectacularly well-stocked private collection than a shop. Ultimo carries both women's and men's clothing, making it one of the rare spots fashion hounds of both genders can shop together. 114 E. Oak St. (between Michigan Ave. and Rush St.). ☏ **312/787-1171.** www.ultimo.com. Subway/El: Red Line to Chicago.

COLLECTIBLES

Quimby's   The ultimate alternative newsstand, Quimby's stocks every kind of obscure periodical, from cutting-edge comics to 'zines "published" in some teenager's basement. Their book selection is also decadently different from your local Barnes & Noble; categories include "Conspiracy," "Politics & Revolution," and "Lowbrow Art." 1854 W. North Ave. (just east of Damen Ave.). ☏ **773/342-0910.** www.quimbys.com. Subway/El: Blue Line to Damen.

Uncle Fun 😊😊 *Finds*   Whenever I'm looking for a quirky Christmas stocking-stuffer or the perfect gag gift, I know Uncle Fun will come through for me. Bins and cubbyholes are stuffed full of the standard joke toys (rubber-chicken key chains and chattering wind-up teeth), but you'll also find every conceivable modern pop-culture artifact, from Jackson Five buttons to Speed Racer's Mach-Five model car. 1338 W. Belmont Ave. (1 block east of Southport Ave.). ☏ **773/477-8223.** www.unclefunchicago.com. Subway/El: Red or Brown line to Belmont.

DEPARTMENT STORES

Barneys New York   The first Midwest outpost of Barneys has the same look and feel of the New York original: minimalist-chic decor, high-priced fashions, and a fair amount of attitude from the sales staff. That said, the store has a stellar—if high-priced—shoe selection, along with always-interesting home accessories and a fun-to-browse cosmetics area full of specialty beauty products. 25 E. Oak St. (at Rush St.). ☏ **312/587-1700.** www.barneys.com. Subway/El: Red Line to Chicago.

Bloomingdale's   Though not as large as the New York original, Chicago's Bloomingdale's appeals to stylish shoppers looking for just a bit of urban edge. The shoe department has a good range (with serious markdowns during semiannual sales), and a special section is devoted to souvenir Bloomingdale's logo merchandise. 900 N. Michigan Ave. (at Walton St.). ☏ **312/440-4460.** www.bloomingdales.com. Subway/El: Red Line to Chicago.

Lord & Taylor   Overall, Lord & Taylor is a more affordable alternative to stores such as Bloomingdale's and Saks Fifth Avenue, with styles geared to women a few sizes larger than waifish fashion models. The shoe department is worth checking out for its good selection and sales. Water Tower Place, 835 N. Michigan Ave. (between Chestnut and Pearson sts.). © 312/787-7400. www.lordandtaylor.com. Subway/El: Red Line to Chicago.

Macy's ⭐⭐⭐ When Macy's took over Marshall Field's—Chicago's best-known "hometown" department store—in 2006, there was much local hand-wringing about what the buyout meant for Field's grand State Street headquarters. Although Field's iconic green awnings and shopping bags have been replaced by Macy's more dreary black, the good news is that the store itself remains impressive. A number of exclusive "miniboutiques" are scattered throughout the overwhelming space, including the 28 Shop, which stocks the latest from hot young designers; beauty stations where you can get a manicure and pick up exclusive products; and a gourmet food department developed by celebrity chef Charlie Trotter. The enormous shoe department is another highlight, with everything from killer high heels (at killer prices) and boots to sneakers and casual sandals.

The Water Tower store, 835 N. Michigan Ave. (© 312/335-7700), is a scaled-down but respectable version of the State Street store. 111 N. State St. (at Randolph St.). © 312/781-1000. www.macys.com. Subway/El: Red Line to Washington.

Neiman Marcus Yes, you'll pay top dollar for designer names here—the store does, after all, need to live up to its Needless Markup moniker—but Neiman's has a broader price range than many of its critics care to admit. It also has some mighty good sales. The four-story store, a beautiful environment in its own right, sells cosmetics, shoes, furs, fine and fashion jewelry, and clothing. The top floor has a fun gourmet food department as well as a pretty home-accessories area. Neiman's has two restaurants: one relaxed, the other a little more formal. 737 N. Michigan Ave. (between Superior St. and Chicago Ave.). © 312/642-5900. www.neimanmarcus.com. Subway/El: Red Line to Chicago.

Nordstrom Nordstrom's spacious, airy design and trendy touches (wheatgrass growing by the escalators, funky music playing on the stereo system) gives it the feel of an upscale boutique rather than an overcrowded department store. The company's famed shoe department is large but not overwhelming; more impressive is the cosmetics department, where you'll find a wide array of smaller labels and an "open sell" environment (meaning you're encouraged to try on makeup without a salesperson hovering over you). 520 N. Michigan Ave., inside Westfield North Bridge mall, 55 E. Grand Ave. (at Rush St.). © 312/379-4300. www.nordstrom.com. Subway/El: Red Line to Grand.

Saks Fifth Avenue Saks Fifth Avenue might be best known for its designer collections—Valentino, Chloe, and Giorgio Armani, to name a few—but the store also does a decent job of buying more casual and less expensive merchandise. Still, the mood here can be somewhat chilly, and the high-fashion clothes on display seem geared toward the super-skinny. The men's department is located in a separate building across Michigan Avenue. Don't forget to visit the cosmetics department, where Saks is known, in particular, for its fragrance selection. Chicago Place, 700 N. Michigan Ave. (at Superior St.). ✆ 312/944-6500. www.saksfifthavenue.com. Subway/El: Red Line to Chicago.

GOURMET FOOD

Fox & Obel ✸✸ The city's top gourmet market is a foodie paradise: from the wide selection of specialty cheeses to the mouth-watering display of desserts. An easy walk to Navy Pier and the lakefront, it's a great place to pick up a picnic lunch or a bottle of wine and some chocolates to enjoy late-night in your hotel room. There's also an in-store cafe if you want to take a break while strolling around the Michigan Avenue area. 401 E. Illinois St. (at McClurg Ct.). ✆ 312/410-7301. www.foxandobel.com. Subway/El: Red Line to Grand, and then 65 Grand bus.

Goddess & Grocer This upscale version of a neighborhood deli stocks everything you need for a mouthwatering lunch or dinner on the go—from specialty sandwiches to chicken and pasta dishes to freshly baked cookies and brownies. There's also a good selection of wine and prepackaged snacks. The same owners run another, smaller, outpost in Bucktown, 1646 N. Damen Ave., at North Ave. (✆ 773/342-3200). 25 E. Delaware St. (at Rush St.). ✆ 312/896-2600. www.goddessandgrocer.com. Subway/El: Red Line to Chicago.

HOME DECOR & GIFTS

Art Effect ✸✸ Classifying this wonderfully eclectic Armitage Avenue shop is no easy task (the owners refer to it as a "modern day general store"). It's got everything from aromatherapy oils and kitchen mixing bowls designed by cookbook author Nigella Lawson to handcrafted jewelry and gag gifts, not to mention a whole room devoted to hippie-chic women's clothing. The merchandise has a definite female slant, with a vibe that's young and irreverent rather than fussy, but the laid-back, friendly sales staff makes everyone feel welcome. 934 W. Armitage Ave. (at Bissell St.). ✆ 773/929-3600. www.art effectchicago.com. Subway/El: Brown Line to Armitage.

Orange Skin ⊕ It may look like an ultracool loft catering only to trendier-than-thou style experts, but don't be intimidated: Orange Skin is one of my favorite places to check out what's new in the world of modern interior design (and the staff is more welcoming than you might expect). From colored clear-plastic dining chairs to bowls made of welded steel wires, browsing here is a good way to gauge what's cool in the world of design. Visit the shop's lower level for smaller tabletop items that make good, one-of-a-kind gifts. 223 W. Erie St. (at Franklin St.). ℭ **312/335-1033.** www.orangeskin.com. Subway/El: Brown Line to Chicago.

MUSIC

Jazz Record Mart ⊕⊕ This is possibly the best jazz record store in the country. For novices, the "Killers Rack" displays albums that the store's owners consider essential to any jazz collection. Besides jazz, there are bins filled with blues, Latin, and "New Music." 27 E. Illinois St. (between Wabash Ave. and State St.). ℭ **312/222-1467.** www.jazz recordmart.com. Subway/El: Red Line to Grand.

Reckless Records The best all-round local record store for music that the cool kids listen to, Reckless Records wins brownie points for its friendly and helpful staff. There are also locations in Wicker Park at 1532 N. Milwaukee Ave. (ℭ **773/235-3727**), and the Loop, 26 E. Madison St. (ℭ **312/795-0878**). 3157 N. Broadway (at Belmont Ave.). ℭ **773/404-5080.** www.reckless.com. Subway/El: Red or Brown line to Belmont.

PAPER & STATIONERY

Paper Source ⊕⊕⊕ The acknowledged leader of stationery stores in Chicago. The store's claim to fame is its collection of hand-made paper in a variety of colors and textures. You'll also find one-of-a-kind greeting cards and a large collection of rubber stamps for personalizing your own paper at home. There's also a location in the trendy Armitage shopping district at 919 W. Armitage Ave. (ℭ **773/ 525-7300**). 232 W. Chicago Ave. (at Franklin St.). ℭ **312/337-0798.** www.paper-source.com. Subway/El: Red or Brown line to Chicago.

The Watermark Chicago socialites come here to order their engraved invitations, but this stationery store also carries a good selection of handmade greeting cards for all occasions. 109 E. Oak St. (1 block from Michigan Ave.). ℭ **312/337-5353.** Subway/El: Red Line to Clark/ Division.

SALONS & SPAS

Art + Science This Lincoln Park spot, just steps from the Armitage Avenue shopping strip, may look a little intimidating from outside, but the ambience inside is welcoming. Stylists can get as creative as you want, but most clients here are young professional women who want the same basic cut as everyone else. There's also another location in Wicker Park at 1552 N. Milwaukee Ave. (② **773/227-HAIR**). 1971 N. Halsted St. (at Armitage Ave.). ② **312/787-HAIR**. www.artandsciencesalon.com. Subway/El: Brown Line to Armitage.

Charles Ifergan   Charles Ifergan, one of the city's top salons, caters to the ladies-who-lunch, and his rates, which vary according to the seniority of the stylist, are relatively high. But if you're a little daring, you can get a cut for the price of the tip on Tuesday and Wednesday evenings when junior stylists do their thing gratis—under the watchful eye of Monsieur Ifergan (call ② **312/640-7444** between 10am and 4pm to make an appointment for that night). 106 E. Oak St. (between Michigan Ave. and Rush St.). ② **312/642-4484**. www.charlesifergan.com. Subway/El: Red Line to Chicago.

Kiva Day Spa ⊙⊙   Kiva is the city's reigning "super spa," and is named for the round ceremonial space used by Native Americans seeking to quiet, cleanse, and relax the spirit. The two-floor, 6,000-square-foot space offers spa, salon, nutrition, and apothecary services, and a nutritional juice-and-snack bar in a setting that evokes its namesake inspiration. Water Tower Place, entrance at 196 E. Pearson St (at Mies van der Rohe Way). ② **312/840-8120**. www.premierspacollection.com. Subway/El: Red Line to Chicago.

Salon Buzz   This hip hair parlor, operated by wizardly stylist Andreas Zafiriadis (who has wielded his scissors in Paris, Greece, New York, and California), is the choice for young women in creative professions. 1 E. Delaware Place (at State St.). ② **312/943-5454**. Subway/El: Red Line to Chicago.

Spa Space ⊙⊙ *(Finds)*   Located in the up-and-coming West Loop, this trendy spa offers the latest skin-care treatments in a stylishly modern building that feels like a boutique hotel. The gender-neutral decor and specialized menu of guy-friendly treatments (including a massage designed for golfers) has given this spa a far larger male clientele than other local spots. 161 N. Canal St. (at Randolph St.). ② **312/943-5454**. www.spaspace.com. Subway/El: Green Line to Clinton.

Urban Oasis *(Finds)*   After a long day of sightseeing, try a soothing massage in this spa's subdued, Zen-like atmosphere. The ritual begins with a steam or rain shower in a private changing room followed by the spa treatment you elect—various forms of massage (including a couple's massage, in which you learn to do it yourself), an aromatherapy wrap, or an exfoliating treatment. Fruit, juices, or herbal teas are offered on completion. There's also another location in a burgeoning retail district a few blocks south of the Armitage Avenue shopping strip at 939 W. North Ave. (© 773/640-0001). 12 W. Maple St., 3rd floor (between Dearborn and State sts.). © 312/587-3500. www.urbanoasis.biz. Subway/El: Red Line to Clark/Division.

SHOES & BAGS

1154 Lill Studio ☆ *Finds*   Purse-a-holics and wannabe designers will find fashion heaven at this custom-handbag shop. Pick a style (which includes everything from evening purses to diaper bags), and then browse the huge selection of fabrics to create your own custom interior and exterior. Your finished creation can be picked up in a few weeks or shipped to your home. 904 W. Armitage Ave. (at Fremont St.). © 773/477-LILL. Subway/El: Brown line to Armitage.

Lori's Designer Shoes ☆☆ *Value*   Lori's looks like a local version of Payless Shoes (shoeboxes stacked on the floor and women surrounded by piles of heels and boots), but the designer names on most of those shoes prove that this is a step above your typical discount store. A mecca for the shoe-obsessed, Lori's stocks all the latest styles, at prices that average 10% to 30% below department-store rates. 824 W. Armitage Ave. (between Sheffield Ave. and Halsted St.). © 773/281-5655. www.lorisdesignershoes.com. Subway/El: Brown Line to Armitage.

SOUVENIRS & MAPS

ArchiCenter Shop ☆☆☆   Stop here for the coolest gifts in town. This bright, sleek shop is part of the Chicago Architecture Foundation, so everything in stock—including photography books, tour guides, stationery, and kids' toys—has a definite sense of style. Whether you're in the market for a $900 reproduction of a vase from Frank Lloyd Wright's Robie House or more affordable black-and-white photos of the city skyline, it's well worth a visit. 224 S. Michigan Ave. (at Jackson St.). © 312/922-3432, ext. 241. www.architecture.org. Subway/El: Red Line to Jackson.

City of Chicago Store   Located in the Water Works Visitor Center right off Michigan Avenue, this is a convenient stop for Chicago-related souvenirs and gifts, including truly one-of-a-kind pieces of retired municipal equipment (although the parking meters we've seen for sale here might be a little hard to stuff in your suitcase). 163 E. Pearson St. (at Michigan Ave.). © 312/742-8811. Subway/El: Red Line to Chicago.

The Savvy Traveller   This Loop specialty store carries just about everything a traveler might need, from guidebooks and maps to rain gear and portable games. 310 S. Michigan Ave. (between Van Buren St. and Jackson Blvd.). ℂ 312/913-9800. www.thesavvytraveller.com. Subway/El: Red Line to Jackson.

SPORTING GOODS
Sports Authority   The largest sporting-goods store in the city, Sports Authority offers seven floors of merchandise, from running apparel to camping gear. Sports fans will be in heaven in the first- and fifth-floor team merchandise departments, where Cubs, Bulls, and Sox jerseys abound. Cement handprints of local sports celebs dot the outside of the building; step inside to check out the prints from Michael Jordan and White Sox slugger Frank Thomas. 620 N. LaSalle St. (at Ontario St.). ℂ 312/337-6151. www.sportsauthority.com. Subway/El: Red Line to Grand.

TOYS & CHILDREN'S CLOTHING
Little Strummer ℛ   This compact store is located in the Old Town School of Folk Music, which offers music classes for children, and stocks every kind of mini-instrument imaginable, from accordions and guitars to wind chimes and music boxes. There's also a good selection of music-related games and kids' CDs. 909 W. Armitage Ave. (at Halsted St.). ℂ 773/751-3410. Subway/El: Brown Line to Armitage.

Madison & Friends   Clothing for kids that's both cute and wearable is the specialty here, from baby-size leather bomber jackets to yoga pants for toddlers. A separate back room caters to older kids and tweens—including a staggering array of jeans. 940 N. Rush St. (at Oak St.). ℂ 312/642-6403. www.madisonandfriends.com. Subway/El: Red Line to Chicago.

Psycho Baby   The opening of this everything-for-baby shop was the definitive sign that Bucktown had gentrified. The prices may sometimes cause a double take ($60 for shoes that your kid will outgrow in 3 months), but the creative selection and happy vibe make it fun for browsing. 1630 N. Damen Ave. (1 block north of North Ave.). ℂ 773/772-2815. www.psychobabyonline.com. Subway/El: Blue Line to Damen.

VINTAGE FASHION/RESALE SHOPS
The Daisy Shop ℛ   A significant step up from your standard vintage store, The Daisy Shop specializes in couture fashions. These designer duds come from the closets of the city's most stylish socialites and carry appropriately hefty price tags. Well-dressed women from around the world stop by here in search of the perfect

one-of-a-kind item. 67 E. Oak St. (between Michigan Ave. and Rush St.). © **312/943-8880.** Subway/El: Brown Line to Sedgwick.

Fox's This no-frills shop near Armitage Avenue offers designer clothing at a steep discount. The downside: Most clothing labels are cut out, so you might not know exactly which A-list name you're buying. 2150 N. Halsted St. (at Dickens St.). © **773/281-0700.** Subway/El: Brown Line to Armitage.

McShane's Exchange ✸✸ *Finds* This consignment shop has a selection that's a few steps above the standard thrift store, and for designer bargains, it can't be beat. I've done plenty of double takes at the price tags here: Calvin Klein coats, Prada sweaters, and Armani jackets all going for well under $100. If that's not tempting enough, you'll also find barely used shoes and purses. McShane's has another location with a similar selection at 1141 W. Webster St. (© **773/ 525-0211**). 815 W. Armitage Ave. (at Halsted St.). © **773/525-0282.** www. mcshanesexchange.com. Subway/El: Brown Line to Armitage.

WINE & LIQUOR

Binny's Beverage Depot *Value* This River North purveyor of fermented libations is housed in a delightfully no-frills warehouse space and offers an enormous selection of wine, beer, and spirits— often at discounted prices. Binny's has a second, smaller location at 3000 N. Clark St. (© **773/935-9400**). 213 W. Grand Ave. (at Wells St.). © **312/332-0012.** www.binnys.com. Subway/El: Red Line to Grand.

House of Glunz ✸✸ *Finds* Not only is this Chicago's oldest wine shop, but it's also the oldest in the Midwest, with an inventory of 1,500 wines dating back to 1811. There's a stock of modern wines from California and Europe, and the knowledgeable owners are able to steer you to the right bottle to fit your budget. 1206 N. Wells St. (at Division St.). © **312/642-3000.** www.houseofglunz.com. Subway/El: Brown Line to Sedgwick.

8

Chicago After Dark

Chicago's bustling energy isn't confined to daylight hours. The city offers loads of after-hours entertainment, all with a distinctly low-key, Midwestern flavor.

The inviting atmosphere at both the Chicago Symphony Orchestra and the Lyric Opera of Chicago is appealing to culture vultures, while Broadway buffs can choose between big-league theaters such as Steppenwolf and Goodman and the scrappy storefront companies springing up around the city. The theater scene here was built by performers who valued gritty realism and a communal work ethic, and that down-to-earth energy is still very much present. Music and nightclub haunts are scattered throughout the city, but Chicago's thriving music scene is concentrated in Lincoln Park, Lakeview, and Wicker Park, where clubs are devoted to everything from jazz and blues to alternative rock and reggae.

For up-to-date entertainment listings, check the local newspapers and magazines, particularly the "At Play" (Thurs) and "On the Town" (Fri) sections of the *Chicago Tribune* and the "Weekend Plus" (Fri) section of the *Chicago Sun-Times;* the weekly magazine *Time Out Chicago,* which has excellent comprehensive listings; and the *Chicago Reader* or *New City,* two free weekly tabloids with extensive listings. The *Tribune*'s entertainment-oriented website, **www.metromix.com**; the *Reader*'s website, **www.chicagoreader.com**; and the local Citysearch website, **http://chicago.citysearch.com**, are also excellent sources of information, with lots of opinionated reviews.

1 The Performing Arts

Chicago is a regular stop on the big-name entertainment circuit, whether it's the national tour of Broadway shows such as *Wicked* or pop music acts such as U2 or the Dave Matthews Band (both of whom sell out multiple nights at stadiums when they come to town). High-profile shows including Monty Python's *Spamalot* and Mel Brooks's stage version of *The Producers* had their first runs here before moving on to New York.

Thanks to extensive renovation efforts, performers have some impressive venues where they can strut their stuff. The **Auditorium Theatre,** 50 E. Congress Pkwy., between Michigan and Wabash avenues (© **312/922-2110;** www.auditoriumtheatre.org), is my pick for the most beautiful theater in Chicago—and it's a certified national landmark, too. Built in 1889 by Louis Sullivan and Dankmar Adler, this grand hall schedules mostly musicals and dance performances. Even if you don't catch a show here, stop by for a tour (for more details, see p. 95).

The city's other great historic theaters are concentrated in the North Loop. The **Ford Center for the Performing Arts/Oriental Theater,** 24 W. Randolph St., and the **Cadillac Palace Theater,** 151 W. Randolph St., book major touring shows and are well worth a visit for arts buffs. The Oriental's fantastical Asian look includes elaborate carvings almost everywhere you look; dragons, elephants, and griffins peer down at the audience from the gilded ceiling. The Palace features a profusion of Italian marble surfaces and columns, gold-leaf accents a la Versailles, huge decorative mirrors, and crystal chandeliers. (If you'd like to get a look at these historic theaters for a fraction of the standard ticket price, guided tours of both start at 11am Sat and cost $10 per person; meet in the Oriental lobby.) The **LaSalle Bank Theatre** (formerly the Schubert Theatre), 18 W. Monroe St., was built in 1906 as a home for vaudeville; today it books mostly big-name musicals and sometimes comedy performers. For show schedules at all three theaters, call © **312/977-1700,** or visit www.broadwayinchicago.com.

CLASSICAL MUSIC

For current listings of classical music concerts and opera, check with the **Chicago Dance and Music Alliance** (© **312/987-1123;** www.chicagoperformances.org).

Chicago Symphony Orchestra 🎭🎭 The Chicago Symphony Orchestra is considered among the best in the world; a legacy of the late maestro Sir Georg Solti. Recently departed musical director Daniel Barenboim—a talented conductor and piano prodigy who left the CSO after the 2005–06 season—proved a worthy successor. (Currently, interim leadership is in place in the form of Bernard Haitink, the CSO's principal conductor; and Pierre Boulez, the CSO's conductor emeritus.) Under Barenboim, the orchestra added more modern works into their repertoire, but crowd-pleasing favorites by Beethoven or Brahms are performed regularly as well.

Like many other orchestras around the country, the CSO has tried to diversify its programming to attract younger audiences. The "Symphony Center Presents" series has recently included some of the top jazz, world beat, Latin, and cabaret artists in the world. Although demand is high, good seats for concerts—turned in by subscribers who can't make it—often become available on concert days. Call Symphony Center, or stop by the box office to check availability. Orchestra Hall in Symphony Center, 220 S. Michigan Ave. ℂ 312/294-3000. www.cso.org. Tickets $25–$110; box seats $185. Subway/El: Red Line to Jackson.

Grant Park Symphony and Chorus (*Value*)   One of the city's best cultural bargains, this music festival offers a series of free outdoor classical music concerts from June through August. The symphony, along with well-known visiting musicians and singers, performs in the Frank Gehry–designed Pritzker Music Pavilion in Millennium Park. Featuring Gehry's signature sinuous lines, the pavilion is surrounded by dramatic ribbons of curved steel. Concerts are held Wednesday, Friday, and Saturday, with most performances beginning at 6:30pm (7:30pm on Sat). Seats in the front of the pavilion are reserved for subscribers, but the back rows are available on a first-come, first-served basis. There's also plenty of lawn seating, so bring a blanket and enjoy a picnic dinner. Pritzker Music Pavilion, Michigan Ave. and Randolph St. ℂ 312/742-7638. www.grantparkmusicfestival.com. Subway/El: Red Line to Washington/State; or Brown, Orange, or Green line to Randolph/Wabash.

OPERA

Lyric Opera of Chicago ☆☆   One of the top American opera companies, the Lyric attracts the very best singers in the world for its lavish productions. Talented musicians and performers satisfy opera devotees, while newcomers are often swept away by all the grandeur (English supertitles make it easy to follow the action).

The Lyric Opera performs in the handsome 3,563-seat Art Deco Civic Opera House, the second-largest opera house in the country, built in 1929. If you're sitting in one of the upper balconies, you'll definitely want to bring binoculars (if you're nice, the regulars sitting nearby may lend you theirs). There's only one problem with catching a show at the Lyric: The season, which runs through early March, sells out way in advance. Single tickets are sometimes available a few months in advance. Your other option is to call the day of a performance, when you can sometimes buy tickets that subscribers have turned in. Civic Opera House, Madison St. and Wacker Dr. ℂ 312/332-2244. www.lyricopera.org. Tickets $31–$187. Subway/El: Brown Line to Washington.

Chicago Opera Theater   The "other" opera company in town, Chicago Opera Theater doesn't get all the big names, but it does make opera accessible to a wider audience with an emphasis on American composers and performers who sing in English. It also helps that tickets are less expensive and more plentiful than the Lyric Opera's. The company performs three operas a year (Mar–May), which usually run the gamut from classical tragedies by Handel to 20th-century satirical works. Harris Theater for Music and Dance, 205 E. Randolph Dr. © 312/704-8414. www.chicagooperatheater.org. Tickets $35–$120 adults, half-price for children and students. Subway/El: Red Line to Washington/State.

DANCE

Chicago's dance scene is lively, but unfortunately it doesn't attract the same crowds as our theaters or music performances. Dance lovers should schedule their visit for November, when the annual **"Dance Chicago"** festival (© 773/989-0698; www.dancechicago.com) is held at the Athenaeum Theatre, 2936 N. Southport Ave., on the North Side. Featuring performances and workshops from the city's best-known dance companies and countless smaller groups, it's a great chance to check out the range of local dance talent.

The major Chicago dance troupes perform at the **Harris Theater for Music and Dance,** 205 E. Randolph St. (© 312/334-7777), in Millennium Park. The 1,500-seat theater feels fairly stark and impersonal—the gray concrete lobby could be mistaken for a parking garage—but the sightlines are great, thanks to the stadium-style seating. Most of the troupes listed below perform there. For complete information on local dance performances, check the Chicago Dance and Music Alliance information line at © 312/987-1123, or visit **www.chicagoperformances.org**.

Hubbard Street Dance Chicago ⊛   If you're going to see just one dance performance while you're in town, make it a Hubbard Street one. Chicago's best-known dance troupe mixes jazz, modern, ballet, and theater dance into an exhilarating experience. Sometimes whimsical, sometimes romantic, the crowd-pleasing 22-member ensemble incorporates a range of dance traditions, from Kevin O'Day to Twyla Tharp (who has choreographed pieces exclusively for Hubbard Street). Although the troupe spends most of the year touring, it has regular 2- to 3-week Chicago engagements in the fall and spring. Office: 1147 W. Jackson Blvd. © 312/850-9744. www.hubbard streetdance.com. Tickets $20–$75.

Joffrey Ballet of Chicago ⓡ While this major classical company concentrates on touring, the Joffrey schedules about 6 weeks of performances a year in its hometown. Led by co-founder and artistic director Gerald Arpino, the company is committed to the classic works of the 20th century. Its repertoire extends from the ballets of Arpino, Robert Joffrey, Balanchine, and Jerome Robbins to the cutting-edge works of Alonzo King and Chicago choreographer Randy Duncan. The Joffrey continues to draw crowds with its popular rock ballet, *Billboards,* which is set to the music of Prince and tours internationally. The company is usually in town in the spring (Mar or Apr), fall (Sept or Oct), and December, when it stages a popular rendition of the holiday favorite *The Nutcracker.* Office: 70 E. Lake St. ⓒ **312/739-0120.** www.joffrey.com. Tickets $25–$130.

THEATER

Some of Broadway's most acclaimed dramas in recent years (the Goodman Theatre's revival of *Death of a Salesman* and Steppenwolf's *The Grapes of Wrath,* to name a couple) hatched on Chicago stages. With more than 200 theaters, Chicago might have dozens of productions playing on any given weekend—and seeing a show here is on my must-do list for all visitors.

The city's theaters have produced a number of legendary comedic actors, including comic-turned-director Mike Nichols *(The Graduate, Postcards from the Edge, Primary Colors),* as well as fine dramatic actors and playwrights. David Mamet, one of America's greatest playwrights and an acclaimed film director and screenwriter, grew up in Chicago's South Shore steel-mill neighborhood and honed his craft with the former St. Nicholas Players, which included actor William H. Macy *(Fargo, Boogie Nights).*

The thespian soil here must be fertile. Tinseltown and TV have lured away such talents as John Malkovich, Joan Allen, Dennis Franz, George Wendt, John and Joan Cusack, Aidan Quinn, Anne Heche, and Lili Taylor. But even as emerging talent leave for higher paychecks, a new pool of fresh faces is always waiting to take over. This constant renewal keeps the city's theatrical scene invigorated with new ideas and energy.

For a complete listing of current productions playing, check the comprehensive listings in the two free weeklies, the *Reader* (which reviews just about every show in town) and *New City;* the weekly *Time Out Chicago;* or the Friday sections of the two dailies. The website of the **League of Chicago Theatres** (www.chicagoplays.com) also lists all theater productions playing in the area.

GETTING TICKETS

To order tickets for many plays and events, call the **Ticketmaster Arts Line** (℃ 312/902-1500), a centralized phone-reservation system that allows you to charge full-price tickets (with an additional service charge) for productions at more than 50 Chicago theaters. Individual box offices also take credit card orders by phone, and many of the smaller theaters will reserve seats for you with a simple request under your name left on the answering machine. For hard-to-get tickets, try **Chicago Ticket Exchange** (℃ 312/902-1888; www.chicagoticketexchange.com) or **Gold Coast Tickets** (℃ 800/889-9100; www.goldcoasttickets.com).

Bailiwick Repertory Theatre Bailiwick gets my vote as the most eclectic theater in the city. Its three stages showcase works both dramatic and light-hearted, some produced by Bailiwick, others by smaller, scrappier start-up troupes. Each year, the theater produces a main-stage series of classics and musicals, the Director's Festival of one-act plays by fresh local talents (in June), and gay- and lesbian-oriented shows during the Pride Performance series, which generally runs over 20 weeks from mid-May to early October. The company's children's theater program produces an original musical for kids each spring. 1229 W. Belmont Ave. (at Racine Ave.). ℃ 773/883-1090. www.bailiwick. org. Tickets $20–$35. Subway/El: Red or Brown line to Belmont.

Chicago Shakespeare Theatre ☞ This group's home on Navy Pier is a visually stunning, state-of-the-art jewel. The centerpiece of the glass-box complex, which rises seven stories, is a 525-seat court-yard-style theater patterned loosely after the Swan Theater in Strat-ford-upon-Avon. But what keeps subscribers coming back is the talented company of actors, including some of the finest Shakespeare performers in the country.

The main theater presents three plays a year, almost always by the Bard; founder and artistic director Barbara Gaines usually directs one show. Shakespeare Theatre subscribers are loyal, so snagging tickets can be a challenge; reserve well in advance if possible. If you have a choice of seats, avoid the upper balcony; the tall chairs are uncomfortable, and you have to lean way over the railing to see all the action onstage—definitely not recommended for anyone with a fear of heights. 800 E. Grand Ave. ℃ 312/595-5600. www.chicagoshakes.com. Tickets $40–$67. Subway/El: Red Line to Grand, and then bus no. 29 to Navy Pier. Discounted parking in attached garage.

Goodman Theatre *ⒻⒻ* The Goodman, under artistic director Robert Falls, is the dean of legitimate theaters in Chicago. Productions at the Goodman are always solid; you may not see anything revolutionary, but you'll get some of the best actors in the city and top-notch production values.

The Goodman's custom-designed home in the North Loop is a rehab of the historic Harris and Selwyn theaters, a pair of rococo former movie houses, but the renovation retained none of the historic bric-a-brac; the new structure has a modern, minimalist feel (the side of the building glows with different colors in the evenings). The centerpiece is the 830-seat limestone-and-glass Albert Ivar Goodman Theatre. Connected to the main theater is a cylindrical, glass-walled building that houses retail operations, the 400-seat Owen Theatre, and the restaurant Petterino's.

Every December, the Goodman stages a production of *A Christmas Carol*, which draws families from throughout the Chicago area and beyond. If you're in town then, it's great fun, but buy your tickets in advance, because many performances sell out. 170 N. Dearborn St. ℭ 312/443-3800. www.goodman-theatre.org. Tickets $10–$68. Subway/El: Red Line to Washington/State or Lake/State; Brown or Orange line to Clark/Lake.

The House Theatre *Finds* If you're looking for the up-and-coming stars of Chicago theater, keep your eyes on the House. This group of young actors takes on big themes (Harry Houdini and his obsession with death; the space-age tales of Ray Bradbury) and turns them into nonstop spectacles of drama, music, and comedy. Despite the usual budget constraints, the sets and special effects are impressive—as is the troupe's energy, imagination, and humor. Office: 4700 N. Ravenswood Ave. ℭ 773/251-2195. www.thehousetheatre.com. Tickets $17–$22. Performances: The Viaduct, 3111 N. Western Ave. Subway/El: Red Line to Belmont, then bus no. 77 (Belmont Ave.).

Lookingglass Theatre Company *Ⓕ* A rising star on the Chicago theatrical scene, Lookingglass produces original shows and unusual literary adaptations in a highly physical and visually imaginative style. (Its location in the Water Tower Pumping Station—just off Michigan Ave. and within walking distance of many downtown hotels—makes it especially visitor-friendly.) The company, founded more than a decade ago by graduates of Northwestern University (including *Friends* alum David Schwimmer), stages several shows each year. Recent offerings included *Metamorphoses*, a sublime and humorous modern recasting of Ovid's myths that became a hit in New York, and *Lookingglass Alice,* an acrobatic retelling of *Alice in Wonderland.* Ensemble member Mary Zimmerman—who directed *Metamorphoses*—has built a national reputation for her creative interpretations of literature, so if she's directing a show while you're in town, don't miss it. 821 N. Michigan Ave. (at Chicago Ave.). © 312/337-0665. www.lookingglasstheatre.org. Tickets $25–$55. Subway/El: Red Line to Chicago.

Neo-Futurists *(Finds* A fixture on Chicago's late-night theater scene, the Neo-Futurists have been doing their hit *Too Much Light Makes the Baby Go Blind* since 1988 (it's now the longest-running show in Chicago). The setting—a cramped room above a funeral home—isn't much, but the gimmick is irresistible: Every night the performers stage a new collection of "30 plays in 60 minutes." The "plays" vary from a 3-minute comedy sketch to a lightning-quick wordless tableau; the mood veers from laugh-out-loud silly to emotionally touching. The show starts at 11:30pm on weekends; get there about an hour ahead, because seats are first-come, first-served, and they do sell out. The late-night curtain attracts a younger crowd, but I've taken 60-something relatives who have had a great time (unlike many improv comedy troupes, the Neo-Futurists don't rely on raunchy or gross-out humor). Admission is random: Theatergoers pay $7 plus the roll of a six-sided die. If you want to feel that you've experienced edgy, low-budget theater—but still want to be entertained—this is the place to go. 5153 N. Ashland Ave. (at Foster Ave.). © 773/275-5255. www.neofuturists.org. Tickets $8–$13. Subway/El: Red Line to Berwyn.

Steppenwolf Theatre Company Once a pioneer of bare-bones guerilla theater, Steppenwolf has moved firmly into the mainstream with a state-of-the-art theater and production budgets to rival those in any big city. The company has garnered many national awards and has launched the careers of several respected and well-known actors, including John Malkovich, Gary Sinise, Joan Allen, John Mahoney (of *Frasier*), and Laurie Metcalf (of *Roseanne*). Famous for pioneering the edgy, "rock 'n' roll," spleen-venting style of Chicago acting in the 1970s and '80s, Steppenwolf lately has become a victim of its own success. No longer a scrappy storefront theater, it now stages world premieres by emerging playwrights, revivals of classics, and adaptations of well-known literary works. While the acting is always high caliber, shows can be hit-or-miss, and unlike in the early days, you're not guaranteed a thrilling experience.

Struggling troupes sometimes perform at Steppenwolf's smaller studio theater, which stages more experimental fare. Tickets $20 to $65. Tickets ($20) go on sale at Audience Services at 11am the day of a performance; rush tickets (subject to availability; main stage half-price, studio $10) go on sale 1 hr. before performance. 1650 N. Halsted St. (at North Ave.). © 312/335-1650. www.steppenwolf.org. Subway/El: Red Line to North/Clybourn.

Victory Gardens Theater *(Finds*   Victory Gardens is one of the few pioneers of off-Loop theater that has survived from the 1970s. The five or six productions presented each season are new works, many developed through a series of workshops. The plays tend to be accessible stories about real people and real situations—nothing too experimental. Even though most shows don't feature nationally known actors, the casts are always first-rate, and the plays usually leave you with something to think about (or passionately discuss) on the way home.

Victory Gardens stages shows at its main stage inside the former Biograph movie theater (known in Chicago lore as the place where the FBI gunned down bank robber John Dillinger in 1934). 2433 N. Lincoln Ave. (1 block north of Fullerton Ave.). © 773/871-3000. www.victory gardens.org. Tickets $30–$45. Subway/El: Red or Brown line to Fullerton.

2 Comedy & Improv

In the mid-1970s, the nation was introduced to Chicago's brand of comedy through the skit-comedy show *Saturday Night Live*. Chicago continues to nurture young comics, affording them the chance to learn the tricks of improvisational comedy at Second City, iO, and numerous other comedy and improv outlets.

iO *(Finds*   The iO improv troupe was founded in 1981 by the late, great, and inexplicably unsung Del Close, an improv pioneer who branched off from his more mainstream counterparts at Second City to pursue an unorthodox methodology (the letters "iO" stand for "ImprovOlympic," the group's original name).

iO offers a nightclub setting for a variety of unscripted nightly performances, from free-form pieces to shows loosely based on concepts such as *Star Trek* or dating. Like all improv, it's a gamble: It could be a big laugh, or the amateur performers could go down in flames. Monday is an off night for most other clubs in town, and iO takes advantage with a show called the Armando Diaz Experience, an all-star improv night that teams up some of the best improvisers in

Chicago, from Second City and elsewhere. Besides Mike Myers, successful alums include the late Chris Farley, Tim Meadows, Andy Dick, and Conan O'Brien's former *Late Night* sidekick, Andy Richter. 3541 N. Clark St. (at Addison St.). © 773/880-0199. www.iochicago. net. Tickets $5–$14. Subway/El: Red Line to Addison.

Second City For nearly 50 years, Second City has been the top comedy club in Chicago and the most famous of its kind in the country. Photos of famous graduates line the lobby walls and include Elaine May, John Belushi, and recent *Saturday Night Live* cast members Tina Fey, Horatio Sanz, and Rachel Dratch.

Today's Second City is a veritable factory of improv, with shows on two stages (the storied main stage and the smaller Second City ETC) and a hugely popular training school. The main-stage ensembles change frequently, and the shows can swing wildly back and forth on the hilarity meter. In recent years, the club has adopted the long-form improvisational program pioneered by iO (Improv-Olympic; see above listing), which has brought much better reviews. Check the theater reviews in the *Reader,* a free local weekly, for an opinion on the current offering. To sample the Second City experience, catch the free postshow improv session (it gets going around 10:30pm); no ticket is necessary if you skip the main show (except Fri). 1616 N. Wells St. (in the Pipers Alley complex at North Ave.). © 877/778-4707 or 312/337-3992. www.secondcity.com. Tickets $8–$25. Subway/El: Brown Line to Sedgwick.

3 The Music Scene

JAZZ

In the first great wave of black migration from the South just after World War I, jazz journeyed from the Storyville section of New Orleans to Chicago. Jelly Roll Morton and Louis Armstrong made Chicago a jazz hot spot in the 1920s, and their music lives on in a whole new generation of talent. Chicago jazz is known for its collaborative spirit and a certain degree of risk-taking—which you can experience at a number of lively clubs.

Andy's Jazz Club Casual and comfortable, Andy's, a full restaurant and bar, is popular with both the hard-core and the neophyte jazz enthusiast. It's the only place in town where you can hear jazz nearly all day long, with sets beginning at noon, 5pm, and 9pm on weekdays; Saturday at 6 and 9:30pm; or Sunday at 5 and 7pm. 11 E. Hubbard St. (between State St. and Wabash Ave.). © 312/642-6805. www.andys jazzclub.com. Cover $5–$20. Subway/El: Red Line to Grand.

Green Dolphin Street ☆ An old garage on the north branch of the Chicago River was transformed, Cinderella-like, into this sexy, retro, 1940s-style nightclub and restaurant. The beautiful, well-appointed crowd shows up here to smoke stogies from the humidor, lap up martinis, and take in the scene (there's also a fine-dining restaurant whose patrons can move on to jazz after dinner without paying the cover charge). Green Dolphin books jazz in all its permutations, from big band to Latin. The main room is closed Monday. 2200 N. Ashland Ave. (at Webster Ave.). ☎ 773/395-0066. www.jazz itup.com. Cover $7–$20. Subway/El: Brown Line to Armitage or Red Line to Fullerton, and then a 10-min. cab ride.

Green Mill ☆ *Finds* Green Mill, in the heart of Uptown, is "Old Chicago" down to its rafters. It became a popular watering hole during the 1920s and 1930s, when regulars included Al Capone, Sophie Tucker (the Last of the Red Hot Mamas), and Al Jolson, and today it retains its speak-easy flavor. On Sunday night, the Green Mill plays host to the **Uptown Poetry Slam,** when poets vie for the open mic to roast and ridicule each other's work. Most nights, however, jazz is on the menu, beginning around 9pm and winding down just before closing at 4am (5am Sat). Get there early to claim one of the plush velvet booths. 4802 N. Broadway (at Lawrence Ave.). ☎ 773/878-5552. Cover $6–$15. Subway/El: Red Line to Lawrence.

Pops for Champagne *Finds* A civilized, elegant way to enjoy jazz, the Pops champagne bar is one of the prettiest rooms in the city, and its River North location makes it a convenient walk from most downtown hotels. 601 N. State St. (at Ohio St.). ☎ 312/266-POPS. www.pops forchampagne.com. Cover $5–$10 Tues–Sat; no cover Sun–Mon. Subway/El: Red Line to Grand.

BLUES

If Chicagoans were asked to pick one musical style to represent their city, most of us would start singing the blues. Thanks in part to the presence of the influential Chess Records, Chicago became a hub of blues activity after World War II, with musicians such as Muddy Waters, Howlin' Wolf, and Buddy Guy recording and performing here. Chicago helped usher in the era of "electric blues"—low-tech soulful singing melded with the rock sensibility of electric guitars. Blues-influenced rock musicians (the Rolling Stones and Led Zeppelin, for example) made Chicago a regular pilgrimage spot. Today, the blues has become yet another tourist attraction, especially for international visitors, but the quality and variety of blues acts is still

Lincoln Park & Wrigleyville After Dark

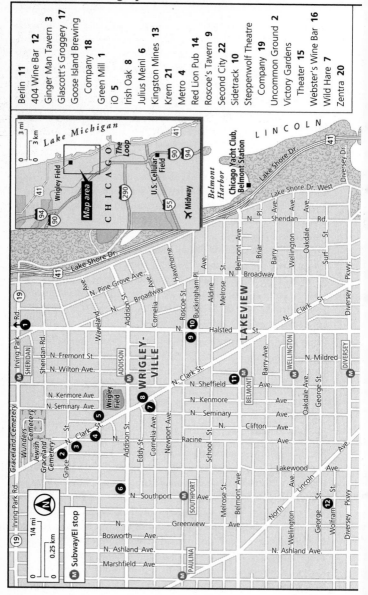

Berlin **11**
404 Wine Bar **12**
Ginger Man Tavern **3**
Glascott's Groggery **17**
Goose Island Brewing
Company **18**
Green Mill **1**
iO **5**
Irish Oak **8**
Julius Meinl **6**
Kingston Mines **13**
Krem **21**
Metro **4**
Red Lion Pub **14**
Roscoe's Tavern **9**
Second City **22**
Sidetrack **10**
Steppenwolf Theatre
Company **19**
Uncommon Ground **2**
Victory Gardens
Theater **15**
Webster's Wine Bar **16**
Wild Hare **7**
Zentra **20**

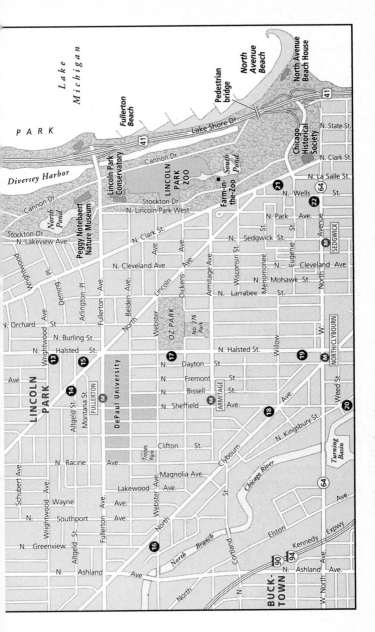

Lake Michigan

Fullerton Beach

PARK

Diversey Harbor

North
Pond

Cannon Dr.

Stockton Dr.
N. Lakeview Ave.

**Peggy Notebaert
Nature Museum**

Stockton Dr.

Cannon Dr.

*Pedestrian
bridge*

*North
Avenue
Beach*

*North Avenue
Beach House*

Lincoln Park
Conservatory

Cannon Dr.

Lake Shore Dr.

41

LINCOLN
PARK
ZOO

Stockton Dr.
N. Lincoln Park West

*South
Pond*

Farm-in-
the-Zoo

**Chicago
Historical
Society**

N. State St.

N. Clark St.

N. La Salle St.

21

N. Wells St.

22

64

Deming
Pl.

Arlington Pl.

N. Clark St.

N. Cleveland Ave.

Fullerton Ave.

Lincoln Ave.

N. Park Ave.

N. Sedgwick St.

Wisconsin

Menomonee

Eugenie St.

St.

Cleveland Ave.

Mohawk St.

North Avenue

SEDGWICK

5

Wrightwood Ave.

V. Orchard St.

N. Burling St.

N.   Halsted   St.

13

Belden Ave.

Webster

North

Dickens

Armitage Ave.

N. Larrabee St.

OZ PARK

No 276
Park

N. Halsted St.

Willow

19

N. Halsted   St.

M

NORTH/CLYBOURN

Ave.

15

Altgeld St.

Montana St.

FULLERTON

14

M

DePaul University

N.   Dayton   St.

N.   Fremont   St.

N.   Bissell   St.

N. Sheffield   Ave.

17

ARMITAGE

M

Ave.

W.

Weed St.

18

20

Schubert Ave.

N. Racine

N. Wrightwood Ave.

Ave.

Clifton St.

*Trebes
Park*

Magnolia Ave.

Lakewood   Ave.

Webster   St.

Clybourn   St.

N. Kingsbury St.

*Turning
Basin*

N.

Wayne

Southport

Ave.

Ave.

Chicago River

64

Ave.

N. Greenview

Altgeld St.

N.   Ashland

16

North

North   Branch

Cortland

Elston

Ave.

Kennedy   Expwy.

90

94

N.   Ashland   Ave.

**BUCK-
TOWN**

W. North Ave.

N.

impressive. Hard-core blues fans shouldn't miss the annual (free) **Blues Fest,** held along the lakefront in Grant Park in early June. See the "Chicago Calendar of Events" in chapter 3 for more on the festival.

Blue Chicago   Blue Chicago pays homage to female blues belters with a strong lineup of the best women vocalists around. The 1940s-style brick-walled room, decorated with original artwork of Chicago blues vignettes, is open Monday through Saturday, with music beginning at 9pm. 736 N. Clark St. (between Chicago Ave. and Superior St.). © 312/642-6261. www.bluechicago.com. Cover $8–$10. Subway/El: Red or Brown line to Chicago.

Buddy Guy's Legends ⟨⟨ *Finds*   A legend himself, gifted guitarist Buddy Guy runs one of the most popular and comfortable clubs in town. Blues paraphernalia, from a Koko Taylor dress to a Muddy Waters tour jacket, decorates the walls of this club near the South Loop. You may catch Buddy onstage when he's in town. (Or, if you're lucky, one of his high-profile friends, such as Mick Jagger, will stop by for an impromptu jam session.) The kitchen serves good Louisiana-style soul food and barbecue. 754 S. Wabash Ave. (between Balbo Dr. and Eighth St.). © 312/427-0333. www.buddyguys.com. Cover $10–$15. Subway/El: Red Line to Harrison.

Kingston Mines ⟨   Chicago's premier blues bar, Kingston Mines, is where musicians congregate after their own gigs to jam and socialize. Celebs have been known to drop by when they're in town shooting movies, but most nights the crowd includes a big contingent of conventioneers looking for a rockin' night on the town. But don't worry about the tourist factor—everyone's here to have a good time, and the energy is infectious. The nightly show begins at 9:30pm, with two bands on two stages, and goes until 4am (5am Sat). The late-night kitchen serves up burgers and ribs. 2548 N. Halsted St. (between Wrightwood and Fullerton aves.). © 773/477-4646. www.kingston mines.com. Cover $10–$15. Subway/El: Red or Brown line to Fullerton.

Underground Wonder Bar   This intimate club on the Near North Side only gets better as the night wears on (it's open until 4am Sun–Fri, until 5am Sat). It's one of the most eclectic live-music spots in town; you'll hear jazz trios, folk singers, and R&B vocalists playing the quirky, compact, and, yep, below-street-level room early in the evening. Things really heat up when co-owner Lonie Walker and her Big Bad Ass Company Band take the stage at 11pm on Friday and Saturday, playing a raucous blues-rock mix. 10 E. Walton St. (at State

St.). ☏ **312/266-7761**. www.undergroundwonderbar.com. Cover $8–$15. Subway/El: Red Line to Chicago.

ROCK (BASICALLY)

In the early 1990s, Chicago's burgeoning alternative-rock scene produced such national names as the Smashing Pumpkins, Liz Phair, Veruca Salt, Urge Overkill, and Material Issue. Although the city's moment of pop hipness quickly faded (as did most of the aforementioned artists), the live music scene has continued to thrive. Scan the *Reader, New City,* or *Time Out Chicago* to see who's playing where.

Here are some bars and clubs that book live music most nights of the week.

Double Door *Finds* This club has capitalized on the Wicker Park/Bucktown neighborhood's ascendance as a breeding ground for rock and alternative music. Owned by the proprietors of Metro (see below), the club has some of the better acoustics and sightlines in the city and attracts buzz bands and unknowns to its stage. When you need to escape the noise, there's a lounge-type area with pool tables in the basement. 1572 N. Milwaukee Ave. (at North Ave.). ☏ **773/489-3160**. www.doubledoor.com. Tickets $5–$20. Subway/El: Blue Line to Damen.

House of Blues The largest location in a national chain of music venues, the House of Blues could more appropriately be called the House of Pop. Although it's decorated with Mississippi Delta folk art, the bands that play here tend to be rock groups, '80s novelty acts, and the occasional hip-hop or reggae performer. This is a great place to see a show—concerts are in a theater that re-creates a gilded European opera house (minus the seats), and the stage views are pretty good no matter where you stand. 329 N. Dearborn St. (at Kinzie St.). ☏ **312/923-2000** for general information, or 312/923-2020 for concert information. www.hob.com. Tickets usually $15–$45. Subway/El: Red Line to Grand.

Metro ☆ Metro is located in an old auditorium and is Chicago's premier venue for live alternative and rock acts on the verge of breaking into the big time. There's not much in the way of atmosphere—it's basically a big black room with a stage—but the place has an impressive history. Everybody who is anybody played here when they were starting out, including REM, Pearl Jam, and local heroes the Smashing Pumpkins. Newer "alternative" bands that are getting attention from MTV and radio stations show up at Metro eventually. Some shows are all-ages, but most require concertgoers to be at least 21. Tickets are sold in person through the adjoining **Metro**

Store (sans service charges), or by phone through Ticketmaster. 3730 N. Clark St. (at Racine Ave.). ℂ **773/549-0203**, or 312/559-1212 for Ticketmaster orders. www.metrochicago.com. Tickets $8–$25. Subway/El: Red Line to Sheridan.

COUNTRY, FOLK & ETHNIC MUSIC

HotHouse *Finds* This "Center for International Performance and Exhibition" schedules some of the most eclectic programming in the city, attracting well-known jazz and avant-garde musicians from around the world. When the heavy hitters aren't booked, you'll see anything from local musicians improvising on "invented instruments" to Japanese blues singers. 31 E. Balbo Dr. (at S. Wabash Ave.). ℂ **312/362-9707**. www.hothouse.net. Cover $10–$25. Subway/El: Red Line to Harrison.

Old Town School of Folk Music ℛ *Finds* Country, folk, bluegrass, Latin, Celtic—the Old Town School of Folk Music covers a spectrum of indigenous musical forms. Best known as a training center offering a slate of music classes, the school also plays host to everyone from the legendary Pete Seeger to bluegrass phenom Alison Krauss. The school's home, in a former 1930s library, is the world's largest facility dedicated to the preservation and presentation of traditional and contemporary folk music. In midsummer it sponsors the popular Folk and Roots outdoor music festival. The school maintains another retail store and offers children's classes at its first location, 909 W. Armitage Ave. 4544 N. Lincoln Ave. (between Wilson and Montrose aves.). ℂ **773/728-6000**. www.oldtownschool.org. Tickets $10–$25. Subway/El: Brown Line to Western.

Wild Hare Number one on Chicago's reggae charts is the Wild Hare, in the shadow of Wrigley Field. After 20 years in business (an eternity in the nightclub world), this spot has kept up with the times by adding a state-of-the-art sound and video systems. Owner Zeleke Gessesse, who has toured with Ziggy Marley and the Melody Makers, books top acts such as Burning Spear and Yellow Man; he also nurtures local talent. With a Red Stripe in hand, you might even forget that it's 20 degrees outside. 3530 N. Clark St. (between Addison and Roscoe sts.). ℂ **773/327-4273**. www.wildharereggae.com. Cover $7–$15. Subway/El: Red Line to Addison.

CABARETS & PIANO BARS

Coq d'Or Whether you're huddled close around the piano or hanging back on the red Naugahyde banquettes, this old-time, clubby haunt in the historic Drake hotel offers an intimate evening of song stylings (it's one of the only downtown hotel lounges that still offers live music). The Coq d'Or claims to be the second bar in

Chicago to serve drinks after the repeal of Prohibition in 1933—and the place hasn't changed much since then. In The Drake Hotel, 140 E. Walton St. (at Michigan Ave.). © 312/787-2200. Subway/El: Red Line to Chicago/State.

Davenport's Piano Bar & Cabaret *(finds)* The youthful hipster haunt of Wicker Park isn't the first place you'd expect to find a tried-and-true piano bar and cabaret venue, but Davenport's does its best to revive a fading art form. The piano bar in front is flashier than the subdued cabaret in back, featuring a singing waitstaff, blue velvet banquettes, funky lighting fixtures, and a hand-painted mural-topped bar. The cabaret's sound equipment is first-rate. 1383 N. Milwaukee Ave. (just south of North Ave.). © 773/278-1830. http://davenports pianobar.com. Cover $10–$20. Subway/El: Blue Line to Damen.

Zebra Lounge *(finds)* The most wonderfully quirky piano bar in town, Zebra Lounge has a loyal following despite (or maybe because of) the campy decor. Just as you would expect, black-and-white stripes are the unifying element at this dark, shoebox-size Gold Coast spot, furnished with black vinyl booths, a small mirrored bar, and zebra kitsch galore. The place is relatively mellow early in the evening, though it can get packed late into the night on weekends. 1220 N. State Pkwy. (between Division and Goethe sts.). © 312/642-5140. Subway/El: Red Line to Clark/Division.

4 The Club Scene

Chicago is the hallowed ground where house music was hatched in the 1980s, so it's no surprise to find that it's also home to several vast, industrial-style dance clubs with pounding music and a mostly under-30 crowd. Given the fickle nature of clubgoers, some places listed below might have disappeared by the time you read this, but there is an impressive list of longtime survivors—clubs that have lasted more than a decade but continue to draw loyal crowds.

Berlin One of the more enduring dance floors in Chicago, Berlin is primarily gay during the week but draws dance hounds of all stripes on weekends and for special theme nights (disco the last Wed of every month, Prince music the last Sun of the month). It has a reputation for outrageousness and creativity, making it prime ground for people-watching. The space isn't much—basically a square room with a bar along one side—but the no-frills dance floor is packed late into the evening. 954 W. Belmont Ave. (at Sheffield Ave.). © 773/348-4975. www.berlinchicago.com. Cover $3–$5. Subway/El: Red or Brown line to Belmont.

crobar A veteran of Chicago's late-night scene, crobar has managed to stay hip since 1991; it's even expanded to locations in New York City and Miami. The warehouse-gone-glam look and thumping sound system give the space a quintessential dance-club feel, and the booth-lined balcony overlooking the huge dance floor is a good spot for people-watching. If you're especially gorgeous—or free-spending—you might make it into the glass-encased VIP room. The soundtrack is mostly hip-hop and house, and the weekend DJs have a strong local following, so you might be fighting for prime dance space. 1543 N. Kingsbury St. (at North Ave.). ✆ 312/266-1900. www.crobar.com. Cover $20 on weekends. Subway/El: Red Line to North/Clybourn.

Le Passage The Gold Coast's swankiest nightclub fits all the prerequisites for chic exclusivity, starting with the semihidden entrance at the end of a narrow (but well-lit) alleyway just steps from Oak Street's Prada and Barneys New York stores. The beautiful, the rich, and the designer-suited come here for the loungy aesthetic. The soundtrack mixes R&B, soul, hip-hop, house, funk, and acid jazz. Another highlight is the stellar French fusion menu and the late-night eats such as mini-cheeseburgers and fries, served well into the wee hours. 1 Oak Place (between Rush and State sts). ✆ 312/255-0022. www.lepassage.tv. Cover $20. Subway/El: Red Line to Chicago.

Reserve No longer just a neighborhood rife with restaurants, the West Loop has also become a hot nightlife destination, thanks to its anchor, Reserve nightclub. The bi-level club became so popular for its ultra-exclusive VIP offerings that it took over as *the* place to rub elbows with visiting celebs, music artists, and athletes alike. Even under-the-radar high rollers splurge here on the bottle service (call ahead to book a table, as they often fill up on weekends.) You can settle in downstairs for a more low-key lounge vibe, or head up to the 5,000-square-foot club to join the throngs of scenesters who can't seem to get enough of the mashed-up music spun nightly. 858 W. Lake St. (at Green St.). ✆ 312/455-1111. www.reserve-chicago.com. Cover $20 on weekends. Subway/El: Green Line to Clinton.

Zentra Club-hoppers often make Middle Eastern and Moroccan-flavored Zentra, which stays open into the wee hours, their last stop of the night. A large four-room space, Zentra banks on the current trend of East meets West, with exotic Moroccan textiles, thick drapes, Indian silks, red lanterns, funky chrome fixtures, and even "Hookah Girls" proffering hits on pipes packed with fruity tobacco blends. Upstairs entertains those who want to move to progressive dance and techno sounds, while downstairs has DJs spinning mostly house and hip-hop. Zentra attracts an eclectic mix of patrons who come to soak in the exotic vibes, do some people-watching, and simply have fun dancing. 923 W. Weed St. (just south of North Ave. at Clybourn Ave.). © 312/787-0400. http://zentranightclub.com. Cover $15–$20. Subway/El: Red Line to North/Clybourn.

5 The Bar & Cafe Scene

If you want to soak up the atmosphere of a neighborhood tavern or sports bar, it's best to venture beyond downtown into the surrounding neighborhoods. Lincoln Park, Wrigleyville, and Bucktown/ Wicker Park have well-established nightlife zones that abound with bright, upscale neighborhood bars. You'll also find numerous dives and no-frills "corner taps" in the blue-collar neighborhoods.

As for hotel nightlife, virtually every hotel in Chicago has a cocktail lounge or piano bar and, in some cases, more than one distinct environment where you can take an aperitif before dinner or watch an evening of entertainment. The piano bars at The Drake Hotel and the Ambassador East Hotel's Pump Room are standouts.

BARS
THE LOOP & VICINITY

Miller's Pub 😭 A true Loop landmark, Miller's has been serving up after-work cocktails to downtown office workers for more than 50 years; it's one of the few places in the area that offers bar service until the early morning hours. There's a full dinner menu, too. Autographed photos of movie stars and sports figures cover the walls; while some might be unrecognizable to younger patrons, they testify to the pub's long-standing tradition of friendly hospitality. 134 S. Wabash Ave. (between Jackson Blvd. and Adams St.). © 312/645-5377. Subway/ El: Red Line to Jackson.

NEAR THE MAGNIFICENT MILE

Cru Café and Wine Bar *Finds* A couple of blocks west of the Mag Mile, Cru draws both discriminating oenophiles and curious tourists with its sleek interior of gold-painted surfaces, a zebra-wood bar, hip light fixtures, and 400-plus wine list. Comfortable and loungy, the cafe also serves a lunch, dinner, and late-night menu of seafood, soups and salads, quiche, caviar, sandwiches, and desserts. A 40-seat alfresco seating area is available in warm weather. 888 N. Wabash Ave. © 312/337-4078. Subway/El: Red Line to Chicago.

Elm Street Liquors In a neighborhood often teeming with tourists, this lounge for locals exudes an urban but laid-back style with its anything-goes attitude. The music is familiar, and the drinks are forward-thinking, boasting champagne cocktails rather than the ubiquitous martinis found at every other nightspot in Chicago. We especially like that you don't have to pay a cover charge to enjoy the party. 12 W. Elm St. (at State St.). ℭ 312/337-3200. Subway/El: Red Line to Clark/Division.

Signature Lounge For the price of a trip to the John Hancock tower observatory ($11, two floors below), you can drink in the view and a cocktail at this lofty lounge. The views are fabulous (especially at sunset), though you'll probably be surrounded by other tourists. It's open until 1am Sunday through Thursday and until 2am on the weekends. 96th floor, John Hancock Center, 875 N. Michigan Ave. ℭ 312/787-7230. Subway/El: Red Line to Chicago.

RIVER NORTH & VICINITY

Brehon Pub Big front windows, a high tin ceiling, and a great antique back bar lend charm to this little neighborhood bar in (often) tourist-packed River North. Brehon regulars hang out weeknights after work and even at lunchtime, when the tavern serves sandwiches and soup. In the 1970s, the *Sun-Times* newspaper set up this spot as a phony bar (appropriately named the Mirage) and used it in a "sting" operation to expose city corruption. 731 N. Wells St. (at Superior St.). ℭ 312/642-1071. Subway/El: Red or Brown line to Chicago.

Clark Street Ale House *(Finds)* A handsome, convivial tavern and a popular after-work spot for white- and blue-collar types alike, Clark Street Ale House features a large open space filled with high tables and a long cherrywood bar along one wall. Better than the atmosphere are the 95 varieties of beer, a large majority of them from American microbreweries. The bar also offers a wide selection of scotches and cognacs. 742 N. Clark St. ℭ 312/642-9253. Subway/El: Red or Brown line to Chicago.

J Bar Yes, this lounge is just off the lobby of the James Hotel, but it's no conventioneer hangout. The low-slung leather couches, seating cubes, and flickering votive candles give it the look of an upscale urban club, and its laid-back vibe has made it a gathering place for stylish locals in their 20s and 30s. One drawback: you have to call and reserve a table if you want to be guaranteed a place to sit into the late-night hours. 610 N. Rush St. (at Wabash Ave.) ℭ 312/660-7200. Subway/El: Red Line to Grand.

10pin A modern interpretation of the classic bowling alley, this lounge is tucked away under the Marina Towers complex on the Chicago River. Everything feels bright and new (even the rental shoes), and there's a full menu of designer beers and upscale snacks (gourmet pizzas, smoked salmon, specialty martinis). A giant video screen overlooks the 24 bowling lanes, and a top-notch sound system gives the place a nightclubby vibe. You don't *have* to bowl—the bar area is a casual, welcoming place to hang out—but I'd certainly recommend giving it a try. 330 N. State St. (between Kinzie St. and the Chicago River). ✆ **312/644-0300.** www.10pinchicago.com. Subway/El: Red Line to Grand or Brown Line to Merchandise Mart.

RUSH & DIVISION STREETS

Around Rush Street are what a bygone era called singles bars—although the only singles that tend to head here now are suburbanites, out-of-towners, and barely legal partiers. Rush Street's glory days may be long gone, but there are still a few vestiges of the old times on nearby Division Street, which overflows with party-hearty spots that attract a loud, frat-party element. They include **Shenanigan's House of Beer,** 16 W. Division St. (✆ **312/642-2344**); **Butch McGuire's,** 20 W. Division St. (✆ **312/337-9080**); the **Lodge,** 21 W. Division St. (✆ **312/642-4406**); and **Mother's,** 26 W. Division St. (✆ **312/642-7251**). Many of these bars offer discounts for women, as loud pitchmen in front of each establishment will be happy to tell any attractive ladies who pass by.

OLD TOWN

The center of nightlife in Old Town is Wells Street, home to Second City and Zanies Comedy Club, as well as a string of reliable restaurants and bars, many of which have been in business for decades. You're not going to find many trendy spots in Old Town; the nightlife here tends toward neighborhood pubs and casual restaurants, filled mostly with a late-20s and 30-something crowd.

Corcoran's Owned by the same family for more than 30 years, this is one of Old Town's favorite local hangouts, and it makes a good stop before or after a show at Second City, which is located right across the street. The cozy, wood-lined interior and hearty pub food (bangers and mash, shepherd's pie, fish and chips) will put you right at ease. In nice weather, check out the beer garden in back, which offers a tranquil retreat from the city traffic. 1615 N. Wells St. (at North Ave.). ✆ **312/440-0885.** Subway/El: Brown Line to Sedgwick.

Goose Island Brewing Company (Finds) On the western fringes of Old Town, the best-known brewpub in the city features its own Honker's Ale on tap, as well as several other beers produced here and at an off-site distillery. Ask for a tasting menu to try them all, or show up on any Tuesday when they give out free samples of the newest weekly release at 6pm. 1800 N. Clybourn Ave. (at Sheffield Ave.). ℭ 312/915-0071. Subway/El: Red Line to North/Clybourn.

Krem A 33-foot "bed" is the highlight of this see-and-be-seen, subterranean Lincoln Park haunt. Part club, part small-plates restaurant, Krem is a "dine and disco" spot filled with white furniture that glows in a blue light. It has also jumped on the bottle service bandwagon; regulars can even reserve their own liquor storage lockers. There is no cover charge, but drink prices approach those of downtown clubs. Dinner is served until 11pm, desserts until midnight. 1750 N. Clark St. (at Eugenie St.). ℭ 312/932-1750. Bus: 22 (Clark St.).

LINCOLN PARK

Lincoln Park, with its high concentration of apartment-dwelling singles, is one of the busiest nightlife destinations in Chicago. Prime real estate is at a premium in this residential neighborhood, so you won't find many warehouse-size dance clubs here; most of the action is at pubs and bars. Concentrations of in-spots run along Halsted Street and Lincoln Avenue.

Glascott's Groggery At the top of any self-respecting Lincoln Park yuppie's list of meeting places is Glascott's, an Irish pub that has been in the same family since it opened in 1937. You'll see groups of guys stopping in after their weekly basketball game, couples coming in after dinner to catch up with their friends, and singles hoping to hook up with old college buddies and meet new friends. 2158 N. Halsted St. (at Webster Ave.). ℭ 773/281-1205. Subway/El: Brown Line to Armitage.

Red Lion Pub ✯ (Finds) An English pub in the heart of Lincoln Park, the Red Lion is a comfortable neighborhood place with a mix of old and young DePaul students, actors, and Anglophiles who feel right at home among the Union Jacks and photos of Churchill. And if you're looking for atmosphere, the British owner even claims the place is haunted. 2446 N. Lincoln Ave. (between Fullerton and Wrightwood aves.). ℭ 773/348-2695. Subway/El: Red or Brown line to Fullerton.

Webster's Wine Bar It's a bit off the beaten track—on the western fringe of Lincoln Park—but the low-lit, sophisticated decor makes Webster's a good alternative to the usual beer blast. The wait-staff can help you choose from a list of dozens of wines by the bottle or glass, or you can hone your taste buds with a flight of several wines. There's also a tapas-style menu for noshing. Step back into the library area to light up a cigar and recline on the couch. 1480 W. Webster Ave. (between Clybourn and Ashland aves.). © 773/868-0608. Subway/ El: Red or Brown line to Fullerton, and then a short cab ride.

WRIGLEYVILLE, LAKEVIEW & THE NORTH SIDE

Real estate in Wrigleyville and Lakeview is a tad less expensive than in Lincoln Park, so the nightlife scene here skews a little younger. You'll find a mostly postcollegiate crowd partying on Clark Street across from Wrigley Field (especially after games in the summer). But head away from the ball field, and you'll discover some more eclectic choices.

404 Wine Bar   One of the most inviting bars in the city, 404 Wine Bar makes you feel as if you've been invited to a party in a private home (it adjoins Jack's, a standard sports-and-beer spot; make sure you go in the entrance on the left side of the building). Tables and soft leather couches fill a series of cozy, low-lit rooms; the laid-back vibe attracts groups of friends and couples rather than on-the-prowl singles. In the summer, tables are set up in an outdoor courtyard; in the winter, fireplaces fill the rooms with a warm glow. 2852 N. Southport Ave. (at George St.). © 773/404-5886. Subway/El: Brown Line to Wellington.

Ginger Man Tavern   Ginger Man definitely plays against type in a row of predictable sports bars across the street from Wrigley Field. On game days the earthy bar has been known to crank classical music in an attempt to calm drunken fans—or at least shoo them away. Pool tables (free on Sun) are always busy with slightly bohemian neighborhood 20-somethings, who have more than 80 beers to choose from. 3740 N. Clark St. (at Racine Ave.). © 773/549-2050. Subway/El: Red Line to Addison.

Irish Oak *Finds*   Owned and staffed by folks from the Old Sod, this is one of the city's nicest Irish bars. The handsome woodwork and collection of antiques give the tavern a mellow, laid-back feel. Irish bands perform once in a while on weekends. There are plenty of whiskeys, stouts, and ales to sip, and the kitchen offers shepherd's pie and other Irish fare. 3511 N. Clark St. (between Cornelia Ave. and Addison St.). © 773/935-6669. Subway/El: Red Line to Addison.

WICKER PARK & BUCKTOWN

For an alternative scene, head over to Wicker Park and Bucktown, where slackers and some adventurous yuppies populate bars dotting the streets near the confluence of North, Damen, and Milwaukee avenues. Don't dress up if you want to blend in: A casually bohemian getup and low-key attitude are all you need.

The Bucktown Pub *(Value* The owners' collection of groovy 1960s and '70s rock-'n'-roll posters and cartoon art is phenomenal. However, most Bucktown patrons are more interested in nursing their pints of imported and domestic microbrews than in gawking at the walls. Other Wicker Park/Bucktown bars try to come off as low-key; this is the real thing, where attitude is firmly discouraged at the door. The psychedelic- and glam-rock-filled jukebox keeps toes tapping, and competition on the skittle-bowling machine can get quite fierce. Credit cards not accepted. 1658 W. Cortland St. (at Hermitage Ave.). *©* 773/ 394-9898. Subway/El: Blue Line to Damen.

The Map Room *(★ (Finds* Hundreds of travel books and guides line the shelves of this globe-trotter's tavern. Peruse that tome on Fuji or Antarctica while sipping a pint of one of the 20-odd draft beers. The Map Room's equally impressive selection of bottled brews makes this place popular with beer geeks as well as the tattered-passport crew. Tuesday is theme night, featuring the food, music, and spirits of a certain country, accompanied by a slide show and tales from a recent visitor. 1949 N. Hoyne Ave. (at Armitage Ave.). *©* 773/252-7636. Subway/El: Blue Line to Damen.

Marie's Riptide Lounge Nothing here looks as though it has been updated since the 1960s (owner Marie is long past retirement age), but personal touches and the retro cool of the place have made it a hip stop on the late-night circuit. A jukebox stocked with campy oldies, a curious low-tech duck-hunting "video" game, and the occasional blast of black light make Marie's a hoot. The owner takes great pains to decorate the interior of the little bar for each holiday season (the wintertime "snow-covered" bar is not to be missed.) 1745 W. Armitage Ave. (at Hermitage Ave.). *©* 773/278-7317. Subway/El: Blue Line to Damen.

CAFES
Julius Meinl *(★* Austria's premier coffee roaster chose Chicago— and, even more mysteriously, a location near Wrigley Field—for its first U.S. outpost. The result is a mix of Austrian style (upholstered

banquettes, white marble tables, newspapers hanging on wicker frames) and American cheeriness (lots of natural light, smiling wait-staff, smoke-free air). The excellent coffee and hot chocolate are served European-style on small silver platters with a glass of water on the side, but it's the desserts that keep the regulars coming back. Try the apple strudel or millennium torte (glazed with apricot jam and chocolate ganache), and for a moment you'll swear you're in Vienna. 3601 N. Southport Ave. (at Addison St.). ✆ **773/868-1857.** Subway/El: Brown Line to Southport.

Uncommon Ground 𝕽𝕽 When you're looking for refuge from Cubs game days and party nights in Wrigleyville, Uncommon Ground offers a dose of laid-back, vaguely bohemian civility. Just off busy Clark Street, the cafe has a fireplace in winter (when the cafe's bowl—yes, bowl—of hot chocolate is a sight for cold eyes) and a spacious sidewalk operation in more temperate months. Breakfast is served all day, plus there's a full lunch and dinner menu. Music fig-ures strongly; the late Jeff Buckley and ex-Bangle Susanna Hoffs are among those who've played the place. Open until 2am daily. 1214 W. Grace St. (at Clark St.). ✆ **773/929-3680.** Subway/El: Red Line to Addison.

6 The Gay & Lesbian Scene

Most of Chicago's gay bars are conveniently clustered on a stretch of North Halsted Street in Lakeview (in what's known as Boys Town), making it easy to sample many of them in a breezy walk.

Circuit It has all the necessary nightclub elements: flashing lights, a killer sound system, the biggest dance floor in Boys Town, and plenty of eye candy. Open until 4am on weekends, Circuit attracts a hard-partying, minimally dressed crowd after all the other local bars have closed. Friday is "girls' night." 3641 N. Halsted St. (at Addison St.). ✆ **773/325-2233.** www.circuitclub.com. $5–$10 cover. Subway/El: Red Line to Addison.

Roscoe's Tavern *Finds* The picture windows facing Halsted make Roscoe's, a gay neighborhood bar in business since 1987, an espe-cially welcoming place. It has a large antiques-filled front bar, an out-door patio, a pool table, and a large dance floor. The 20- and 30-something crowd is friendly and laid-back—except on weekends when the dance floor is hopping. The cafe serves sandwiches and salads. 3356 N. Halsted St. (at Roscoe St.). ✆ **773/281-3355.** Cover after 10pm Sat $4. Subway/El: Red or Brown line to Belmont.

Sidetrack *(Finds)* If you make it to Roscoe's, you'll no doubt end up at Sidetrack. The popular bars are across the street from each other, and there's a constant flow of feet between the two. Sidetrack is a sleek video bar where TV monitors are never out of your field of vision, nor are the preppy professional patrons. Don't miss Show Tunes Night on Sunday, Monday, and Friday, when the whole place sings along to Broadway and MGM musical favorites. 3349 N. Halsted St. (at Roscoe St.). © **773/477-9189.** Subway/El: Red or Brown line to Belmont.

Index

See also Accommodations and Restaurant indexes below.

ACCOMMODATIONS

RESTAURANTS

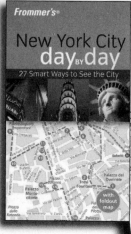
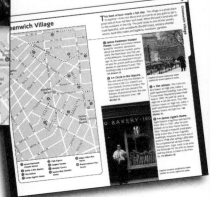

FROMMER'S® COMPLETE TRAVEL GUIDES

FROMMER'S® DAY BY DAY GUIDES

PAULINE FROMMER'S GUIDES: SEE MORE. SPEND LESS.

FROMMER'S® PORTABLE GUIDES

Acapulco, Ixtapa & Zihuatanejo
Amsterdam
Aruba, Bonaire & Curacao
Australia's Great Barrier Reef
Bahamas
Big Island of Hawaii
Boston
California Wine Country
Cancún
Cayman Islands
Charleston
Chicago
Dominican Republic

Florence
Las Vegas
Las Vegas for Non-Gamblers
London
Maui
Nantucket & Martha's Vineyard
New Orleans
New York City
Paris
Portland
Puerto Rico
Puerto Vallarta, Manzanillo &
Guadalajara

Rio de Janeiro
San Diego
San Francisco
Savannah
St. Martin, Sint Maarten, Anguila &
St. Bart's
Turks & Caicos
Vancouver
Venice
Virgin Islands
Washington, D.C.
Whistler

FROMMER'S® CRUISE GUIDES

Alaska Cruises & Ports of Call

Cruises & Ports of Call

European Cruises & Ports of Call

FROMMER'S® NATIONAL PARK GUIDES

Algonquin Provincial Park
Banff & Jasper
Grand Canyon

National Parks of the American West
Rocky Mountain
Yellowstone & Grand Teton

Yosemite and Sequoia & Kings
Canyon
Zion & Bryce Canyon

FROMMER'S® WITH KIDS GUIDES

Chicago
Hawaii
Las Vegas
London

National Parks
New York City
San Francisco

Toronto
Walt Disney World® & Orlando
Washington, D.C.

FROMMER'S® PHRASEFINDER DICTIONARY GUIDES

Chinese
French

German
Italian

Japanese
Spanish

SUZY GERSHMAN'S BORN TO SHOP GUIDES

France
Hong Kong, Shanghai & Beijing
Italy

London
New York
Paris

San Francisco
Where to Buy the Best of Everything.

FROMMER'S® BEST-LOVED DRIVING TOURS

Britain
California
France
Germany

Ireland
Italy
New England
Northern Italy

Scotland
Spain
Tuscany & Umbria

THE UNOFFICIAL GUIDES®

Adventure Travel in Alaska
Beyond Disney
California with Kids
Central Italy
Chicago
Cruises
Disneyland®
England
Hawaii

Ireland
Las Vegas
London
Maui
Mexico's Best Beach Resorts
Mini Mickey
New Orleans
New York City
Paris

San Francisco
South Florida including Miami &
the Keys
Walt Disney World®
Walt Disney World® for
Grown-ups
Walt Disney World® with Kids
Washington, D.C.

SPECIAL-INTEREST TITLES

Athens Past & Present
Best Places to Raise Your Family
Cities Ranked & Rated
500 Places to Take Your Kids Before They Grow Up
Frommer's Best Day Trips from London
Frommer's Best RV & Tent Campgrounds in the U.S.A.

Frommer's Exploring America by RV
Frommer's NYC Free & Dirt Cheap
Frommer's Road Atlas Europe
Frommer's Road Atlas Ireland
Retirement Places Rated